Comparative Information Technology

Languages, Societies and the Internet

Globalisation, Comparative Education and Policy Research

12-volume Book Series (Springer)

Series editor: Joseph Zajda (Australian Catholic University, Melbourne Campus)
http://www.springeronline.com/sgw/cda/frontpage

Book series overview

The *Globalisation, Comparative Education and Policy Research* book series aims to meet the research needs of all those interested in in-depth developments in comparative education research. The series provides a global overview of developments and changes in policy and comparative education research during the last decade. Presenting up-to-date scholarly research on global trends, it is an easily accessible, practical yet scholarly source of information for researchers, policy makers and practitioners. It seeks to address the nexus between comparative education, policy and forces of globalisation, and provides perspectives from all the major disciplines and all the world regions. The series offers possible strategies for the effective and pragmatic policy planning and implementation at local, regional and national levels.

The book series complements the *International Handbook of Globalisation and Education Policy Research.* The volumes focus on comparative education themes and case studies in much greater scope and depth than is possible in the Handbook.

The series includes volumes on both empirical and qualitative studies of policy initiatives and developments in comparative education research in elementary, secondary and post-compulsory sectors. Case studies may include changes and education reforms around the world, curriculum reforms, trends in evaluation and assessment, decentralisation and privatisation in education, technical and vocational education, early childhood education, excellence and quality in education. Above all, the series offers the latest findings on critical issues in comparative education and policy directions, such as:

- Developing new internal strategies (more comprehensive, flexible and innovative modes of learning) that take into account the changing and expanding learner needs
- Overcoming 'unacceptable' socio-economic educational disparities and inequalities
- Improving educational quality
- Harmonizing education and culture
- International cooperation in education and policy directions in each country

For other titles published in this series, go to
www.springer.com/series/6932

Joseph Zajda • Donna Gibbs
Editors

Comparative Information Technology

Languages, Societies and the Internet

Springer

Editors
Prof. Joseph Zajda
Australian Catholic University
Melbourne Campus
Australia

Prof. Donna Gibbs
Macquarie University
Australian Centre for Educational Studies
Sydney
Australia

ISBN 978-1-4020-9425-5 e-ISBN 978-1-4020-9426-2
DOI: 10.1007/978-1-4020-9426-2

Library of Congress Control Number: 2008943990

Printed on acid-free paper

springer.com

To Rea, Dorothy, and Nikolai

Preface

Comparative Information Technology: Languages, Societies and the Internet, which is the fourth volume in the 12-volume series *Globalisation, Comparative Education and Policy Research*, offers a critique of the nexus between ICT and its impact on society, individuals and educational institutions. One of the most signification dimensions of globalisation has been the rapid development of information and communications technologies (ICTs). Our lives have been changed by this in numerous ways and the implications for education are enormous. The ICTs have transformed the linguistic, cognitive and visual dimensions of human communication, as well as our perceptions of the self, and social identity in the global culture. The ICTs have facilitated the development of new dimensions of digital literacy, such as blogging and sms messaging. In this sense, cyberlanguage continues to evolve by borrowing and adapting familiar words, coining new expressions, and embracing particular styles (Gibbs & Krause, 2006, 2007).

However, information technology can be both empowering and disempowering. Individuals use the Internet, notebooks, and their BlackBerries and communicate via email. If clothing is an extension of one's skin, then the ICT has become an extension of our bodies. In a globalised world, linked through the Internet, a net-formed identity can lead to a multiplicity of identities, some contradictory to each other, and some taking place primarily in the virtual communities of cyberspace. The proliferation of the Internet, as both a tool for communication and a site of new forms of community and identity, has the power to influence our mind, our consciousness, and our perceptions of reality.

Despite the fact that we live in the information rich, and Digital Society, information technology is not always integrated effectively in schools, and traditional teaching techniques and styles are employed in the classroom. Furthermore, a new digital divide between the 'info-rich' and 'info-poor' societies has now been added to the traditional social stratification divide between the 'haves' and the 'have-nots' (McIntosh, 2005). Thus, from the equality of access and social justice perspectives, increasing access to ICT should be a key factor in any authentic and quality-driven education reforms (Zajda et al., 2006).

This book is devoted to the study of the impact information technology has made on learning in the global context. It provides directions in education, and policy research, relevant to transformational educational reforms in the twenty-first century. Various book chapters critique the dominant discourses and debates pertaining to ICT, cultural identity and pedagogy (see also Zajda et al., 2008). The book draws upon recent studies in the areas of ICT, cultural identity and pedagogy, set against the background of dominant ideologies in information technology and education (Zajda, 2005). The general intention is to make *Comparative Information Technology: Languages, Societies and the Internet* available to a broad spectrum of users among policy-makers, academics, graduate students, education policy researchers, administrators and practitioners in the education and related professions. The book is unique in that it:

- Examines recent research dealing with ICT, cultural identity and pedagogy
- Explores conceptual frameworks and methodological approaches applicable in the research of ICT, globalisation and pedagogy
- Demonstrates ideological imperatives of technodeterminism affecting cultural identity and pedagogy
- Provides strategic education policy analysis on recent developments in information technology and cultural identity research
- Gives suggestions for directions in education and policy changes, relevant to democratic and empowering pedagogy in the twenty-first century

We hope that you will find *Comparative Information Technology: Languages, Societies and the Internet* useful in your teaching, future research and discourses concerning information technology, pedagogy, social justice and educational reforms in the global culture.

Joseph Zajda
Australian Catholic University (Melbourne Campus)

References

Gibbs, D. & Krause, K-L. (2006) (Eds.). *Cyberlines: Languages and Culture of the Internet*. Melbourne: James Nicholas Publishers.

Gibbs, D. & Krause, K-L. (2007) (Eds.). *Cyberlines 2.0: Languages and Culture of the Internet*. Melbourne: James Nicholas Publishers.

McIntosh, C. & Varoglu, Z. (Eds.) (2005). *Perspectives on Distance Education: Lifelong Learning & Distance Higher Education*. Paris: UNESCO.

Zajda, J. (2005) (Ed.). The *International Handbook of Globalisation and Education Policy Research*. Dordrecht: Springer.

Zajda, J., Majhanovich, S., and Rust, V. (2006) (Eds.) *Education and Social Justice*. Dordrecht: Springer.

Zajda, J. (2008). Technodeterminism. In G. McCulloch & D. Crook (Eds.), *The International Encyclopedia of Education*. London: Routledge

Zajda, J., Biraimah, B., & Gaudelli, W. (2008). (Eds.), *Education and Social Inequality in the Global Culture* (pp. xvii–xxvii). Dordrecht: Springer.

Acknowledgements

We wish to thank the following individuals who have provided invaluable help, advice and support with this major research project:

Harmen van Paradijs, Publishing Editor, Springer

Bernadette Deelen, Springer Marianna Pascale, Springer

Dorothy Murphy, Assistant Editor, *Educational Practice and Theory*, James Nicholas Publishers

We also want to thank numerous reviewers who were prepared to review various drafts of the chapters. These include:

Helena Allahwerdi, University of Finland

John P. Anchan, University of Winnipeg

Ari Antikainen, University of Helsinki

Alberto Arenas, University of Arizona

Jill Blackmore, Deakin University

Malcolm Campbell, Bowling Green State University

Paul Carlin, Australian Catholic University (Melbourne Campus)

David Gamage, University of Newcastle

Yaacov Iram, Bar Ilan University

Erwin Epstein, Loyola University Chicago

Kyu Hwan Lee, Ewha Womans University (South Korea)

Kas Mazurek, University of Lethbridge

Christopher McIntosh, UNESCO Institute for Lifelong Learning

Caroline Smith, Australian Catholic University (Melbourne Campus)

Nikolai Zajda, Guest Editor, *Information Technology Education and Society*, of James Nicholas Publishers

Rea Zajda, Managing Editor, *Information Technology Education and Society*, of James Nicholas Publishers

Contents

Contributors

David Butt is Director of the Centre for Language in Social Life, in Linguistics at Macquarie University. Dr. Butt's research projects include discourse studies in contexts of surgical care, in the Conversational Model of psychiatry, and in various other forms of technical register. A particular focus of his work has been the relations between literary forms and the investigations of scientists, for instance, the "thought experiments" of modernist poetry and of physics. He has also conducted research into the changing demands of school curriculum.

Jennifer Fergusson (Macquarie ICT Innovations Centre) has been a primary school teacher and assistant principal, a facilitator of teacher professional development in Technology in Learning and Teaching (TILT), and a school district technology advisor. Currently a director of the Macquarie ICT Innovations Centre, she is pursuing her interest in the capacity of ICT to enhance learning and completing her master's degree.

Donna Gibbs (Macquarie University) is an Associate Professor in the School of Education at the Australian Centre for Educational Studies, Macquarie University. She teaches in the area of curriculum studies, curriculum change theory, and the implications of technology for education, with a particular focus on effective pedagogies. Dr. Gibbs' research interests range from Elizabethan love poetry to children's literature to cyberculture. Her latest edited book is *Cyberlines 2: Languages and Cultures of the Internet* (coedited with K. Krause), James Nicholas Publishers (2006).

Gerard Goggin (University of Queensland) is an ARC Australian Research Fellow in the Centre for Critical and Cultural Studies, University of Queensland, where he is researching mobile phone culture, policy, and regulation. Dr. Goggin is coauthor of *Disability in Australia* (University of NSW Press, 2005) and *Digital Disability: The Social Construction of Disability in New Media* (Rowman & Littlefield, 2003); and editor of *Virtual Nation: The Internet in Australia* (University of NSW Press, 2004). He is currently writing a book entitled *Cell Phone Culture: Mobile Technologies in Everyday Life* (Routledge, 2006).

Maree Gosper (Macquarie University) is a Senior Lecturer in academic development (e-learning) in the Centre for Professional Development and the Institute of Higher Education Research and Development, Macquarie University. Dr. Gosper has particular research interests in integrating information and communications technologies (ICTs) into the curriculum, matching cognitive processes underpinning learning with cognitive enabling features of technologies, and the development of effective and sustainable learning communities and e-learning environments. She has been involved in a number of cross-sector and university-wide research and development projects related to educational programs, teaching and learning resources, and organizational capacity in e-learning.

Ichiro Kobayashi (Ochanomizu University, Tokyo) is an Associate Professor in the Department of Information Sciences, Faculty of Sciences, at Ochanomizu University. Dr. Kobayashi was also a researcher from 2000 to 2005 at the Brain Science Institute of RIKEN where he furthered his research in the study of Intelligence Systems Computing, based on natural language. He is a specialist on the modelling of complex and fuzzy systems and a member of the Editorial Board of the *Journal of Advanced Computational Intelligence and Intelligent Informatics.*

Ellen Mandinach is a Senior Research Scientist and Senior Project Director at the CNA Corporation in Alexandria, VA, USA. She received her Ph.D, in educational psychology from Stanford University in 1984. She has done extensive work in the field of educational technology first at Educational Testing Service and then at the Educational Development Center's Center for Children and Technology. Dr. Mandinach's research has focused on the implementation and impact of technology-based learning environments on teaching, learning, and classroom dynamics. She has published widely in the area of educational technology, including *Classroom Dynamics: Implementing a Technology-Based Learning Environment* and *Data-Driven School Improvement: Linking Data and Learning*. She was elected president of the educational psychology division of the American Psychological Association for the 2008/2009 year and is currently serving as president-elect.

Patrick McAndrew (The Open University, Milton Keynes, UK) is a Senior Lecturer in the Institute of Educational Technology (IET) at The Open University. Before joining The Open University, Dr. McAndrew was Manager of the Institute for Computer Based Learning at Heriot-Watt University where he was involved in a large number of research and development projects including HIPERNET (RACE), LEVERAGE (ACTS), and ASTEP (MMTF action). His main research interests are in ways to structure material for reuse and approaches to enabling learning and sharing knowledge using networks.

Robyn Philip (Macquarie University) is an educational Project Manger at the E-Learning Centre of Excellence at Macquarie University. Her background is in educational development, online learning, and distance education and her research has centerd on the effective use of online technologies. She recently coordinated the education research for a project about the integration of educational IT systems and repositories of learning objects. This is reported on in a forthcoming book, *The COLIS Project*, which she has coedited with Professor James Dalziel and Jonathan Clare.

Cher Ping Lim (Nanyang Technological University, Singapore) is an Assistant Professor of Learning Sciences and Technologies in the Centre of Research in Pedagogy and Practice at Nanyang Technological University, Singapore. Dr. Ping Lim is the principal investigator of two large-scale projects on 3D gaming and digital literacies in schools. He also works closely with schools nationally and internationally (Inter-American Development Bank, UNESCO and Commonwealth of Learning) in the integration of technologies. He has published widely internationally in different areas of ICT in education, namely designing ICT-mediated learning environments, and emerging technologies and systemic processes to support schools in integrating ICT.

Makoto Sasaki (Aichi Gakuin University, Nagoya) has been central in the network of linguists in Japan (JASFL) who have developed functional approaches to language in education and in registers of technology and artificial intelligence. Having studied first with Fred C. Peng at I.C.U. in Tokyo, Makoto's more recent work has been in the applications of the functional linguistics of M.A.K. Halliday. He has also written materials for computing in classrooms, as well as a stylistic study of transitivity in different translations of The Tale of Genji.

Karunamay Subuddhi is an Associate Professor in the Department of Humanities and Social Sciences, Indian Institute of Technology, Mumbai, India. He has worked elsewhere in other leading postgraduate technology institute in India such as in School of Planning, Centre for Environmental Planning and Technology (CEPT) as a faculty in sociology and worked in number of research projects sponsored by World Bank and UNICEF and Government of India on various programs relating to education, health care delivery in rural areas, Command Area Development involving small, medium, and large-scale irrigation projects. He has published papers in leading national and international journal on issues relating to ICT, science and technology for rural development, and on environmental issues.

Myint Swe Khine (Nanyang Technological University, Singapore) is an Associate Professor in Learning Sciences and Technologies in the Centre of Research in Pedagogy and Practice at Nanyang Technological University, Singapore. He teaches instructional technology, pedagogy, and education research methods courses in teacher education programs and has published widely on these topics in international journals.

Joseph Zajda holds BA (Hons), MA, M.Ed. and Ph.D. from Monash University. He coordinated M.Ed. programs, the School of Education, Australian Catholic University for the February 2007–June 2008 period (Melbourne Campus), and teaches core courses, including: Development and Learning (EDFD446), EDFD528, Studies of Society & Environment (EDSS322) and Humanities & SOSE Curriculum (EDSS503). In 2003 he received the Vice-Chancellor's Award for *Excellence in*

Teaching, Australian Catholic University. He was chair/co-chair of the Publications Standing Committee of the World Council of Comparative and Education Societies (WCCES) for the 2006–2008 period. He has written and edited 24 books and over 100 book chapters and articles in the areas of education policy, curriculum and education reforms, social justice, and decentralization and privatization in education. His recent monographs and edited books include: *Decentralisation and Privatisation in Education* (Springer, 2006), *Education and Social Justice* (Springer, 2006), *Schooling the New Russians* (James Nicholas Publishers, 2006), *Society and Environment*, and *Curriculum, Culture and Teaching* (James Nicholas Publishers, 2006), *Education and Social Inequality in the Global Culture* (Springer, 2008), *Comparative and Global Pedagogies: Equity, Access and Democracy in Education* (Springer, 2008), *Nation-Building, Identity and Citizenship Education: Cross-cultural Perspectives* (Springer, 2008). He is editor of the *International Handbook of Globalisation, Education and Policy Research* (Springer, 2005). He is also the editor of the 12-volume book series *Globalisation, and Comparative Education* (Springer, 2008).

Chapter 1
Comparative Information Technology: Languages, Societies and the Internet

Joseph Zajda and Donna Gibbs

1.1 Information Technologies, Virtual Identities and Global Learning

As far back as the time of the penning of *The Communist Manifesto* by Marx and Engels, published in 1848, the view that globalisation would bring with it a fundamental change in human affairs was being voiced.[1] At the beginning of the twenty-first century confirmation of this remarkable prophecy is everywhere apparent in the political, economic, and social life of human societies. Recently, McLaren and Farahmandpur (2005) have applied relevant dimensions of Marxist and critical theory in their critique of forces of globalisation (McLaren & Farahmandpur, 2005). One of the most important engines of the evolving phenomenon of globalisation has been the rapid development of information and communications technologies (ICTs). Our lives have been changed by this in manifold ways and the implications for education are enormous. The ICTs have transformed the linguistic, cognitive and visual dimensions of human communication, as well as ideas on what particular attributes define social identity in the global culture (see Gibbs & Krause, 2007).

Globalisation as a new dimension of political economy and culture has depended on a fusion of capitalism and advanced technologies, leading to 'technodeterminism' (Zajda, 2008), and what Kellner (1991) has called 'techno-capital' (see also Langman & Morris, 2007). Sassen (1998) and Castells (2001) have argued that one of the essential moments of globalisation consists of vast flows of electronic information. The rapid and ubiquitous proliferation of ICT has resulted in profound changes in society and culture, especially those affecting social identity (Morris & Langman,

[1] For a discussion of the history of this idea, see, for example, Friedman, Thomas, L. (2005). The World is Flat: A Brief History of the Twenty-First Century. New York: Farrar, Straus & Giroux.

J. Zajda
Australian Catholic University, Melbourne

D. Gibbs
Macquarie University

J. Zajda and D. Gibbs (eds.), *Comparative Information Technology*,
DOI: 10.1007/978-1-4020-9426-2_1, © Springer Science+Bussiness Media B.V. 2009

2005; Gibbs & Krause, 2007; Zajda, 2008). Castells (2001) notes that the Internet facilitates the structured aspects of the network society. Yet, Antikainen (2005) argues that in a network society the power and influence of traditional political institutions are weakened (Antikainen, 2005, p. 53).

The modern notion of globalisation is rife with unresolved tensions and ambiguities. Globalisation is not an easy term to define. There are numerous competing and contested definitions of globalisation. The problem lies not so much in defining globalisation, but rather in understanding and critiquing its intended and unintended consequences on nation-states and individuals around the world. Definitions of globalisation have varied from one author to another. Some have described it as a process, while others, a condition, a system, a force or an age. In most cases, scholars bring their own critical approach to the intersection of globalisation and their particular discipline and methodology (Zajda et al., 2008). Globalisation can be viewed as having the beneficial effects of breaking down national, geographic frontiers and facilitating processes of international trade. But it can also be seen as having the undesirable effects of increasing the potential of large multinational corporations to carry out unscrupulous exploitation of markets and of cheap sources of labour – an extension of the kind of capitalistic exploitation that Marx and Engels were attacking.

1.2 ICTs and Hegemony

One of the unresolved moral and political dilemmas is the contested relationship between technology, power and hegemony. ICT, as a manifestation of the post-industrial society, global economy, the knowledge revolution and the information age, has been accepted, uncritically, as a dominant ideology of progress, development and technological change. Perceiving technology as 'good' in itself, as the 'right thing' to do, is problematic. For one, we tend to accept implicitly the natural dominance of technological revolution, without critiquing the hegemony of technology. Such hegemony is based on power, control and domination. It also reinforces socio-economic divisions in society, based on an unequal distribution of socially valued commodities such as income, education and cultural capital.

Using a critical theory approach, one could argue that the hegemonic dimension of technology creates a new divide based on technologically rich and technologically poor nations, where technology is used to evaluate nations and their economic progress and well-being. Some scholars have argued that the Internet has provided, with its modes of virtual realms, 'moments of hegemonic process' that contribute to alienation and social fragmentation. Langman and Morris (2007) suggest that the problematics and ideological complexities, surrounding dominant discourses of social identity, can be seen in 'various debates over hegemony, resistance, social fragmentation, identity politics, or youth cultures' (Langman & Morris, 2007, pp. 10–11). Here, Marx's concepts of *alienation* and *reification* are particularly relevant to contemporary discourses of social identity. Langman and Morris (2007) also examine an ambivalent nexus between the Internet, identity and commodification:

> Moreover, insofar as consumer based identities are dependent on commodities and commodified forms of selfhood, we can see how reification has moved from the production of commodities to the realms of identity giving rise to new postmodern articulations of alienation...in a globalized world, linked through the Internet, those identity formations that sustain contemporary hegemony, do so at the cost of alienated subjectivities. (Langman & Morris, 2007, p. 11)

As Langman and Morris (2007) explain, Gramsci (1971) understood how the power of collective rituals, sustained hegemony, namely the ideological control of culture to frame consciousness in power of particular historic blocs to make their rule, seem normal:

> For Gramsci, structures of domination depended less on force than the control of cultural understandings to produce "spontaneous assent" to a particular historic bloc, eg the cadres of economic, political and cultural power and control. Thus as Gramsci (1971) understood, hegemony depends on the construction and mediation of identities that accept the legitimacy of social arrangements that sustain certain historic blocs. This is as true today as it was several millennia ago.

Similarly, Castells (1996) claimed that Internet-mediated identities serve to legitimate social identities through the various forms of Net-mediated events of today.

In the sphere of education, technological innovations bring with them powerfully influential – even transformative – opportunities for changing educational practice. They enable new ways of thinking and behaving, of acquiring, passing on, sharing, and storing knowledge. By their very nature ICTs have the potential to link people together, creating new communities across boundaries of time and space, boundaries that in the past would have prevented this kind of communication and collaboration. This was already shown by Poster (2001), where the Internet is perceived to be both a tool and a cyber community. An example of this is cyberactivism and social movement networks, which have developed through the Net (Morris & Langman, 2005; Gibbs & Krause, 2007). Furthermore, the Internet has made once private information available to a greater number of individuals around the world. Yet, as Wong (2006) points out in her discussion of the cyberself, the tag 'world wide' when referring to the web is still unwarranted, and English, if not American English, remains the dominant language. Those without access to technologies are, of course, effectively excluded and marginalised, a matter of increasing concern for educators.

1.2.1 The Net Identities and the Virtual Communities of Cyberspace

We could extend Castells' model of identity and networks, as Langman and Morris (2007) have done it, to examine the problematics of identity, as refracted 'through some of the cultural moments of globalisation, particularly the emergence of cyberspace' (Castells, 2000; Langman & Morris, 2007). Langman and Morris (2007) are questioning whether social identities articulated on the Net in fact are meaningful, central and salient to the individual in the information society:

> Do some users fashion a variety of virtual identities with voices disconnected from their real gender/age/status, etc. … Castells (2001) suggests that many of these virtual identities are embraced by teen-agers exploring their own identities—a typical activity for people of that age. Further, in that online net use surveys find that the most common use of the net is email. (Langman & Morris, 2007, p. 1)

One could argue, using a post-structuralist paradigm, that the post-modern subject, the 'saturated self' (Gergen, 1991), is located in a number of often contradictory subject positions (Langman & Morris, 2007, p. 3). The Net may well be able to manufacture a multiplicity of identities, some contradictory to each other, some taking place primarily in the virtual communities of cyberspace (Turkle, 1995). Recent research in the ICTs increasingly examine culture, intercultural communication and communities in cyberspace (Zajda, 2007). Annette Wong's work on cyberself, where she analyses the nexus between social identity, language and stylisation on the Internet, is such an example (Wong, 2006). Internet technology and the vast cyberspace image production are some technological changes which affect the processes of cultural identity formation, and the important role of language and stylisation. The Internet has given rise to 'default identities' and 'bodilessness' (Gibbs & Krause, 2007, p. 7). Using their analysis of cyberpunk communities and hacker subcultures, Gibbs and Krause argue that while the Internet facilitates interaction and connection 'across previously immutable barriers of time, space, language and ethnicity, these pathways are not always as smooth and unimpeded as they may seem' (Gibbs & Krause, 2007, p. 7).

A major problem for educators that has emerged in the wake of these developments is that most of the technology they employ in their teaching and learning has been designed by technicians and others with very little contribution from the educational community. All too often the Giant of Technology goes striding forward, leaving behind it the kowtowing figure of Education clinging bravely to its coat-tails, determined to stay in the race. This situation must be altered so that educational principles and philosophies, rather than new technologies, can shape the design and development of learning technologies and systems. Systems that meet global standards are interoperable with other systems, and yet encourage pedagogical richness need to be developed in consultation with educators if there is to be a sea change in our learning futures (Gibbs & Gosper, 2006). Ways in which educators might solve some of the problems that have arisen from this upside-down world order provide an important thematic concern in this volume.

Other issues of concern that recur across the chapters of this book include how the various digital divides ('haves' and 'have nots'; 'information rich' and 'information poor', 'digital natives' and 'digital immigrants' and so on) created by technologies and globalisation can be minimised; how understandings of cultural difference can be taken more fully into account in a wired world; what policies are appropriate and adequate for educators operating within a globalised community; how technologies can be used to improve teaching, and what needs to happen to make this a sustainable and effective option; what kind of leadership and management works best in this rapidly changing arena; how funding priorities can be identified and ordered; and how we as a society need to keep abreast of, and critically responsive to, the changes we are making, and that in turn are making us.

1.2.2 The Digital Divide Pedagogical Issue

Recent OECD and UNESCO studies show that those without access to ICTs and without ICT skills are less and less capable of participating in the knowledge-based society and may experience a new inequality of the *digital divide* kind (UNESCO, 2004; Zajda, 2005). The highest percentage of households possessing a PC was in Denmark (63%), the USA and Australia were almost equal with 50%, and Italy was 20%. The access to Internet was 46% for White and 23% for African-American households in August 2000, and as few as 3% of poorer households were on line, compared with 48% of the more affluent households (OECD, 2001, *Education Policy Analysis*, p. 86).

Some 400 million people use the Internet, which represents only '7 per cent of the world's population' (UNESCO, 2004, p. 8). One of the conclusions drawn is that education policies are not sufficient to address the equity issue, and that 'social inequalities existing outside the education system contribute to educational inequalities in terms of access, opportunity, process and outcomes' (p. 92). Despite the impressive expansion of participation in education, a relatively large part of the population, especially people from low-income families, remains excluded from access to education and ICTs (Zajda, 2005, 2008). Education policies to promote equal learning opportunities for all 'can therefore hardly be seen as successful' (OECD, 2001, *Education Policy Analysis*, p. 92).

The digital divide is particularly applicable to China, India, Pakistan and the Philippines, to name a few. For instance in the Philippines, much of the country lacks even the most basic technological infrastructure to implement ICT-based pedagogy. Without electricity, there is little that can be done to power the technology. In some counties, students are forced to go to Internet cafés to complete their homework (Mandinach, 2007, p. 59).

E-learning, the use of electronic means to facilitate teaching and learning, is a significant new field in education and is the subject of several chapters in this volume. E-learning as an adjunct to the classroom, as part of a blended learning programme, or as a sole means of transmitting education is currently being employed in schools and tertiary institutions in most parts of the world. The individual student in a classroom using the Internet to find information, and groups of students from around the world learning together in a virtual environment, are all engaged in e-learning. Initially many institutions saw e-learning as a time and money saver that would transform the way education was delivered, banishing physical classrooms and creating a learning space without boundaries. Experience has changed this view to some extent: experiments in e-learning have proved both demanding and costly and it is now clear that if educators are to realise its full potential, they have much to learn about this new environment: the role of teacher and student changes dramatically; the design and way software is chosen for the delivery of learning radically affects the nature of the learning that takes place; and the pedagogies that are required in an electronic environment are quite different from those that work successfully in the classroom.

Tool innovations are seen as simultaneously material (matter has to be crafted), biological (they require and result from the faculties of an organism), social (they happen in group environments, and are thereby incrementally modified, or improved) and semiotic (they are carried, as meaning bearing behaviour, to other groups and generations). The interest and drama of tools in the twentieth and twenty-first centuries result from the fact that they offer a new level of mental or abstract tools. Computers, for example, now offer an extension of the range of quality of mental activities (not just the multiplication of lower-level tasks); a new division of labour between the human knowing subject and the externalised repositories of knowledge (in data bases and libraries); and a heightened sense that interlocking tools of information might have a life of their own, with human beings unable to predict the emergent properties of the systems that they have set in train.

The ICTs have facilitated the development of new dimensions of digital literacy, such as blogging and SMS messaging. In this sense, cyberlanguage continues to evolve by 'borrowing and adapting familiar words, coining new expressions, and embracing particular styles' (Gibbs & Krause, 2006, p. 2). Lengel (2008) notes that despite the fact that we live in the information-rich and Digital Society, information technology is not always integrated effectively in schools, and that traditional teaching techniques and styles are employed:

> Despite various attempts that have been made to integrate technology and new educational reforms into our nation's schools, Warschauer (2006) argues that American high schools are "still organized much as they were a century ago – students sitting quietly in rows and listening to teachers lecture in 50-minute periods". (Lengel 2008, p. ix)

More importantly, even when technology is being used, many students continue to remain passive learners. Recent research has revealed, according to Lengel (2008), that technology is frequently underused, poorly integrated into classrooms and seldom impacts or alters teachers' regular teaching practice (Cuban, 2001; Hennessey et al., 2005). Furthermore, Wallace (2004) demonstrates that educational studies have been 'slow to include research on using technology in classrooms in service of teaching subject matter' (Wallace, 2004, p. 449).

This book is devoted to study of the impact information technology has made on learning in the global context. In this opening chapter, Donna Gibbs (Macquarie University) and Joseph Zajda (Australian Catholic University) discuss emerging trends in the ICTs globally and their impact on digital literacy, identities and classroom pedagogies.

In 'Abstract Tools and Technologies of Learning: An Evolving Partnership', David Butt (Macquarie University, Sydney), Ichiro Kobayashi (Ochanomizu University, Tokyo) and Makoto Sasaki (Aichi Gakuin University, Nagoya) journey to the very heart of how technological developments are transforming social, educational and cultural practices. They discuss the human use of tools in an evolutionary context and argue that tool innovations are hard-won cultural events, usually involving felicitous conditions.

In 'E-Learning in Schools: Making Successful Connections', Jennifer Fergusson, Donna Gibbs, Maree Gosper and Robyn Philip (Macquarie University) examine some twenty-first century examples of online projects developed through collaborations between technical support staff and academic staff from a range of centres and disciplines at an Australian University; technical and teaching staff from schools in New South Wales; and research staff from organisations such as the Australian Centre for Astrobiology (ACA), National Aeronautics and Space Administration (NASA) in America, and the Centre for Astronomy and Science Education (CASE) at the University of Glamorgan. Through analysing the nature and effectiveness of four very different projects that link students together across traditional classroom boundaries, the authors are able to identify a timely and detailed list of suggestions about what needs to be taken into account if collaboration through e-learning is to work effectively.

Patrick McAndrew (The Open University, Milton Keynes, UK) turns his attention to the area of higher education and discusses emergent trends in methods being used to develop and deliver e-learning programmes for a global market. In 'What Is Needed for Global E-Learning in Higher Education' he throws light on factors that have contributed to the failure of several global e-learning programmes. Armed with these insights, he analyses design approaches that draw on learning objects, learning design and learning patterns currently being used to produce more flexible online courses. He argues that at this early stage of the evolution of e-learning there are no obvious solutions and no easy recipe for success, but that building knowledge of developments and the trends and methods that show promise in this area, and learning about innovative practices undertaken by institutions that have already experimented in this field, is a way forward. His detailed and perceptive account of up-to-date examples of ways to approach online teaching and learning provides encouragement and wise advice for those reflecting upon current practices or implementing the delivery of new global e-learning programmes.

The mobile learning practices made possible through technologies are explored by Gerard Goggin (University of Queensland) in his chapter 'Mobile Learning: The Significance of New Mobile and Wireless Communications Technologies for Education'. Goggin describes the phenomenal diffusion of mobiles around the world, including in many developing countries, and the directions now being taken with the convergence between mobiles, the Internet and computing. What he finds striking about this pervasive and far-reaching new mode of ICTs is the comparative lack of attention being accorded to its potential for education. In surveying the use of mobile phones in educational practices and institutions across a number of countries, especially Australia, Hong Kong, the USA and the Nordic countries, he finds that issues of control and regulation have tended to overshadow consideration of their possible educational uses or benefits. He argues that the censorious tone that imbues discourses surrounding the use of mobile phones needs to be seen in the larger context of moral panics about mobiles (or 'mobile panics'), which like other classic moral panics and 'folk devils' appear to be closely associated with the regulation of subcultural groups by more dominant groups. Against this background Goggin elucidates what is distinctive about mobile learning and identifies some of the major issues educational theorists and practitioners will need to pursue if their use is to be fruitfully integrated into education.

A different kind of collaboration enabled by ICTs is that between schools in the Asia Pacific region with their local and wider communities. Cher Ping Lim and Mykint Swe Khine (Nanyang Technological University, Singapore) in 'Connecting Schools to Their Communities: The South-East Asian Experience' describe examples from schools in Indonesia, Malaysia, Singapore and Thailand of positive responses to, and enthusiastic uptake of, the use of ICTs to improve home/school and school/communities interaction. They explore the nature of the education systems in each of these countries and examine how technology is being used to establish beneficial linkages between its stakeholders and the wider world. The tangible benefits they observe from these initiatives include increased improvements in home/school connections and parental involvement; stronger support and achievement from parents and communities where programmes require changed attitudes; and a strengthening of students' personal and social development.

José Luis Rodríguez Illera (Universidad de Barcelona) and Mónica Kaechele (Universidad Católica de Temuco), in 'Digital Literacy and Activity Systems in Adolescents', examine the schooling and digital literacy of young adolescents, whose technological practices represent a challenge for schools today. They examine the concept of digital literacy as a social practice and present the results of an empirical study conducted in two distinct contexts of practice: a secondary school and a *locutorio* (telephone/Internet café). They conclude that digital literacy in the global culture and the information age, and knowledge society understood as a cultural practice, encourages the development of distinct skills according to the social contexts in which young people are immersed using technology. The authors suggest that schools not only need to court more technology, but more particularly they need to understand learning and pedagogies in a different way, so that information technology is integrated within the system, in order to facilitate the development of the necessary digital literacy skills.

In 'Digital Literacy and Using Online Discussions: Reflections from Teaching Large Cohorts in Teacher Education', Anne Scott and Josephine Ryan, Australian Catholic University, Melbourne Campus, analyse their research findings from 6 years' use of online discussions as an integral component of the pedagogical design in a compulsory literacy education unit undertaken by approximately 200 primary pre-service teachers during 2002–2007. The authors discuss their findings in terms of the prerequisites needed to set up online discussions with a large cohort of participants and present both positive and negative outcomes of their experiences. The authors believe that given our role as educators in the twenty-first century, when our lifestyles often depend on the efficient use of ICT, it is important that we continue to seek ways to prepare prospective teachers for teaching digital literacy in the digital age.

In 'Development of IT-Infrastructure for Rural Connectivity: A Pro-poor Approach to E-Governance for Rural Development in India', Karunamay Subuddhi (Indian Institute of Technology, Bombay: Mumbai) suggests that the ICT and web technologies have made possible the creation of a network society establishing 'rural peoples' right to connectivity and enhancing their abilities to participate more actively and effectively in economic, social and political activities. The author argues that ICT and digital literacy have become an effective tool for rural development in India and elsewhere in the developing world.

As globalisation impacts on educational communities around the world, it is becoming increasingly important to understand and appreciate the differences and similarities among countries as they continue to implement ICT solutions to their pressing digital literacy needs and pedagogical applications. In 'Context Is Everything: An International Perspective of, and Its Challenges to, Research and the Evaluation of Educational Technology', Ellen B. Mandinach (The CNA Corporation) reviews the international technology literature and describes a methodology based on the principles of systems thinking as a potential way to gain a richer contextual understanding of the complex process of implementing technology in educational settings.

The increasingly rapid development and ubiquitous proliferation of information and communication technologies, under the sign of globalisation, are forcing rapid social, cultural and technological changes in education and society. A new digital divide between the 'info-rich' and 'info-poor' societies has now been added to the tradition social stratification divide between the 'haves' and the 'have-nots' (McIntosh, 2005, p. 3). Thus, from the equality of access and social justice perspectives, increasing access to ICTs should be a key factor in any quality education reforms, and authentic and effective global pedagogy strategies for the future.

References

Antikainen, A. (2005). Transformation of a Nordic Leaning Society: The Case of Finland. *Information, Technology, Education and Society*, 6(2), 47–63.

Castells, M. (2000). *The Rise of the Network Society*. Malden, MA: Blackwell.

Castells, M. (2001). *The Internet Galaxy: Reflections on the Internet, Business and Society*. Oxford: Oxford University Press.

Cuban, G. (2001). *Oversold & Underused: Computers in the Classroom*. Cambridge, MA: Harvard University Press.

Gibbs, D. & Krause, K.-L. (2006) (Eds.). Cyberlines: Languages and Culture of the Internet. Melbourne: James Nicholas Publishers.

Gibbs, D. & Krause, K.-L. (2007) (Eds.). Cyberlines 2.0: Languages and Culture of the Internet. Melbourne: James Nicholas Publishers.

Gibbs, D., Gosper, M. (2006). The Upside-Down-World of E-learning. *Journal of Learning Design*, 1(2), 46–54.

Gramsci, A. (1971). *Prison Notebooks*. New York: International Publishers.

Hennessy, S., Ruthven, K., Brindley, S. (2005). Teacher perspectives on integrating ICT into subject teaching: Commitment, Constraints, Caution and Change. *Journal of Curriculum Studies*, 37(2), 155–192.

Langman, L. Morris, D. (2002). The Net and the Self: Cyberactive Versus Ludic Identities. *Information, Technology, Education and Society*, 3(1&2), 23–46.

Langman, L. Morris, D. (2005). Networks of Dissent: A Typology of Social Movement in a Global Age. *Information, Technology, Education and Society*, 6(2), 5–25.

Langman, L. & Morris, D. (2007). Globalization, Cyberspace and Identity. Unpublished paper.

Lengel, L. (2008). Adolescent Literacy and Online Discussion: Enhancing Learning Opportunities in the English Classroom. Unpublished paper.

Love, K. Isles, M. (2006). 'Welcome to the online discussion group': Towards a diagnostic framework for teachers. *Australian Journal of Language and Literacy*, 29(3), 210–225.

McIntosh, C. & Varoglu, Z. (Eds.) (2005). Perspectives on Distance Education: Lifelong Learning & Distance Higher Education. Paris: UNESCO.

McLaren, P. Farahmandpur, R. (2005). *Teaching Against Global Capitalism and the New Imperialism*. Lanham: Rowman & Littlefield.
Sassen, S. (1998). *Globalization and its Discontents: Essays on the New Mobility of People and Money*. New York: New Press.
UNESCO (2004). Higher Education in a Globalized Society. UNESCO Education Position Paper. Paris: UNESCO.
Vess, D.L. (2005). Asynchronous Discussion and Communication Patterns in Online and Hybrid History Courses. *Communication Education*, 54(4), 355–364.
Turkle, S. (1995). *Life on the Screen*. New York: Simon & Schuster.
Wallace, R. (2004). A Framework for Understanding Teaching With the Internet. *American Educational Research Journal*, 41(2), 447–488.
Warchauer, M. (2006). *Laptops and Literacy: Learning in the Wireless Classroom*. New York: Teachers College Record.
Wong, A. (2007). *Cyberself: Identity, Language and Stylisation on the Internet*. In D. Gibbs & K. Krause (Eds.), Cyberlines 2.0: Languages and Cultures of the Internet. Melbourne : James Nicholas Publishers.
Zajda, J. (2005) (Ed.). The International Handbook of Globalisation and Education Policy Research. Dordrecht: Springer.
Zajda, J. (2008). Technodeterminism. In G. McCulloch & D. Crook (Eds), The International Encyclopedia of Education. London: Routledge.
Zajda, J., Biraimah, B. & Gaudelli, W. (2008a). (Eds.). *Education and Social Inequality in the Global Culture*. Dordrecht: Springer.
Zajda, J., Davies, L. & Majhanovich, S. (2008b) (Eds.). *Comparative and Global Pedagogies: Equity, Access and Democracy in Education*. Dordrecht: Springer

Chapter 2
Abstract Tools and Technologies of Learning: An Evolving Partnership

David Butt, Ichiro Kobayashi, and Makoto Sasaki

2.1 Tools, Mental Tools, and Teaching Tools

This discussion begins by placing the human use of tools in an evolutionary context. This helps in understanding the many ways educationists need to think about the meaning of 'tools' and of 'technology', especially in relation to a drift towards globalised delivery of training and knowledge. For, while it is a straightforward step to think of the material form of tools – from the Olduvai Gorge technology of 2 million years ago to the robotic tools of contemporary medicine – the essence of a tool is the goal-directed thought behind the material form. Tools imply goals, and staging or planning. And planning implies group-based semiotic behaviour. This is to say, to be mindful of tools (so as to be able to make them), humans have needed a social network and the meaningful behaviour of that group.

In fact, human language is itself the primary human tool in that it enables other forms of tool use; and it is language that provides the medium within which innovation (whether fortuitous or by human design) can be retained and refined, thereby overcoming the need for continuous reinvention. In many registers of technology, language is commonly recruited to create heuristic tools – abstract ideas that take on a role as placeholders in elaborate webs of calculation and concept. Such abstract tools may never really 'materialise'. Think here of ideas like irrational numbers, infinitesimals in calculus, the quark in physics (a word originally lifted from James Joyce by the physicist Murray Gell-Mann) and 'black holes' (which were predicted by theory decades before any possible instances were isolated).

'Tool', then, is a complex notion. And those who have seen most clearly the complexity of its multiple meanings include Lev Vygotsky (1895–1933) and Richard Gregory. Both these very different scholars emphasised the role of mental

D. Butt
Macquarie University, Sydney

I. Kobayashi
Ochanomizu University, Tokyo

M. Sasaki
Aichi Gakuin University, Nagoya

J. Zajda and D. Gibbs (eds.), *Comparative Information Technology*,
DOI: 10.1007/978-1-4020-9426-2_2, © Springer Science+Bussiness Media B.V. 2009

tools and the symbiotic character of human behaviour, namely, that humans are typically extending their potential through the employment of a scaffolding of props and devices (Vygotsky, 1978, Ch 1; Gregory, 1984, Ch 2). Vygotsky also proposed a further distinction, a notion of tools which applies specifically to the practice of teaching. Vygotsky emphasised the role of 'pedagogic tools' in utilising the zone of proximal development – the area of potential between what a student could achieve with relevant support (from teacher and tools of culture) and what the same child might achieve independent of such pedagogic scaffolding. This zone, according to Vygotsky, varies independently of IQ or other measures of performance (see the discussion below in Section 2.8).

Teachers employ 'pedagogic tools' to explain the legacy of the culture in which they work. The idea of pedagogic tools is central to the argument and illustrations of this discussion: teachers develop their professional repertoire of explanatory tools, which is pedagogically efficacious in their field. Teachers are typically under greatest pressure to produce or adapt such tools when they are explaining the core ideas (or mental tools) of the given field of knowledge, or when the channels for delivering the curriculum undergo dramatic change (as is the case under the competitive globalisation of would-be 'knowledge-based economies'). Vygotsky's mental tools were part of a general account of the development of higher mental functions. The metaphors of scaffolding through mental tools were also clear in the earlier work of Nietzsche (1874, as discussed in Vaihinger, 1925, p. 345, and in Butt, 1989 [1985], pp. 81–83), who regarded the central concepts of human cultures as tools or 'useful fictions' (in the sense that 'points' or 'parallel lines' are constructions of our minds rather than observed entities).

The habit of using 'tool' in referring to a manual implement obscures the fact that the majority of crucial tools are actually mental or abstract tools. The 'information era' and the 'digital age' are terms that correct the oversight, but which, in turn, understate the continuous expansion of knowledge over the last 2,500 years (Lloyd, 1999 [1979]). This expansion has been dramatic in the way that cultures have lent structure to the thinking and problem solving of their individual members. Teachers have been the mediators of this evolutionary expansion and diversification. Their institutional practices have been developed and chronicled, for example, in traditions of rhetoric, mathematics, religion, statecraft and practices involving measurement.

A critical case of such chronicling concerns the other term of immediate relevance: technology. The word *techne* in Classical Greek turns up across a broad spectrum of situations where it would be rendered today in English as 'skill' or 'craft' or 'training', and was therefore distinct from *episteme*, which referred to a more general 'understanding'. The word was central to perhaps the first titanic debate in the West on the nature of 'mother tongue' teaching: when Socrates challenged leading sophists to explain what techne their students might expect to have mastered when they have completed and paid for their classes. Socrates used the comparison of sending a young man to work with a shipwright (for an extended investigation of this still 'current' debate, see Roochnik, 1996).

'Technology', like the word 'tool', has had to do service on many fronts, ranging from material to mental phenomena. Like 'tool', within the domain of mental experience, 'technology' is used to refer to both the practice that must be mastered and the pedagogical techniques for passing on that mastery.

This chapter focuses on the cultural implications and the linguistic details of pedagogic techniques for explaining mental tools. It focuses on the teacher's tools for expounding the culture's abstract tools. Sections 2.2, 2.3 and 2.4 highlight different aspects of the evolutionary and historical contexts of tool use. Sections 2.5, 2.6 and 2.7 investigate specific instances of teacher explanatory technique in relation to multi-dimensional concepts – life cycles, the solar system, representing three dimensions on two (in maps or art), graphing change, government and weather systems on the scale of El Niño. Section 2.8 reviews the findings and implications of the enquiry. Section 2.9 uses contemporary Japan as a basis for interrogating current patterns of tool use, including the social perturbations created by technological change.

The discussion offers one kind of context for other papers in this volume, each of which addresses fundamental issues of change in the media, organisation, and interpersonal proximities by which knowledge is carried from teacher to taught.

2.2 From *Homo Habilis* to Contemporary Teaching

The human use of tools has been criterial in our theories of what separates humans from other species and, indeed, what in our activities should be passed on through culture, especially in the training of children. When the work of Raymond Dart and the Leakey family supported the view that hominids originated in Africa, the first binomial containing 'homo' was proposed: *homo habilis* – the 'handy man' or 'tool maker'. The notion of 'tool' is not, however, a straightforward category with defined boundaries and an unequivocal place in human affairs. The complexities are brought into focus when we reflect on the most crucial tool devised in evolution, namely, language. Language is our 'second nature'. As Monod, the great biologist, expressed the relation between this tool and humans: 'It is language which created humans rather than humans language' (cited in Jakobson, 1973, p. 57). As tools direct changes in human activities, they direct the drift of evolution; they are not merely the spin-off of pre-existing cognitive organs. Following Monod also, we need to investigate how our most fundamental tool continues to shape our 'evolving nature' and how this relationship between humans, symbolic processes and tools (material and mental) is mediated by the talk of the group most responsible for the continuities of tool use in a culture, namely, professional teachers.

This discussion, therefore, briefly sketches the current social and educational role of tools, with a special emphasis on what may be distinctive today about the experience of technology for children, parents, and teachers. The argument includes the findings of earlier work – an Australian Research Council project conducted by Butt, Cloran and Hasan in 1990–1992: The Development of Abstract Tools through Classroom Talk. The project focused on teachers' explanations of culturally critical abstractions: the core ideas that provide the basis of mental tools (like maps, models, mathematical predictions, generic forms and machines). The present discussion reviews the findings and implications of the earlier study in order to ask how the classroom talk of teachers may need to be re-evaluated under the conditions of the current decade, at the beginning of a new century of technological intensification.

In data drawn from the 1990–1992 study, the textual patterns employed by the teachers did not correspond simply with any of the highly visible ‘units’ of either theoretical or folk linguistics. Rather, they were remarkable patterns of unremarkable patterns, or of patterns which have been changing in their probabilities across many registers of English, as English has been changing to manage complexities of experience that encompass phenomena (such as ‘genes’ and ‘black holes’) that were previously outside the spectrum of direct human apprehension.

Example 1 displays just such a pattern – in this case, one that falls close to what was a canonical form for teachers. The summarising, double-embedded equation (in clauses 316–318) is a grammatical motif often employed at the outset and/or as the concluding QED in the chain of the teacher’s reasoning. Along with this linguistic equation, there is the balancing of qualifiers in the interrupting clauses, < < ... > >, and the revising elaborations (clause 316.1.2 appears to be a second go at 316.1.1, with the teacher redesigning the *agentless passive* form into an *explicit active* one).

Example 1 (Speaker: Teacher)

<table>
<tr><td>316</td><td>316.1</td><td>[[Well what happens</td></tr>
<tr><td></td><td>316.1.1</td><td>[[... when the eggs are laid</td></tr>
<tr><td></td><td>316.1.2</td><td>||when the mosquito lays the eggs ...]]]] (IS)..</td></tr>
<tr><td></td><td>316.2</td><td>[[the eggs start to develop, <<ok>></td></tr>
<tr><td></td><td>316.3</td><td>||and they actually – the little mosquito, <<if you want to call it that>>, inside the egg starts to eat the shell of the egg.]]</td></tr>
<tr><td>317</td><td></td><td><<ok>></td></tr>
<tr><td>318</td><td></td><td><<if you want to call it that>></td></tr>
<tr><td>319</td><td></td><td>Now, << as it eats >> it grows, gets bigger.||</td></tr>
<tr><td>320</td><td></td><td><<as it eats>>||</td></tr>
<tr><td>321</td><td></td><td>It then goes into life of a wiggler||</td></tr>
<tr><td>322</td><td></td><td>which is the next ... part of the cycle.||</td></tr>
<tr><td>323</td><td></td><td>Like we start off as little babies||</td></tr>
<tr><td>324</td><td></td><td>and we get to your age now||</td></tr>
<tr><td>325</td><td></td><td>then eventually you get to my old decrepit age,||</td></tr>
<tr><td>326</td><td></td><td>Ok?||,</td></tr>
<tr><td>327</td><td></td><td>So you get older.||</td></tr>
<tr><td>328</td><td></td><td>So the little mosquito changes into a larva,||</td></tr>
<tr><td>329</td><td></td><td>From the larva it goes into the next stage||</td></tr>
<tr><td>330</td><td></td><td>which is a pupa,||</td></tr>
<tr><td>331</td><td></td><td>Like baby, then you have .. um .. child ||</td></tr>
<tr><td>332</td><td></td><td>The pupa’s like a teenager ||</td></tr>
<tr><td>333</td><td></td><td>which you people are nearly getting to ||</td></tr>
<tr><td>334</td><td></td><td>and then you get to adults, like myself, ||</td></tr>
<tr><td>335</td><td></td><td>Ok?||</td></tr>
<tr><td>336</td><td></td><td>So they have a similar cycle of young to children, teenagers, and adults. ||</td></tr>
<tr><td>337</td><td></td><td>And everything does all that,||</td></tr>
<tr><td>338</td><td></td><td>even plants go through that ||</td></tr>
<tr><td>339</td><td></td><td>You have the seed, ||</td></tr>
<tr><td>340</td><td></td><td>then you have the small ... seedlings small plant,||</td></tr>
<tr><td>341</td><td></td><td>then you have a maturing plant ||</td></tr>
</table>

(continued)

Example 1 (continued)

342 then you're going to say a mature plant ||
343 which could be a tree,||
344 Ok?||
345 So it's grows up through those stages. ||
346 Right, so we've come to a conclusion [[that all animals go through a life cycle.]]

Key: Each numbered line is a main clause or message; || *= clause boundary; [[...]] = embedded clause (indicated in the numbering by .1, .1.1, etc.) ; << ... >> = interrupting clause*

Such rhetorical choreography is a hallmark of the experience and professional skill of teachers. It is, therefore, important that the structures and their linguistic patterns are brought out of the implicit background of classrooms and recognised for their fundamental role in the cognitive transformation of students. While these verbal ensembles are themselves crucial in the liminal role of teachers – namely, in their role of bringing people into the 'mysteries' of our community – they do also involve a steep semantic climb for most children. To significant groups of students, the semantic challenge is too forbidding and these particular rhetorical strategies may never become 'second nature' to them in their transactions, whether at school or later at work (Bernstein, 1996, pp. 91–133; Hasan & Cloran, 1990; Hasan, 1996, pp. 165ff; Williams, 2001). For this reason too, our explanations with children always require interpretation from multiple perspectives.

2.3 Innovation

Tool innovations are hard-won cultural events. They are extensions of 'mindedness' (Noble & Davidson, 1996, pp. 14 & 227) and, as such, they demand not only discoveries but also a community that is motivated to share in and pass on the increase in behavioural potential. Typically, they involve felicitous conditions (if we take the observations made of other primate groups as evidence for early hominids; see Rogers, 1997, pp. 81–88 on tool use in non-human animals). Skills also demand concentrated effort and apprenticeship within a group: researchers who have tried to emulate the stone technologies of early humans take several months to develop the technique for fashioning the stone tools of *Homo erectus* (Toth cited in Leakey, 1994, pp. 47–54). Tools, then – whether implements, boats or arts (like bone carvings or parietal/cave painting) – are a complex of events. They are material, since matter has to be crafted; they are biological, since they require and result from the faculties of an organism; they are social in that they can only happen in group environments, and are thereby incrementally modified, or improved; and they are semiotic in that they can be carried, as meaning bearing behaviour, to other groups and generations.

'Tools' are now so diverse in their forms and so subtle in their cultural mediation that they are best characterised as a 'family resemblance' category – they cannot be described by a single definition. This is well illustrated in the transcript (in Example 10 in Section 2.7 below) of a teacher trying to clarify for primary school children the difference between tools and machines. The 10-year-olds sense that the distinction is 'fuzzy' (in the technical sense of this term: see for example the discussion of the work of Michio Sugeno in Kosko, 1994, pp. 170–171). It is often difficult to separate out the ideas of the human user (the tool as mental or abstract conceptualisation) from the materials recruited to be the realisation or instrument of those ideas (the tool as material object). Also, there are often competing accounts of what constitutes the source of energy or power for a tool under consideration by the class (this being the distinction that the teacher makes in Example 10: 'quite often machines have some sort of power or energy', whereas with tools, 'we normally … do the work').

Modern computers extend the ambiguities of this divide – between the tool as concept and the tool as instrument. There is a dialectic between the software and the hardware. Advances in the one change the conditions of operation and the cultural potential for the other. Consequently, the cultural role of computing can change dramatically as innovation from the conceptual or from the material may initiate a 'cascade' of changes in the tool and in the function that the tool may have across communities and different classes of user. In particular, think of the 'do it yourself' potential among non-experts (for instance, in accountancy, or in desktop publishing). This process is encapsulated in descriptors like 'personal computer' and 'iBook'. The dialectic, or reciprocation, between mental and material is the point made by Monod in the above quotation. And the phenomenon of cascading changes has been associated with many of the innovations of technology across human history, from weaponry to writing. We should note that earlier mental tools (such as calculus or trigonometry) extended human mental power in the same dramatic way that we currently associate with the coming of computers and the information era, but with much longer 'take up' times (see Kline, 1972[1953], pp. 247–268, on calculus). It is important to interrogate the claims of novelty and innovation in order to ascertain what does, in fact, differentiate the current experiences of our community from changes in preceding cultures.

2.4 From Literacy to 'Technacy'

Because tools can now *talk* to each other without human mediation, technology can be rationally thought of as taking on an 'animus' of its own. This 'intelligent' realm now competes with family and neighbourhood for a child's psychical attention. Clearly, it is a new realm with which children must exchange an increasing proportion of meanings, as illustrated by contemporary social patterns in Japan (see Section 2.9 below).

Teachers, at any stage of a child's cultural apprenticeship, might wish to put all exchanges on the basis of reciprocating comprehension – children require a 'theory' of the meaning potential of cultural tools, particularly as the tools themselves are being reconceptualised to anticipate the precise characteristics of their typical user (thereby creating whole environments or 'smartspaces'). This adaptive relation between children and tools provides a basis for the concept of 'technacy'

(Jenkins, 1996, p. 287). Preceding communities and individuals could exercise some discretion (i.e. as to whether or not they wished to engage with innovations). But tools now extend our mental powers in the way that previous tools mainly extended our control over physical properties. And our actual choices have been modified along with this shift, so that non-use of an available tool is penalised or treated, hegemonically, as the marked option (e.g., bank customers who choose counter service over electronic banking accumulate financial penalties as a result of this choice). Computers now involve:

(a) A change in the quality of abstract activities simulated (not just a multiplication of lower level tasks)
(b) A new division of labour between the human knowing subject and the externalised repositories of knowledge (in databases and libraries)
(c) A heightened sense that interlocking systems of information might have a 'life of their own', with human beings unable to predict the emergent properties of the systems of systems that they have set in train

All three observations (a–c) here can be exemplified by the methods that people devise to report on these systems of systems. Such reports are necessary to diminish the chances of a 'crash' – whether of a train, or of an economic system.

A model for economic forecasting in Japan (as proposed by Kobayashi & Sugeno, 2002, and Kobayashi, 1997) is illustrative. Expert, human opinion is factored into the model's predictions. But it is just one factor. An enormous array of measures and derivations from such measures are also factors. For anyone plotting future investments, the expectation may be that a forecast is the product of an expert mind whose personal knowledge is the basis for projecting trends and probabilities. In fact, such an expectation suggests a limited understanding of the technological environment. More typically, a large number of automated tools are brought to bear on statistics supplied (again automatically) from a number of indices. These statistics are transformed into graphs and histograms which do invite comparisons and projections by human agents. But even the wordings appropriate to the transforming data may be generated automatically, rather than supplied by a human subject. In fact, we must regard many of the quantities invoked in modern living as artefacts with a controversial relationship to the underlying processes they purport to describe. Consider, for example, 'intelligence quotient' (as critiqued by Rose et al., 1984); 'viral load' in the care of patients with human immunodeficiency virus (HIV) (Moore, 2003, pp. 8ff); and the way 'risk' is reified and quantified for a variety of specific contexts (e.g. Reason, 1997, Ch. 6 & pp. 224ff).

Heuristic models, whether in economics, in risk management or in other fields, illustrate the shift towards 'knowledge without a knowing subject' – the agency of non-human repositories of learning (Popper, 1972, pp. 159ff). Work in modern societies depends more and more on what Popper calls 'World 3': the knowledge, procedures and concepts which exist exo-somatically, i.e. in storage outside of individual human brains and personalities. The evolutionary significance of this situation was brought out dramatically by Gregory (1970) over 30 years ago, in relation to human vision, language and our mental tools:

> Until recently, men in all cultures handled rather similar objects and used them for similar ends. But with the development of technology, for large parts of the day one man may be concerned with the queer properties of electronic circuits, another with magnetic fields and a third with zero gravity. ... These situations demand different skills: different ways of ordering, handling and seeing objects. As abstract and queer object properties become more important, we may expect languages to develop with deep structures to reflect the worlds which we discover and create: worlds which so far as we know are uniquely human. We are being cut off from the biological past which moulded the eyes and the brains and the speech of our ancestors. The Intelligent Eye is for the first time confronted with an essentially unpredictable future, where present object hypotheses are bound to fail. As we create so we must adapt to what we have created. (Gregory, 1970, p. 166)

While a whole team of humans may have invented the intellectual tools behind the process of economic forecasting, it is not clear that any single human ‘knows’ all the facts that the tools generate, or that anyone is in a position to appreciate the possibly changing relation between the programs devised and the underlying economic realities which the programs purport to represent. It is reasonable to claim then that, in such a context, the machines are leading people, not the other way round.

Humans are all now, as Dennett (1996, pp. 100ff) claims, ‘Gregorian creatures’ (after the mind tool theory of the neuroscientist Richard Gregory, quoted above). Humans are all now modified by mental tools, not just assisted by them. And with respect to mental tools, teachers need to take stock of the current state, and direction, of that symbiotic relationship. More recently, in ‘Natural-Born Cyborgs’, Clark updates this theme of ‘non-biological props and scaffolds’ and the degree to which human experience is a ‘cognitive hybrid’ of human and machine activity (Clark, 2004, p. 77).

Certain pedagogical implications of this new intensity in cultural and human evolution are examined below, in particular, the discourse strategies which the new semantic pressures engender from the teachers themselves: How have teachers been bringing young children to understand the greater role of tools? How is that most fundamental of cultural tools – language – being organised by teachers in order to meet the new demands?

2.5 Teaching for Mental Tools

The examples in this section are taken from 70 ‘new topic’ explanations from late primary and early high school – just that period when children are asked to convert their primary school practice into the discourse of separate disciplines (with discipline specific teachers). For instance, when we can operate with algebra, we understand number operations quite differently (Vygotsky, 1986 [1962], pp. 202–203). There is, in a sense, no going back to our previous way of seeing and understanding. Similarly, when one can solve a problem both algebraically and geometrically, there is a further stepping up in interpretation of the problem. As Gregory Bateson has pointed out in his idea of double seeing, the dual perspective on a problem produces a deeper insight: for example, if the problem of expanding $(a + b)^2$ is displayed geometrically as well as algebraically (as in Fig. 2.1), it is immediately clear why the expansion must produce 2ab as well as the a^2 and b^2 (Bateson, 1980, pp. 79ff).

$(a+b)^2 = a^2 + b^2 + 2ab$

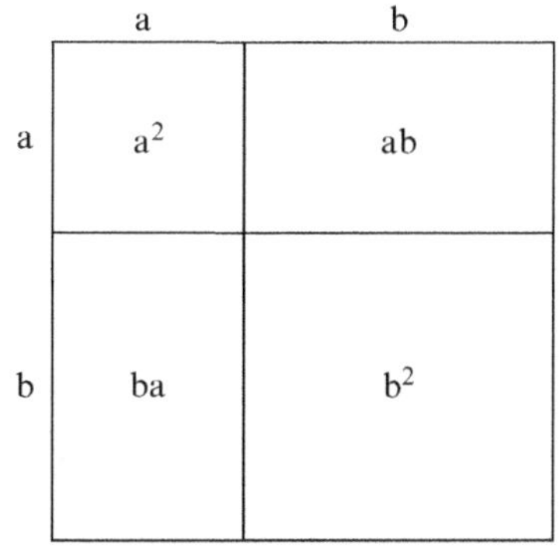

Two regions – ba and ab – to be accounted for also

Fig. 2.1 Dual perspectives on the same problem (following Bateson, 1980)

These two simple mathematical steps illustrate what is meant by abstract tools: there is a principle from which the procedures can be themselves generated when the principle is understood – for example, literally making a 'square' (or rectangle) of sides (a + b). Then on to 'cubing': (a + b) × (a + b) × (a + b) and so on.

Maps, particularly topographical maps, are another useful example of what is meant by a mental or abstract tool. Maps model reality, but at the same time they misrepresent it. A flat map, like a Mercator's projection or a Peter's projection, gives us a clearer notion of the shape and relative size of landforms, respectively (Turnbull, 1989). On the other hand, a globe captures other aspects of reality while being quite unsuitable for most of the human purposes of map carrying. With maps, one can do calculations and solve problems. As long as one understands the conventions by which the model has 'selected' from the reality, one can read off 'knowledge' which is not stored away in the mind of individuals. Thus it is these conventions – knowing how a tool is arrived at – that underpin 'technacy': an adaptive, working familiarity with our environments of tools.

A table of logarithms, or a map, or any intellectual procedure by which new information can be derived by operating upon old or given information, is a cultural tool. Such cultural tools can be viewed as separate instances of problem solving, or more plausibly as parts of an extended system of more localised systems of doing and thinking. Some of our cultural tools depend so closely on others that there is the impression of interlocking procedures. Between others, there appears less of a connection, and if we were ourselves to 'map' this system of cultural tools, we would find a very pluralistic, uneven structure. Some would be tied together by direct lines of dependency, whereas other domains may be loosely related by, say, a shared metaphor (e.g. the way 'valency' is shared across chemistry and linguistics, and the way tropes from atomism are used in most analytical procedures). There is an isomorphism between the image of World 3 presented above and the pluralism of language as reflected in register variation – a system of systems for saying (and thinking!), a confederation of variously interdependent language activities in changing social configurations (Halliday, 1978; Halliday & Hasan, 1985).

The essence of a mental tool is the way it literally 're-presents' the problem – i.e. gives to it an alternative symbolic form. In this light, contemporary concern for the basic metaphors or tropes within a discipline is well motivated (see Hesse, 1980, pp. 111ff; Miller, 1986; Black, 1962; Goodman, 1978). We can understand an abstract tool by examining the function it plays in the discourse of problem solving, how it changes the meanings being exchanged.

2.6 The Semantic Choreography of Teachers

Before an idea can take taught as a mental tool, or a 'meme' (Dawkins, 1989, pp. 192ff), it must be articulated in a natural language. Insights can only be exchanged by first meeting the conditions and opportunities presented by the specific modes of meaning in a spoken or written tradition. Such traditions will be themselves further circumscribed by the social setting and shared experience of the group in a given discussion. The texture of a teacher's explanation carries students from the strangeness of a new intellectual phenomenon over to its naturalisation in the working habits of a specific group of students. This complex 'recontextualisation' is a semantic *tour de force* that deserves study in its own right as a pedagogical tool – the tool that carries us through our cultural apprenticeship in mental tools.

One of the less abstract explanatory strategies can be seen in Example 2 – an attempt to explain the El Niño effect. This explanatory step is strong on how the phenomenon is recognised, but low on integrating that recognition with what drives or motivates the El Niño 'reversal of ocean currents'.

Example 2 (Speaker: Teacher)

70	and that drought scientists believed was caused by what is called the El Niño effect
71	and the El Niño effect is the reversal of ocean currents
72	and this links in to what we're going to do today
73	so I want everyone paying attention.
74	The El Niño effect is –
75	Just say we've got Australia on our map here.
76	and we have over here South America on the other side of the Pacific Ocean
77	On the west coast of South America there is a desert
78	and it is the Atacama desert
79	The Atacama desert is the driest desert in the world
80	They go sort of five years without a drop of rain
81	The current ocean – or the general pattern of ocean currents in the Pacific Ocean is something like this
82	You have your equator running through here
83	and the ocean currents move in that direction
84	[?being] that we get warm currents coming down the east coast of Australia
85	They then move down to the southern part of the Pacific Ocean
86	and move across the Pacific Ocean
87	and < < 88 > > they are cold ocean currents
88	as they come up the west coast of South America
89	Now the El Niño effect is simply the reversal of those currents

A 'critical' aspect of a 'critical' explanation is the self-consciousness it produces about the form of representation. It may be the power of multiple representations which lies behind problem-solving abilities, creative insights and the kind of understanding that is pursued in higher education. The point is to achieve a productive mastery of an idea. Examples 3 and 4 display two strategies used by the same teacher in guiding students towards such a mastery of coordinate graphs. First, in Example 3, the teacher makes the general value of the new representation explicit – the fact that one can use a graph to represent and read off a lot of detail at once. Then, in Example 4, the teacher gives this general value a localised context (and therefore localised value) for the students, by discussing an 'everyday' use of this kind of abstraction in relation to sporting events.

Example 3 (Speaker: Teacher)

24	Yes, to compare,
25	and also, if you've got information in graph form,
26	it's very easy to read.
27	Rather than… wade through a lot of figures,
28	and then work it out in your head,
29	if you put down in the form of graphs,
30	it's like a picture,
31	and you can tell instantly.
32	This is a different type of graph.
33	It's called using coordinates.
34	And these are the two coordinates.
35	What do you think we should name this column?
36	We've got – from the information you've got there,
37	You've got one, two, three, four, five, six, seven, eight.
38	What should we name that column, do you think?
39	What d– E.?

Example 4 (Speaker: Teacher)

140	Ye – that's a very good example, Ts.
141	You where they – when you see the one-day cricket –
142	they start with no overs, no runs,
143	and then they record each over and the runs,
144	and you can see it with the graph,
145	and you can see how the two sides are going against each other;
146	it's a perfect example of a coordinate graph.
147	Yes, um S.?

Representing a problem in a number of different symbolic modes – for example, verbally, iconically, numerically, geometrically and musically – sets up opportunities for seeing new aspects of experience much in the way that stereoscopic vision does. The two 'pictures' we receive from our eyes set up a situation of slight discrepancy, or comparison, thereby providing us with the basis of the human experience of depth, a world that is not merely two dimensional or flat (Bateson, 1980, pp. 79–80). Every comparison of symbolic forms creates the chance for what Bateson has called 'news of difference'. And it is news of difference that can be turned to understanding from first principles. Example 5 also displays the clarity achieved by using two semantic directions in counterpoint; in this case one direction is towards the difficult abstraction of government and the other, towards the local realisation in 'mum and dad'.

Example 5 (Speaker: Teacher)

60	Ok, [[what you are doing ‖ what you are doing]] **is** [[you're thinking about Government ‖as being a person or a place]]
61	But if you read that through,
62	you'll notice that it is not one person
63	and it's not one place
64	it is a group of people
65	and it is a group of people that come together
66	and they talk about how our country is going to be run,
67	what the laws are going to be,
68	how they are going to spend taxes they've collected from your mum and dad or from anyone who works
69	the taxes that they collect when um we buy goods in–
70	there are– there's a tax that you have to pay on them
71	so all of these things have to happen

The emerging 'drift' of these discourses is further clarification of the semantic core in this cultural activity: the more *abstract* notion or procedure has to be 'naturalised' into a recognisable type of *local* knowledge. This is no particular surprise. But its corollary is not so overt, and possibly more significant to the higher learning upon which the children have embarked. The teachers' skills have to work in both directions – not only to ground the general, but to denaturalise the common sense, so that the conventional arrangements which underpin our intellectual tools are laid bare, and thereby offered up for negotiation to these new members of the 'guild'.

2.7 Typology and Rhetorical Strategy

Critical abstractions give students the power to go beyond the information given; i.e. there is a potential to 'read off' new facts from the way that the phenomenon has been represented or modelled. A clear instance of this comes from a composite class (Years 5/6) in which the solar system is being discussed and drawn. The teacher is clarifying the relationship between the proximity of a planet to the sun, the time taken to orbit the sun, and the earthly notion of 'year' (and 'leap year'). In Example 6, the teacher draws explicit attention to the way new information will be produced through the transformation of data the students already have.

Example 6 (Speaker: Teacher)

70	We're going to work out some new information
71	Using the facts [[that I've already given to you]]
72	We should be able to work this out from the other information on the table.

The problem is how to encompass in one's imagination the relation between the 88-day orbit of Mercury and the 248-year orbit of Pluto. This emerges for some children (see message 175) when the teacher turns to the scale of iconic representation they are considering (i.e. when they turn from the charts); the relevant talk is shown in Example 7.

Example 7 (Speakers: T = teacher; C = children)

170	T	So even our scaled drawing on the board does show us quite nicely what we are trying to visualise;
171		but we can't even get it as big as it should be.
172		If we really wanted it to show the true relationship
173		we'd need a much bigger board
174		and I'm sure you can imagine if we draw a big circle right would take for the planet to represent two hundred and two hundred and forty eight years...
175	C	It wouldn't even [?]

The children realise some important facts about the semiotic form of the 'pictures' of the solar system with which they are familiar. Firstly, the scale of a diagram could not consistently represent the two extremes, Mercury and Pluto. And second, that the notion of a year is based on experience, but in an arbitrary way – other phenomena could be used as a basis for organising 'time'. Since planets rotate at different rates and orbit over different distances around the sun, our notions of 'day' and 'year' are very earthbound perspectives. This is not to say, of course, that every Year 5/6 student would appreciate how these facts make measures of time semiotically interesting. Rather, these examples show how the combination of verbal explanation, tables of comparative measures, and a diagram 'to scale' all work to clarify a phenomenon. The potential for insight is a product of the cross-calibration of symbolic types – verbal, numeric, iconic.

The critical abstraction brings out what one might call the imperative of representation: 'we can't even get it as big as it should be'. The modulation here is the necessity of Popper's World 3 – the symbolisation itself makes demands because it has its own conditions of use. This kind of imperative is evident even in kindergarten discourse (Butt, 1989). It is often introduced as steps in an action; for example, as a teacher begins a class discussion on shape, she asks the children to sit around in a circle: 'maybe our circle is not as round as it should be' (i.e. to achieve the criteria of true 'circleness'). This grammatical balance of conation (want/try), modality (can't, need, should, would), mental process (imagine), conditionals and actions by symbols (drawings as Doers, etc.) is the form of the grammar which schools the students in World 3; it is the grammatical texture which sets out all the nuances and constraints, all the conditions of use, between the human subjects and the formal demands of the evolving symbolic order.

Critical abstractions relating to mathematics have a broad range of variation and a relatively discrete, overt expression. In the data from the 1990–1992 study, it was noteworthy how often the mathematics addressed issues of meaning and wording. For example, in Year 5, teachers might set a problem and not want the solution. Rather, the central task was the 'rewording' of the details in order to remove any terms which were superfluous – if the problem began with 'if the world's fastest snail moved 84 cms in 4 minutes', it was important that the students saw that the whole 'snail' nominal group could be set aside.

In another Year 5 group, the first crucial learning requires a 'guess' or an 'estimate' of the answer. An inventory of alternatives follows – counting, multiplying, using tables, remembering the answer from a previous day, using an array or diagram and, finally, using the calculator with 'constant function'. The elucidation is remarkable for some students who advise the teacher that applying the constant function would **not** work with the number 504 because 'constant function' soon would not be practicable; see Example 8.

Example 8 (Speaker: child)

73	You'd only be able to do it a few times
74	because it'd go off

The child realises that the small digit display on her calculator would limit the application of the constant function. This is analogous to recognising that the whole wall of the classroom still would not be sufficient to represent the relationship between Mercury and Pluto. In fact, the child has a clear understanding of the calculator as a tool in that she can recognise the limits of its power to represent even though the problem of constantly adding 504 can go on and on. The teacher enhances the point (but complicates matters) by saying that some calculators involve one less press; see Example 9.

Example 9 (Speaker: Teacher)

152	... so it's one less actually on those calculators, the old-fashioned kind.
153	You might have a different answer on that particular kind of calculator there Brian...

As with rhetorical concepts in general, there is difficulty in sorting out the linguistic account of the teaching strategy: there are crucial aspects (1) in the contextual parameters, (2) in the generic structure, (3) in the semantic specification of discourse elements, and (4) in the grammatical texture. Hence, there are at least four kinds of linguistic statement that need to be made to establish the visibility (the non-latent character) of this symbolic phenomenon. First of all, teachers do not gain sufficient recognition for their profession's techniques. But bringing out the visibility of the notion would also assist in training. In the following discussion of 'tools and machines', again from Year 5, the teacher asks for the names of some of the tools – 'not machines' – that are found around the home. The inventory she receives (including screwdriver, glue, paintbrush, and knives and forks) is organised around the issue of function: 'What kind of problems would the tool – a knife and fork – solve?' The conceptual difficulties arise, however, when the teacher tries to support the earlier strong boundary between tools and machines.

Example 10

325	We normally with our tools do the work
326	even though it's easier with the tools.
327	Quite often machines have some sort of power or energy

The ideas become more contentious as the notional distinction disappears at message 433: 'I want you to write the name of your more complex tool-machines. ... I mean things like tractors, cassettes, cars, calculators'. These are to be brought into a three-column chart: the name of the 'complex tool or machine', the fuel it uses, and the problem it solves. At this blending of the ideas of tool and machine the overall argument becomes baffling. The teacher's creativity and effort lose their direction because she is not herself clear about the semiotics of her argument – she sets out from a strong distinction between machines and tools, explains this distinction in a qualified way, and then appears to dissolve it without explanation. The teacher is not operating with a global schema of her argument and, consequently, in her verbal elaboration, there is a slippage. The result must be a sense of contradiction for the students since the valuable local points made in the discourse are not consistent at the higher levels of relationship. This would be immediately apparent if the basically verbal presentation had used a taxonomic tree diagram. The switch to iconicity (with definite exclusions and branching) would supply the global schema required – the semiotic nub becomes apparent as soon as the issues are 'recoded' or 'reformulated' so that there is more than one mode of symbolic representation. We are back to Bateson's idea of double seeing, his example of algebraic and geometric proofs.

In fact, the critical insights offered by students were typically associated with the articulation of the problem in a number of symbolic forms, each with its own conditions of use and its own opportunities and constraints. In this way, different representations of a problem can be regarded as different versions of a state of affairs which, while comparable, are not synonymous. The creative insight comes from the 'news of difference' of the comparison. The non-synonymy of different versions is a key to the critical, productive, comprehension of the representational conventions which are often shared across disciplines. For instance, mapping, painting and geometry all share the issues of representing three dimensions on two dimensions; so too, calculus, movies and almost all model builders, from social sciences like linguistics to physical sciences like thermodynamics, have shared the problem of representing change – sometimes by the illusion of multiples of smaller and smaller slices of a static reality: 'infinitesimals', 'moving' pictures and 'synchronic' linguistics.

2.8 Testing Claims in Classroom Discourse

An early, provisional review of the classroom material exemplified above suggested that critical tropes of explanation are:

(a) Often concerned with the re-coding of one symbolic form in terms of another: translating different kinds of maps; turning alphabetic/numeric values into iconic forms (pie graphs, bar graphs); stripping a problem of irrelevant details
(b) Centrally concerned with the representation of phenomena rather than with the phenomena themselves – the nub of critical abstraction is the status of the information given; and this comes only from seeing behind the conventions of representations in the subject
(c) Different in relation to the subject matter of each of the school disciplines under consideration (Natural Science, Social Science, Mathematics, Language), but often producing an interdisciplinary formulation

(d) Given by some teachers explicitly, by others through a diffuse (non-discrete) method, and by certain teachers not at all
(e) Particularly problematic in the area of language teaching for English
(f) Typically involved with different locutions – expressions of judgement/tendency; reports of other opinions, evaluation; processes of identification (with complex terms in verbal equations); and heuristic expressions (to do with an 'as if' mode) and
(g) Amenable to enhancement for the students and teachers

As a latent aspect of a teacher's resources, critical explanatory strategies are important because they address something latent in the students also. While most school tests try to measure individual performance on set tasks, they would better address what students can do when appropriately guided in a particular kind of apprenticeship relation. In the first we have the pattern of standardised tests (namely 'intelligence quotient'). In the second, there is Vygotsky's concept of 'zone of proximal development' (ZPD) – what the subject can achieve when given some selective, pertinent guidance from the teacher, master, *sensei*. These two kinds of ability vary independently of one another (Vygotsky, 1978; Brown & Ferrara, 1985). The 'sensei relation' is crucial to problem solving in the classroom and in the workplace. And critical explanatory strategies are the central element in that interdependence.

Linguistically, the critical explanations of teachers across curriculum areas were not so much marked by new jargon as they demonstrated the way general resources of the grammar and rhetorical traditions of English were brought into a new relation (a new ensemble of semantic choices). These choices prioritised:

(a) Verbal equations (as first and last moves)
(b) Embedded information (in the equations) and long interpolations which hold the students over for a sustained elaboration between a first move and a final, quasi-QED
(c) The objectification of mental tools and ideas as agents in their own right, as if free of human motivations
(d) The construal of ideas as conscious entities with their own Platonic strivings or imperatives (*should*, *ought*, and *trying to*)
(e) Dramatic shifts between school-based knowledge and popular culture (e.g. graphs from televised cricket) and
(f) Complex references to the teacher's own explanatory strategy as it is being delivered ('you see what I'm doing now is …')

None of these is unique or novel in itself. What seems to be noteworthy is the ensemble effect and how it semanticises the technological order as a profound, almost numinous, dimension of our shared experience. Given the evolutionary significance of tools, the teachers' explanations are probably well motivated in this regard – the realms of Pythagorean mysteries, over 2,500 years ago, have now become assumptions of our daily experience; not the assumptions of the modernist 'machine age', but of a realm from which we are used to seeing ideas blaze out into ephemeral, applied forms then soon to fall back, superseded by cognate or novel ingenuities.

Like the religious assumptions with which most communities have lived up to the present era, the technological 'background' with which children now have to come to terms has a heterogeneous appearance. No one can know it all. Much has to be taken on trust. Much cannot be related to finite experience or human scales (e.g. nanotechnology; 'string theory' in cosmology; or the 40 gigabyte iPod that children can slip into a pocket). Neophytes can only hope that they will be trained in those strands of technique which will not soon become obsolete. And training often means only enhanced preparation for becoming a customer, i.e. for becoming a buyer rather than a master or maker.

When we consider the child of 2000 by contrast with a child born in Australia, Japan or North America in 1950, a number of the changing characteristics of abstract tools and of material technology merit interpretation. First of all, it is astonishing the degree to which the technological background has been naturalised for children and adults – popular assumptions concerning robots and speech synthesis, for instance, far outstrip the actual progress in these technically difficult areas. Many people, especially schoolchildren, are brought up to such a 'faith' in technology that our human tools appear to have been reallocated from our physics to our metaphysics. This can be seen particularly in the mumbo jumbo disseminated around the humane genome and its description – entrepreneurial forces within science have played on the public belief that all human problems (criminality, disease, body fat, etc.) are 'hard-wired' or 'in the genes'.

The problems discussed in the community, and in schools, now have different degrees of displacement in time and space. Topics like global warming and the hole in the ozone layer can be abstract in that their existence has been so publicly contested. The messages from science are, however, 'act now' in order to ensure the state of earth in 2050 and beyond. Such global topics differ from the personal focus of earlier warnings about tobacco, about atomic testing and even about atomic war (as in the Cuban missile crisis of 1961). The collapse of the Soviet Empire from 1989 may have had some aspects in common with the collapse of the Austro-Hungarian Empire (1914–1918), but the access children have as witnesses was quite different between the two periods. A typical television weather report on SBS, Australia's multicultural television network, encapsulates this shift from local meaning, if not the conceptual consequences of such a shift on the psyches of schoolchildren: one began 'Storms threaten over Nandi (Fiji)' and ended 2 min later with 'Clear over Vancouver'.

2.9 Japan: A Global Future?

The current experiences of Japanese children in relation to technology are an important benchmark for evaluating the linguistic and pedagogical practices of schools against the broader front of social changes. Japan is, perhaps, the country in which electronic and machine technologies are worked most widely and evenly into the fabric of family and community activities. From the train system to the mobile phone, the dependency on (and the convenience of) daily electronic transactions is marked by comparison with the less concentrated urban densities of the USA and Australia. The integrated timetable for the various train lines of Tokyo is a remarkable feat of human organisation and of public literacy. The mobile phone has become an electronic instrument for individuating and maintaining one's network of adolescent contacts – albeit with a communicative mode that facilitates wide, shallow and recurrent contacts rather than tight, intimate and sustained interactions.

This diminution of sustained interactions has become topical in Japanese academic and press circles. Most at issue has been the *otaku* or 'stay at home' children. The term has been applied to those with a mania for electronic games and cartoons (*anime*), and other obsessions that obstruct their progress out into society and into the (shrinking) options for work. In fact, some wider community empathy for *otaku* values – namely, keeping to oneself – has produced a form of what might be called 'geek chic'. There is also a new recognition that the *otaku* are a powerful consumer network in themselves. The empathy has been exemplified in a popular movie – *Densha Otoko: A Man in the Train*. This story, a blend of minor heroism and love, dramatises a young man's inability to declare his love, and the plot follows his use of other 'otaku groups' for support.

With new desktop personal computers at around US$350 (and good, second-hand laptops at under US$200), few Japanese households will be shut out of computer ownership (65.7% of homes had a PC in March 2004). But the mobile phone is even more influential (85.1% of homes, March 2004), with the latest models subsuming many of the amusement functions of once unrelated equipment like Nintendo Gameboy or Playstation. One concern in Japan has been the power of such communicative hardware to be used so as to avoid communication. While the *otaku* can watch *anime* and inhabit a virtual world, with current mobile phones, adolescents can be electronically preoccupied in class, at shopping centres and while eating out. Furthermore, the parents of current adolescents were themselves, in Japan, the first generation which grew up with the 'mania' for electronic diversions. Even outdoor activities – kids meeting after school – were not uncommonly centred on electronic games and a power cable. Consequently, children of the current 'second' generation can share the fields of technological interest and the modes of electronic interaction with one or both parents. Technology and digital semantics have been the background assumptions of many homes, not a marked or strange innovation. On the other hand, the technological changes in Japan provide an interesting counterpoint to the traditional and even conservative social and schooling patterns that children may have been processing 'in parallel' with the assumptions of a digital economy. From the outsider's perspective, at least, the situation can appear contradictory. Alternatively, one might predict that complementary pressures of technology and conformity are inexorable as logical extensions of globalisation.

Despite some growing understanding of the forces acting on children because of, and through, technology, various university figures have dramatised the situation with book titles like 'A Fear of Game Brain' (Mori, 2002) and 'Children Killed by IT' (Mori, 2004). IT news columns have also begun to stress the negative effects of emailing from mobile phones. Like Mori's work, the public discussions (at least in the popular press) relate to understimulation of the frontal lobe and resulting poor concentration and restive behaviour. Fear of the current shift towards electronically mediated interactions has resonated with certain public reactions to recent patterns of crime and of suicides. In particular, group suicide of lovers in contact with each other over the Internet has been cited as an index of a new form of social problem. What is science and what is hysteria in these public debates, as elsewhere in the world, can only emerge with a systematic evaluation of claims, whether concerning brains or suicide rates.

What cannot be denied, however, takes us back to the fundamental concepts from which this discussion set out, namely:

(a) The tool power of our culture has changed to an exponential degree in the last 30 years
(b) This change has direct consequences for our primary tool – language – which has directed both the physiological and cultural evolution of humans
(c) That cultural evolution, for some technologised communities at least, has modified the role of face-to-face interaction in the social repertoire of community members, in particular, for those undergoing training or 'apprenticeship' as adolescents
(d) The changed role of face to face interaction has to be interpreted against the increased accessibility of technical information and an increase in the ways such information can be transformed and displayed for personal understanding and re-activation

Evidence from the 1990–1992 study (drawn from 16 schools across Sydney) exemplifies the ways in which teachers' talk has been meeting the demands of the current intensification of abstract tools in children's lives. First of all, at the lower level of analysis, we might say that the teachers recruited existing resources of English grammar, but with changing probabilities of complex structures (e.g. the embedded clause complexes in summarising verbal equations, discussed in relation to Example 1). More crucially, the grammatical and lexical selections were themselves realising a higher-order rhetorical structure: a variety of explanatory 'tropes' or arguments. These arguments are made up of a set of strategic moves by which claim, exemplification and qualifications are balanced in a unit of 'critical abstraction'. Such critical abstractions are the nub of insight by which one can take over the management of the tool, whether it be a map, a model, a diagram, a graph, a genre, a calculation or an enabling concept, like 'government'. The 'tropes', or arguments, employed the varieties of rational moves that are generally associated with established traditions of rhetorical structure, grammar and public debate.

2.10 Conclusion

We should not be surprised that, in the midst of change, we see innovations managed by the deepest continuities of our semiotic selves. On the other hand, it is clear that even the common community talk currently surrounding sport has been technologised in ways that would have been 'unthinkable' (literally) 50–80 years ago.

In 2009, classrooms may be undergoing reorganisation around a principle distinct from the teacher's power for 'critical abstraction'. Or perhaps the 'critical abstraction' will soon be seen built into the anticipatory wisdom of the electronic delivery to individuals online (on or off a campus, but not 'in' a classroom). Increasingly, it is a question of 'where our ICT tools will take us'.

References

Bateson, G. (1980). *Mind and Nature: A Necessary Unity*. Great Britain: Fontana/Collins.

Bernstein, B. (1996). *Pedagogy, Symbolic Control and Identity: Theory, Research, Critique*. London: Taylor & Francis.

Black, M. (1962). *Models and Metaphors*. Ithaca/London: Cornell University Press.

Brown, A. L., and Ferrara, R. A. (1985). Diagnosing Zones of Proximal Development. In J. V. Wertsch (Ed.), *Culture, Communication and Cognition: Vygotskian Perspectives* (pp. 273–305). Cambridge: Cambridge University Press.

Butt, D. G. (1989 [1985]). *Talking and Thinking: The Patterns of Behaviour*. Oxford: Oxford University Press.

Butt, D. G. (1989). The Object of Language. In R. Hasan and J. R. Martin (Eds.), *Language Development: Learning Language, Learning Culture*, Vol. XXVII: Advances in Discourse Processes (pp. 66–110). Norwood, NJ: ABLEX.

Clark, A. (2004). Natural-Born Cyborgs. In J. Brockman (Ed.), *Science at the Edge* (pp. 67–77). London: Weidenfeld & Nicolson.

Dawkins, R. (1989). *The Selfish Gene*. Oxford: Oxford University Press.

Dennett, D. C. (1996). *Kinds of Minds. Towards an Understanding of Consciousness*. London: Weidenfeld & Nicolson.

Goodman, N. (1978). *Ways of Worldmaking*. Great Britain: Harvester Press.

Gregory, R. L. (1970). *The Intelligent Eye*. New York: McGraw Hill.

Gregory, R. L. (1984). *Mind in Science*. London: Penguin.

Halliday, M. A. K. (1978). *Language as Social Semiotic: The Social Interpretation of Language and Meaning*. London: Edward Arnold.

Halliday, M. A. K., and Hasan, R. (1985). *Language, Context and Text: Aspects of Language in a Social-Semiotic Perspective*. Victoria: Deakin University Press.

Hasan, R. (1996). Speech Genre, Semiotic Mediation, and the Development of Higher Mental Functions. In C. Cloran, G. Williams, and D. Butt (Eds.). *Ways of Saying, Ways of Meaning: Selected Papers of Ruqaiya Hasan*. London/New York: Cassell.

Hasan, R., and Cloran, C. (1990). A Sociolinguistic Interpretation of Everyday Talk between Mothers and Children. In M. A. K. Halliday, H. Nichols, and J. Gibbons (Eds), *Learning, Keeping and Using Language: Selected Papers from the 8th World Congress of Applied Linguistics, Sydney, 16–21 August 1987* (pp. 67–99). Amsterdam: Benjamins.

Hesse, M. (1980). *Revolutions and Reconstructions in the Philosophy of Science*. Bloomington/ London: Indiana University Press.

Jakobson, R. (1973). *Main Trends in the Science of Language. London:* Allen & Unwin.

Jenkins, E. (1996). *Electronic Language*. Unpublished Ph.D. thesis, Macquarie University, Sydney.

Kline, M. (1972 [1953]). *Mathematical Thought from Ancient to Modern Times*. New York: Oxford University Press.

Kobayashi, I. (1997). Modality and Information Fusion. Presentation at the Multimodal Workshop, University of Sydney, December 1997.

Kobayashi, I., and Sugeno, M. (2002). An Approach to a Dynamic System Simulation Based on Human Information Processing. *International Journal of Uncertainty, Fuzziness and Knowledge-Based Systems*, 10(6), 611–633.

Kosko, B. (1994). *Fuzzy Thinking*. London: Flamingo.
Leakey, R. (1994). *The Origins of Humankind*. London: Phoenix.
Lloyd, G. E. R. (1999 [1979]). *Magic, Reason and Experience. Studies in the Origins and Development of Greek Science*. London: Gerald Duckworth & Co.
Miller, A. I. (1986). *Imagery in Scientific Thought: Creating 20th Century Physics*. Cambridge: MIT Press.
Moore, A. (2003). *The Discursive Construction of Treatment Decisions in the Management of HIV Disease*. Unpublished PhD thesis, Macquarie University, Sydney.
Mori, A. (2002). *A Fear of Game Brain*. Tokyo: NHK Shuppan.
Mori, A. (2004). *Children Killed by IT.* Tokyo: Kodausha.
Noble, W., and Davidson, I. (1996). *Human Evolution, Language and Mind: A Psychological and Archaeological Enquiry.* Cambridge: Cambridge University Press.
Popper, K. (1972). *Objective Knowledge: An Evolutionary Approach*. Oxford: Clarendon Press.
Reason, J. (1997). *Managing the Risks of Organizational Accidents*. Hants: Ashgate.
Roochnik, D. (1996). *Of Art and Wisdom: Plato's Understanding of Techne*. Pennsylvania: The Pennsylvania State University Press.
Rogers, L. J. (1997). *Minds of Their Own. Thinking and Awareness in Animals*. Australia: Allen & Unwin.
Rose, S., Lewontin, R. C., and Kamin, L. J. (1984). *Not in Our Genes. Biology, Ideology, and Human Nature.* England: Penguin.
Turnbull, D. (1989). *Maps are Territories. Science is an Atlas*. Geelong: Deakin University Press.
Vaihinger, H. (1925). *The Philosophy of 'As if'. A System of the Theoretical, Practical and Religious Fictions of Mankind*. Translated by C. K. Ogden. New York: Harcourt, Brace & Co.
Vygotsky, L. S. (1986 [1962]). *Thought and Language*. Cambridge: MIT Press.
Vygotskv, L. S. (1978). *Mind in Society: The Development of Higher Psychological Processes*. Cambridge: Harvard University Press.
Williams, G. 2001. Literacy Pedagogy Prior to Schooling: Relations between Social and Semantic Variation. In A. Morais, I. Neves, B. Davies, and H. Baillie (Eds.), *Towards a Sociology of Pedagogy: The Contribution of Basil Bernstein to Research*. New York/Oxford: Peter Lang.

Chapter 3
E-Learning in Schools: Making Successful Connections

Jennifer Fergusson, Donna Gibbs, Maree Gosper, and Robyn Philip

3.1 Making Connections in Schools

Many schools in our globalised world have not yet realised the potential of e-learning or experimented with how it might effectively be employed in classrooms, at home or elsewhere. Lack of technical readiness within school systems to support e-learning and low levels of staff readiness to experiment with new methods often perpetuate this situation. Teachers tend not to hear much about the variety of ways e-learning is being used in classrooms around the world, and often have little idea as to how they might employ it in their own contexts. Nevertheless e-learning – the use of electronic means to facilitate the process of teaching and learning – is being more rapidly adopted by educational institutions than previously (McLean, 2001) and is 'destined to become a larger part of the educational experience of children in years to come' (Kalantzis, 2004, p. 22).

This chapter aims to provide a snapshot of a selection of online projects carried out within the last 5 years in order to describe the diversity and range of practices that the medium of e-learning can facilitate and to identify the factors most likely to contribute to their success or failure. Four online projects that shared the goal of aiming to improve learning opportunities for school students through the use of e-learning are discussed. The projects represent a series of initiatives hosted by three different Centres (The Centre for Flexible Learning, the Macquarie University ICT Innovations Centre and the Macquarie University e-Learning Centre of Excellence) located within an Australian University. They involve collaboration between staff from these Centres with technical support staff and academic staff from a range of disciplines at Macquarie University, Australia; with technical and teaching staff from schools in New South Wales; and with

J. Fergusson
Macquarie University ICT Centre

D. Gibbs
Australian Centre for Educational Studies, Macquarie University

M. Gosper
Institute of Higher Education Research and Development, Macquarie University

R. Philip
Macquarie e-Learning Centre of Excellence

J. Zajda and D. Gibbs (eds.), *Comparative Information Technology*,
DOI: 10.1007/978-1-4020-9426-2_3, © Springer Science+Bussiness Media B.V. 2009

research staff from organisations such as the Australian Centre for Astrobiology (ACA), National Aeronautics and Space Administration (NASA) in America and the Centre for Astronomy and Science Education (CASE) at the University of Glamorgan.

Although the projects shared a common goal, they were undertaken for quite specific, individual purposes. They differed from each other in relation to educational aims, pedagogies employed, subject areas covered, technical tools and applications, numbers of staff and students contributing and number of institutions taking part. It is argued here that these diverse experiences provide important lessons about how to approach, develop and implement e-learning programmes in schools and school partnerships operating in a global context.

3.2 School Partner Project in Online Learning[1]

The *School Partner Project in Online Learning* was an initiative of Macquarie University and two local high schools. The project had two main goals. The first was to provide a positive online teaching and learning experience for staff and students, and the second was to enable a greater understanding by school staff of the technical, design and pedagogical issues underpinning the development and delivery of online learning. Previous to this project neither the staff nor the students had experienced online teaching and learning as a formal part of the curriculum at the two schools.

The scope of the project covered four modules of study in Physics, Software Design, Ancient History and Legal Studies, each delivered over a 4-week period. The design of each of the modules was quite different and was determined by statutory curriculum requirements (in this instance, mandated by the New South Wales Board of Studies), the needs of the students and the contribution that could be made by Macquarie University academics.

A key design requirement was that each module contained an online element which was delivered through WebCT, the learning management system adopted by Macquarie University. This was achieved through a variety of strategies including: the provision of web sites containing content developed in a variety of presentation formats (text, audio, graphics) to supplement the class textbooks, links to relevant freely available web resources, and the use of discussion and collaboration tools. The tasks required of students varied from module to module and included contributions to open un-moderated and focused discussions around a topic or a problem, online critiques of group assignments, small group research projects, group problem-solving tasks, quizzes, web searches and site visits, external to the school, followed by discussion activities.

The delivery of each module of work also varied depending on the particular classroom context in each of the schools. Variations ranged from full integration

---

[1] Two of the authors, Maree Gosper and Robyn Philip, were part of this project. They would like to acknowledge the contributions from the academics, staff from the Centre for Flexible Learning and the School Partner Program at Macquarie University; and the two High School Principals, Maurice Brunning and Neville Warren, and the participating teachers from their schools.

into classroom and assessment activities, to stand-alone activities supervised by the classroom teacher, to independent study operating in parallel with normal classes. Each module had particular strengths and weaknesses which will not be discussed here. Instead, a discussion of the effectiveness of the initiative as a whole and factors influencing its implementation will be undertaken.

Overall, students indicated that they were willing to try new methods, as long as they provided them with a reasonable learning experience. The features they valued most about the online approach were the opportunities for discussing and sharing ideas and different perspectives with others, and having access to resources and expertise that would not normally have been available to them.

On reflection, there were four factors that emerged which were critical to ensuring the success of the online experience. The first factor is the importance of high-quality instructional design. In this project, a particular design aim was to develop a meaningful learning experience, not one that was technology driven and devoid of an obvious educational rationale. Hence, considerable effort was made to present students with an online experience that was well-integrated into the existing curriculum, including the assessment processes. Nevertheless, the requirement for an online presence in each of the modules did, in fact, have a major impact on the ensuing instructional design and it is recognised that in some instances the activities could have been more easily executed in a classroom setting. However, there were activities that were well received by students which were only possible because of the online medium. For example, the physics students appreciated access to additional Internet-based materials, as well as being able to read the assignments from other groups; the software design students enjoyed the online discussions and contacts made through industry visits; the legal studies students liked the online case studies and the opportunity to discuss opposing points of view; and the ancient history students valued the discussion and accompanying photographs from experts who had been on archaeological digs.

While the online environment supported these new experiences, the key to their success was their ability to support learning. For the students, the medium of delivery was of secondary importance, although it did provide an initial motivation for them to undertake the activities. Hence, the curriculum requirements should be a major driver in the design of a learning experience; decisions should not be based solely on the technology that is available.

The second factor is the provision of adequate support for and monitoring of the learning process. Because today's teenagers are regarded as being technology savvy, there is a danger of underestimating the support they need for online learning. This was evident in this project. Although, the students from both schools had computer skills and a high level of computer home ownership, the application of their skills to the learning context still needed guidance and support. Students had to become familiar with the technology (WebCT), as well as the new approach to teaching and learning that accompanied its use. The acquisition of the technical skills was easily accommodated; the learning skills required more attention. Students required direction in the form of clear guidelines and expectations. For example, guidelines were required for the collaborative group work undertaken online, and for online discussions in a formal academic mode, as opposed to the informal recreational mode of expression commonly used by teenagers. For all students, but particularly those students working independently, it was important that expectations were made clear from the outset so they could become independent learners, progressing at their own rate, following their own interests and at the same time meeting the requirements of the module.

The need for careful monitoring of the learning process to identify usage patterns and to detect learning difficulties and unacceptable behaviour is incontestable in an educational context. However, the reality is that the provision of such support is both a resource and a professional development issue. In an ideal situation it would be desirable that online initiatives were matched with the technical and pedagogical expertise of the staff involved. However, this was not the case in this project, and although a staff development programme was put in place for the participating teachers, their understanding of the extent and the type of support required for students was not fully realised at the beginning of the trial. As is the case with most innovations, it was only through experience that an understanding of the true nature and requirements of the online environment were developed. Teachers recognised that more learning support and increased monitoring of activities should be factored into future initiatives.

The third factor is reliable and equitable access to stable technical infrastructure. The project team was well aware that the technology could easily get in the way of student learning. Nevertheless, despite their best efforts to ensure the technical infrastructure was stable and working, unforeseen difficulties still arose because of network configurations and other glitches. Examples included a minor upgrade of previously functional software which resulted in problems at the schools because of their firewalls, students having difficulty in accessing audio files, and students having intermittent problems accessing quizzes. Although these were attended to reasonably quickly, the short delays caused inconveniences and influenced the students' reactions to the online environment.

These experiences highlighted the importance of careful and consistent monitoring of technical systems to ensure seamless and reliable access. While the advantages of monitoring go without saying, the real issue in this case was the provision of the support required for these monitoring activities, and then having the resources and expertise available to spontaneously rectify any problems that were detected. The provision of just-in-time support is necessary to deal with the inevitable glitches that will arise.

Not only is access paramount to success, but the equity of the access is also provided. In this project, the online activities were developed on the basis that students would have adequate access to computers during class and/or in their free time at school. However, students could also access the web sites from home. This raises the question of equity. Were those students with home access, which in some instances was easier to organise and more reliable than the school access, being unduly advantaged? Technical capacity, in a 7 × 24 online environment has implications for both the design and the implementation of online programmes. If, for instance, equitable access cannot be assured for all participating students, then consideration should be given to avoiding design elements that require an interactive online presence.

The fourth factor is the presence of an organisational environment which can support new approaches to teaching and learning. The *School Partner Project in Online Learning* was about initiating change. In this case it was the introduction of online learning and understanding the implications for teaching and learning, as well as the supporting infrastructure. In many ways, the biggest challenges were faced by teaching staff and the organisational environment in which they worked. In contrast, for students, the technology used was part of their generational experience and it was met with enthusiasm, optimism and even a sense of 'it's about time'.

The experience of teachers in developing and implementing the four modules highlighted a number of differences in the online environment compared to traditional contexts including differences in the conceptualisation and design of teaching resources and strategies, the time required for producing and coordinating the development of resources and teaching methodologies and the provision of support for learning. Teachers were required to learn new skills related to use of the WebCT, and the design of curricula and facilitation of learning in an online environment. Although the accompanying staff development programme covered some of these new skills and resulted in a workable level of familiarity with the online environment, it was only through experiencing the reality of teaching online that the teachers began to understand and be able to deal with the new context in a practical and meaningful way. Teachers recognised that they needed the time to explore and experiment with new approaches. They also needed the collective support of their colleagues through, for example, the establishment of learning communities to generate ideas and solve problems.

In this project, the scope and extent of the infrastructure required to support the project was beyond the existing capability of the schools at that time; hence, the development and delivery infrastructure (WebCT) was provided by the University. Apart from establishing and maintaining a WebCT server which was secure and reliable, there were administrative functions such as creating the online units and creating and maintaining student accounts that had to be attended to. In addition, the planning and production of web sites and resources involved a team of instructional designers, web developers, computer programmers and content experts which was coordinated by the Centre for Flexible Learning. Unfortunately this type of external support is not always available which means that the establishment of new approaches to teaching and learning, such as this, will require parallel changes in existing infrastructure support systems.

In conclusion, given the steep learning curve for the teachers in grappling with technical infrastructure problems, developing technical skills, preparing curricula and teaching in an online environment, the results of the trial were encouraging and suggest that students would be open to further online experiences. However, to move beyond project status, to the establishment of sustainable, quality online learning within schools, consideration needs to be given to the entire organisational context which encompasses educational, technical and organisational issues.

3.3 Macquarie ICT Innovations Centre Projects

The Macquarie ICT Innovations Centre, a partnership between Macquarie University and the NSW Department of Education and Training, aims 'to develop, implement and evaluate innovative ways of enhancing learning through the application of dynamic and emerging information and communication technologies'. Located on the university campus, the Centre is able to bring teachers from schools together with academics to create projects for students. The two projects discussed below involve incorporating e-learning into science education.

3.3.1 The NOAMA Project

The *NOAMA Project* (NASA Oceanographic Analogue Missions Activity Project), undertaken jointly by the Macquarie ICT Innovations Centre and Macquarie University's Australian Centre for Astrobiology (ACA) in 2003, employed ICT to facilitate collaborative scientific research. Twenty-four Year 10 students from ten high schools close to Macquarie University joined – virtually – a mission to investigate life in the extreme environments of hydrothermal vents 1–3 km deep in the Atlantic and Pacific Oceans. The students had to research and plan an experiment to be carried out on their behalf by researchers aboard the research vessel, *Keldysh*, during the October 2003 mission of the NOAMA programme. There is a requirement for the Stage 5 Science syllabus in New South Wales, Australia, for students to undertake an individual research project to give them first-hand experience of scientific investigation. The *NOAMA Project* was ideally suited to help them achieve this curriculum goal.

The students worked with scientists from the ACA and a science teacher to define the requirements for life in extreme environments. Their goal for the mission was to investigate the presence of microbial life on the surface of, or even in, a hydrothermal vent chimney. If, as some scientists suggest, life on Earth began in extreme environments such as those found around submarine hydrothermal vents, it is possible that life may very well have formed at similar structures on other planets. This was surprising for the students who had not expected to be working on a submarine mission with NASA, a space agency.

The majority of the collaborative research for the project was conducted online, although students had 3 days of on-campus activities for orientation and collaboration with ACA scientists. Internet access was crucial to the project so that students could locate, access and share current information, since much of the research in this area is very recent and not published elsewhere. WebCT was used to create an online learning environment, although the site contained very little 'content' for students. The discussion forum was by far the most frequently used part of the site as it provided the means for the students, teachers and scientists to share ideas and resources.

By working alongside practising scientists, the students were able to gain an insight into the way science is really carried out. For many this was different from the impression they had gained of science from their classroom experiences. The teaching of science in high schools is often limited by traditional methods or by directed projects in which the outcome, unlike science, is predetermined. The fact that the scientists admitted that they did not know the answers to some of the students' questions allowed them to experience the uncertainty of cutting-edge scientific research.

Written and verbal feedback suggested there were two key aspects that had universally engaged the students – using authentic data and coming into contact with the true nature of the processes of science. Although the project was not an assessable part of the students' school work, the WebCT data showed that they logged in frequently and spent considerable time on the site. They continued to log in and post long after this was necessary, indicating the project's success in creating a community of learners. In response to a questionnaire completed at the end of the mission, two thirds of the group said that the project had influenced their choices of science subjects for Year 11. Significantly, two students reversed a decision to end their science education in Year 10.

One of the factors affecting the success of the *NOAMA Project* was the partnership, coordinated by the Macquarie ICT Innovations Centre, which created an environment where new approaches to teaching and learning were possible. The partnership provided the students with access to scientists they would not normally meet and work with, and to resources that would not normally be available in a school.

The presence of the scientists in the project enabled a new approach to teaching and learning and brought about a change in the roles of both teacher and students. At times during the project the scientists, teacher and students were co-learners and researchers. At other times, the scientists were experts, the students and the teacher were learners and the teacher was also a facilitator of learning, helping the students to make connections with the curriculum context. The use of communication tools in the online learning environment supported the change of the teacher's role from instructor to facilitator of learning very well.

The learning management system, WebCT, was made available to the project through the university and the online environment was managed by the Macquarie ICT Innovations Centre. This freed the teacher from the need to acquire the technical skills involved in setting up a learning management system and enabled him to assume the role of online moderator and discussion facilitator, a role he quickly adapted to as it was similar to his classroom teaching style. The students also adapted quickly to the online discussion forum when they realised that student activity on the site was closely monitored. There was a noticeable improvement in the quality of student postings over the life of the project. The positive effect that this small project had on students' motivation to study science encouraged collaboration on future projects that could achieve similar results on a larger scale.

3.3.2 The Are We Alone? Project

For this project the Macquarie ICT Innovations Centre, the Australian Centre for Astrobiology (ACA), the NASA Astrobiology Institute, NASA Learning Technologies and the Centre for Astronomy and Science Education at the University of Glamorgan joined forces to develop a student project based on research being carried out by ACA scientists in the Pilbara region of Western Australia. The Pilbara is an internationally recognized area hosting the best known examples of the earliest evidence of life on Earth. Few educational materials based on the current scientific exploration in the region exist, in spite of its scientific and cultural significance. The success of this ongoing project which began in 2004 will depend on combining the individual partners' distinctive contributions into integrated learning experiences that lead to the achievement of the goals as a whole.

The *Are We Alone? Project* is closely aligned to the curriculum and addresses outcomes in the New South Wales Board of Studies syllabus for Stage 5 Science. These outcomes will also be applicable to similar-aged students in other states of Australia, the UK and the USA. Using innovative learning technologies, the *Are We Alone? Project* aims to provide access to experiences not otherwise feasible for large numbers of students. The project utilises interactive multimedia to create activities which allow students to experience the scientific process, as conducted by research scientists searching for evidence of early life on Earth and life on other planets.

On a virtual field trip to the Pilbara, students explore lines of evidence confirming or not the biogenicity or abiogenicity of 3.5 billion-year-old fossils. They are scaffolded in the formulation of hypotheses and the testing of these against the evidence they gather. The project supports the students' research by providing electronic research tools from NASA Learning Technologies and other sources, information in the form of maps, graphs and microscope specimens, and a library of primary source material from current Astrobiology literature.

In the *Are We Alone? Project*, students view and use animations, simulations and videos to gain essential background knowledge and to grasp some of the higher-level understandings which are beyond the scope of the Stage 5 science syllabus, but necessary for this project. Research indicates that such interactive multimedia resources, by increasing visual impact, can improve scientific understanding (Huppert et al., 2002; Trindade et al., 2002).

An important aspect of the work of scientists involves communicating ideas and findings and seeking constructive evaluation by peers. The *Are We Alone? Project* encourages students to collaborate and exchange ideas with other students. It also provides a link to the Australian Centre for Astrobiology so that students can seek feedback from practising scientists, a strategy which proved so valuable in the NOAMA project. The culmination of the project takes the form of a seminar where students present their findings to their peers using electronic presentation tools.

Trials conducted with teachers to date indicate that the success of this project is dependent on an understanding of the changing role of the classroom teacher from instructor to facilitator. The change from a teacher-centred classroom to a more student-centred approach is being driven in part by the knowledge explosion. Because knowledge is burgeoning and being superseded at an unprecedented rate, it is important that teachers encourage students to develop good inquiry learning strategies and that they model these for their students. This is particularly important in science where research is constantly leading to new knowledge. For this reason it is not expected that teachers have prior knowledge of the scientific content contained in this project, rather that they will model the scientific inquiry skills of a scientist. To assist staff, a teacher's DVD will accompany the student DVD. It will consist of curriculum support materials, a description of the research project, literature addressing the change of role of the teacher and a range of suggestions for making the most of the facilitation role.

As with the NOAMA project, the contribution of each of the partners to the project is fundamental to its success. In this case the scientists provide the authentic, current data and their research experience, the teachers involved in the project's development provide advice on the curriculum and classroom context, and the software designers provide the learning tools and electronic resources. The learning design and the scaffolding for the student research project are the result of the combined experience of all the educators involved.

By using the expertise of the project partners to provide both the resources and the student research project on DVD, the project overcomes a previously identified factor inhibiting the success of online learning in schools, namely the lack of teacher experience and skill in the creation of high-quality, online learning materials.

3.4 The Use of the Learning Activities Management System in Schools

Learning Activities Management System (LAMS) is a web-based Learning Design system that enables the creation and sharing of collaborative, activity-driven learning sequences. It has been available as open source software since February 2005. Although LAMS was developed in Australia at Macquarie University, Kemnal Technology College in the UK was the first school to trial the LAMS software in the classroom. In 2004/2005 the Macquarie E-Learning Centre of Excellence (MELCOE) and the Australian Centre for Educational Studies (ACES) began a programme of evaluations of the use of LAMS in schools. (In the UK, the Joint Information Services Committee [JISC] has sponsored a trial involving up to 20 universities and 20 vocational colleges, and the Specialist School Trust, in conjunction with the UK Department for Education and Skills, has sponsored a trial for up to 100 schools.) The first stage of the Macquarie trials involved a research visit to Kemnal in the UK to interview the teachers using it there, and to observe their work with students. The second stage involved setting up a pilot project to trial the use of LAMS in five Australian schools. The focus of the evaluations was documenting what teachers thought about the educational usefulness and significance of the software.

LAMS allows teachers to construct learning designs using a simplified visual authoring interface that emphasises learning processes, communication and student engagement. These designs or templates are activated for learners whose progress as they work through the activities can be viewed, recorded and stored. The software can be used with learners together in a common space either synchronously or asynchronously, or at a distance from one another. Templates of sequences can be imported or exported so that a database of lesson plans in any subject area can be readily created. Sequences can be individualised, saved for future use and shared or exchanged with colleagues.

3.4.1 LAMS in the UK

Kemnal is a boys' secondary comprehensive school, located in Kent, with approximately 1,200 pupils aged from 11 to 19. The students are from relatively low socio-economic backgrounds. The staff of Kemnal wanted to see how e-learning might be employed as part of a wider set of strategies to:

- Help raise standards
- Reduce teacher workload and
- Address teacher shortages

LAMS was initially employed by teachers across Key Stages 3, 4 and 5 in the subjects of Maths, Technology, Science, Geography and History.[2]

The dramatic and consistent improvement of Kemnal's position on the league tables over the last few years has been attributed by the school to the comprehensive range of strategies they introduced which included the introduction of LAMS to the classroom. Interviews with the teachers involved on site in 2004 suggest that part of the success of using LAMS came from its playing an important part in a whole school plan. The teachers worked together as a group to identify in what ways, for what purposes, and how often LAMS would be employed in their different subject areas. The particular improvements in teaching and learning identified in the interviews with the teachers were that, in general, using the technology:

- Helped to overcome the physical and temporal limitations of a classroom by allowing all learners to contribute simultaneously, to have quick access to the opinions of others, and to be actively involved in learning for longer periods of time
- Motivated students to contribute their opinions in ways they were often not prepared to do in a classroom setting, particularly when contributions were anonymous, which led to improved participation rates
- Was welcomed as a medium for learning by learners who are often very comfortable with using technologies for other purposes outside the classroom. Using the technology appeared to give them added confidence and a sense of ownership of what they were learning
- Provided ready access to the work of their peers that created excellent scaffolding for their own learning
- Enabled learners to engage in multiple activities using a variety of pedagogies in a comparatively short time frame which encouraged the development of higher-order cognitive skills and
- Changed the classroom dynamics considerably so that individuals dominated less and more collaborative student activity could be well supported

Three factors were of particular importance in the success of the e-learning in these trials. The first is that e-learning was not just adopted for the sake of using technology in the classroom: it was adopted for a particular set of identified educational purposes. These purposes were linked to the overarching goal of the successful delivery of curriculum.

Secondly, the adoption of e-learning was implemented as part of a whole school plan. Kemnal's plan was developed, and strongly supported by the school executive under the guidance of the Principal, who had the strong support of the staff. Those staff members who adopted LAMS were clearly achieving higher levels of learning

[2] Key Stage 3 in the UK includes years 7–9 (ages 11–14); Key Stage 4 includes years 10–11 (ages 14–16) and Key Stage 5 includes year 12 (ages 16+).

than they had previously and this achievement acted as a catalyst for more staff to learn how to introduce e-learning into teaching and learning.

The school's success also owes something to the way schools operate in the UK where there is considerable independence from the Government in terms of decisions about how funding can be used, who can be employed, and school governance. Kemnal, for example, chose to build staff morale by raising funds to provide technology, and to employ teachers' helpers and community members for lower order duties to free up time for teachers to devote to their teaching. The sharing of resources and acquisition of a bank of reusable teaching materials enabled by LAMS was also an effective strategy for conserving teacher time.

The third factor was that the e-learning software enabled the teachers to produce high-quality instructional materials relatively easily. The features commented on by the teachers included the intuitive, easy-to-use nature of the software; its suitability for developing thinking skills; that it could be used for individual tasks, small group or whole class resource-based or collaborative activities; and that it combined readily with traditional classroom work.

3.4.2 LAMS in Australian Schools

The second stage of the project involved the evaluation of the implementation of LAMS at three Australian schools. Teachers were asked by the Macquarie researchers to design a sequence of online lessons using LAMS for their students. Evaluation data was gathered by the researchers through classroom observation, from the LAMS 'virtual classroom' monitoring interface, questionnaires, individual and group interviews and the teachers' personal journals. In order to determine the teachers' views on the educational usefulness and significance of LAMS, they were asked to answer questions in relation to the design and implementation of their sequence/s, the adaptability of the system in their context, the quality of outcomes they achieved, and their view of the potential of the software for future use. Table 3.1 shows the year level, subject areas and topics chosen for study by the three participating classes.

Responding to questions about the educational usefulness of LAMS, the Australian teachers commented on the high level of student engagement observed in students while using LAMS. While there may be a novelty effect in using the new technology, observational data and participants' comments indicate that students nonetheless enjoyed the activities and e-learning environment and worked well in small groups during the activities, on and off line.

The Australian school trials also corroborate the UK experience that LAMS is an enabling technology, helping to focus and scaffold student discussions where ideas need to be unpacked gradually, assumptions or propositions questioned, or ambiguity probed and justified. Teachers in the trial acknowledged the support the technology gave for the process of brainstorming ideas, and encouraging all students to contribute their opinions.

The simplicity of user interface, both for authoring the lesson plans and from the student perspective was observed to have contributed to its acceptance and adaptability in the K-12 context. For example, the teacher of the Year 5/6 primary students

Table 3.1 Year level, subject area and topics chosen by the participating classes in the trial

Class	*Subject area*	*Topic used in LAMS sequence*
Year 4/5 Primary: 28 students from a co-educational class of primary students from a NSW government school; relatively computer literate students	Science; Human Society and its Environment	Weather (Science) and Athletics in relation to the Olympic Games (Human Society) Completed in class and (by some students) as homework
Year 7 High School: 10 female students from a class of Gifted and Talented students at a NSW non-government school; relatively computer literate students	English	A Media Studies extension activity focussing on the phenomenon of Barbie dolls Completed independently at home, out of school hours
Year 11 High School: 6 male students from a New South Wales government secondary school; highly computer literate	Software, Development and Design	Discussion and testing of student understanding of four modulesset for study on the Higher School Certificate syllabus
		Completed primarily in class

used the discussions in LAMS as a follow-up activity for work done in class on the theme of the Olympics. Students followed the Olympic sporting events of 2004 with great interest. The teacher developed a LAMS discussion asking students to think about their favourite athlete, and to consider the notion of fame and media treatment of celebrity in relation to their chosen athlete. Her comment about the LAMS interface was that she really liked its lack of 'bells and whistles' because this reduced unnecessary distractions and helped to keep students on task.

The achievement of satisfactory (and sometimes very pleasing) student outcomes was attributed by the teachers primarily to ease of use of the software, the transparent nature of the pedagogical concepts underpinning the technology, the possibilities of collaboration for the students, and the ease of customising the learning designs for individual contexts.

The teachers also identified some frustrations with their e-learning experiences. None of these were viewed as insoluble and all were resolved in some way either with the support of the university, or by the teachers devising a way through the difficulty. Nevertheless hindrances of this kind were temporarily frustrating. They included:

- Censorship issues: Some schools were concerned about students being given unrestricted access to the internet from within their school.
- Technical difficulties: There were some cross-platform compatibility issues reported such as the software not displaying as expected. Problems with institutional network restrictions were also reported. Institutional firewalls sometimes limited full access to LAMS which, for example, caused problems when using the chat tool function.

- Lack of institutional support: Support was variable for the trial within schools as it tended to be seen as an individual's project. Teachers managed to overcome any lack of support through their own initiatives but it is clearly an advantage to have a broader support base.

The educational impact of this technology can be measured in part by the willingness of the teachers to continue with its integration into the curriculum (Baggott La Velle et al., 2003). All of these teachers are continuing to use the software with new classes and have recommended it to other colleagues who are now planning their own learning sequences. The main factors contributing to the success of this e-learning initiative in schools would appear to be:

- That the teachers involved were enthusiastic, experienced and reflective and were keen to experiment with new ways of teaching
- That the teachers were either ready technically to take on the challenge of the new learning system or were provided with sufficient support to help them overcome any difficulties
- That the LAMS software facilitated good pedagogical practice and
- That teachers enjoyed the control they had of the software and appreciated the way it allowed them to individualise what they were doing

3.5 Conclusion

The diverse e-learning programmes described here involved schools from different locations working in partnership with outside institutions, some located in other countries, within a digital environment. It is clear from analysing these varied e-learning experiences that factors can be identified that are likely to influence the success or failure of educational e-learning programmes. The factors that appear crucial in building a context where successful e-learning will be sustainable include:

1. Adopting an appropriate whole school, organizational or partnership approach that identifies a shared vision of the outcomes that are required. This enables the creation of a climate that can capitalize on the range of expertise and support made available to assist in achieving those outcomes.
2. Creating an organizational environment that is developed by professionals and meets the administrative and educational needs of those working within it. This includes providing an effective technical infrastructure that is monitored regularly. If the infrastructure is not given high priority and made stable and reliable it can build frustration, destroy motivation and interrupt learning, eventually leading to disillusion and failure. Support needs to be available for educators from technicians in a timely as well as an ongoing way. Open communication lines between those using the technology to teach and those building and maintaining the system in operational terms is a vital part of this process.
3. Ensuring that management appreciates that curriculum requirements should drive the design of the online learning experiences that are provided for students.

Teachers need time to experiment with design issues and to learn from and build on their experiences.

4. Recognising that a digital environment has an impact on the roles teachers and learners will assume. Teaching online is different from teaching face to face and learning to understand this difference involves learning about online pedagogies and acquiring the technical skills to facilitate these. Provision for time release and training opportunities (that include expert input in relation to pedagogies) to develop these understandings and skills are vital. Establishing learning communities where issues are discussed and experiences can be shared is a strategy that can foster confidence in this new environment. The provision of ongoing support to enable teachers to keep up-to-date with developments in the ever-changing world of technological change is another important element to consider.
The role of the learner is being redefined to some extent as new ways of accessing information and collaborative learning cultures gain ground. Learners may adapt very naturally to this mode of learning as they are often 'digital natives' rather than 'digital immigrants' (Prensky, 2001, 2006). Yet, however technically proficient learners are, they invariably need guidance and support as to how to use a digital environment productively, effectively and efficiently to achieve the range of educational purposes they are pursuing. Students may also need help with adjusting to the different monitoring and assessment processes that online learning enables.
5. Building understanding in the wider community about the changing nature of the role of the teacher and the student in a digital environment, and about the nature of the paradigm shift they are witnessing. Traditional expectations that the teacher is the single expert who controls what and how a student learns are not appropriate in this context. There needs to be recognition of a shift away from this notion to that of the teacher as a facilitator and initiator who locates expertise and resources and teaches learners the skills they need to engage with these, and to pursue their own learning in individual as well as collaborative ways.

   Strategies for making the community more responsive to this change in culture might include public dissemination of information through showcasing students' achievements; modelling the new approaches that are being used; and identifying what e-learning can help learners to do and to achieve that is not possible through other methods.

Any educational institution that aims to be viable and successful in the digital age needs to take factors of the kind described here into account. This will assist the development of a culture that will sustain and support teachers as they find new ways to teach and learn, and enable informed choices to be made about how, why and when to employ technologies for the benefit of learning communities.

References

Baggott La Velle, L., McFarlane, A., & Brawn, R. (2003). Knowledge Transformation Through ICT in Science Education: A Case Study in Teacher-Driven Curriculum Development. *British Journal of Educational Technology*, 34(2), 183–199.

Huppert, J., Lomask, S.M., & Lazarowitz, R. (2002). Computer Simulations in the High School: Students' Cognitive Stages, Science Process Skills and Academic Achievement in Microbiology. *International Journal of Science Education*, 24(8), 803–821.

Kalantzis, M. (2004). Diversity, New Technologies and New Learning. Papers from the International Conference on Computers in Education, RMIT, Melbourne, Victoria, November 30 to December 3, 2004.

McLean, N. (2001) Interoperability Convergence of Online Learning and Information Environments. *New Review of Information Networking*, 7(1), 1–19.

Osborne, J. & Hennessy, S. (2003). Literature Review in Science Education and the Role of ICT: Promise, Problems and Future Directions. NESTA Futurelab Series, Bristol: NESTA Futurelab. Retrieved July 30, 2005, from http://www.nestafuturelab.org/research/reviews/se01.htm

Prensky, M. (2001). Digital Natives, Digital Immigrants. On the Horizon, 9(5). Retrieved July 30, 2005, from http://www.twitchspeed.com/site/Prensky%20-%20Digital%20Natives,%20 Digital%20Immigrants%20-%20Part1.htm

Prensky, M. (2006). Digital Natives, Digital Immigrants: Origins of Terms. Retrieved July 30, 2007, from http://www.marcprensky.com/blog/archives/000045.html

Trindade, J., Fiolhais, C., & Almeida, L. (2002). Science Learning in Virtual Environments: A Descriptive Study. *British Journal of Educational Technology*, 33(4), 471–488.

Chapter 4
What Is Needed for Global E-Learning in Higher Education

Patrick McAndrew

4.1 Introduction

This chapter examines the nature of emergent trends in methods being used to develop and deliver e-learning programmes by higher educational institutions for a global market. As a starting point global e-learning programmes that have been involved in large-scale failure for economic reasons are analysed and the reasons behind their lack of success discussed. An account of the design approaches that are currently helping produce more flexible online courses and ways in which these can be shared among practitioners is provided in order to throw light on the advantages and disadvantages of these approaches. The model used by the Open University in the UK for distance education in the global arena is also considered in some detail particularly in relation to the insights it offers about dealing with cultural bias in global e-learning programmes. Comparison of approaches to providing online courses that draw on learning objects, learning design and learning patterns is made and the chapter concludes with reflections on lessons learned and advice that could be offered to those considering the provision of online courses for a global audience.

4.2 Operating Globally

The Internet offers us the ability to reach anyone in the world connected to it and thus it is easy to envisage global courses where the education provider in one part of the world offers courses without being restricted by their location. These opportunities for operating globally through the Internet have been apparent for several years and in the period 2000/2001 the education sector was a participant in the dot. com explosion (Howcroft, 2001). Large investments were made in online-only

---

P. McAndrew
Institute of Educational Technology, The Open University, Milton Keynes, UK

J. Zajda and D. Gibbs (eds.), *Comparative Information Technology*,

DOI: 10.1007/978-1-4020-9426-2_4, © Springer Science+Bussiness Media B.V. 2009

education providers that planned to operate globally to satisfy requirements for learning more cheaply, more quickly, more flexibly and more efficiently than existing higher education. Market estimates were high and the aim was to make larger profits while also providing access to 'the best education in the world'. Those involved were a combination of government-backed initiatives, businesses, entrepreneurs and established traditional universities. At the same time many smaller initiatives also aimed to extend their provisions to the world through opening up access and adjusting requirements and methods. These smaller initiatives have met with mixed successes as have the larger initiatives. But it is the large-scale failures that are of particular interest here as they act as a warning and throw light on how and why ambitions can remain unfulfilled.

4.2.1 E-Learning Failures

The changing nature of Internet business in the early twenty-first century means that it is not difficult to find examples of economic failure in online operations. This seems particularly true for education. Examples of scaled-back ambitions include UNext (http://www.unext.com) and Fathom Knowledge Network Inc. (http://www.fathom.com), while the UKeUniversity (UKeU) has now been wound up as a commercial entity.

The UK Commons report on the UKeU (House of Commons, 2005) identified the main failure as marketing. In particular the UKeU had taken a supplier view of what was needed rather than a customer-led position, or as the report stated, 'UKeU failed largely because it took a supply-driven, rather than demand-led approach'. This was undoubtedly true in terms of selecting provisions across a range of universities without commissioning subjects or parts of the curriculum where there were established markets, e.g. business and technology at a master's level. However, there is other evidence that there are more subtle contributors to the failure. Analysis supported by the e-Learning Research Centre at Southampton University (Conole et al., 2005) and by Jonathan Darby, former Chief Architect at the UKeU, suggests that many of the component courses that were part of the UKeU are now successfully being offered within their originating institutions, so it was not a failure of individual courses or a lack of market need for those courses in isolation, but rather a failure of the UkeU as an institution or entity. The position of an 'eUniversity' presented by the UKeU was that it could bring benefit for all; however, the benefit of e-learning has only been demonstrated in particular cases and the universal benefit has not been apparent (Parr, 2004). By 2004 the market was aware of this and consequently was wary of e-learning as a solution for education. In attempting to establish a large organisation with new technology and short timescales the Commons report commented that the 'UKeU set itself an impossibly ambitious business model'. That the UKeU failed at a cost of over £60 million does not mean that all such ventures are bound to fail. It does suggest, though, that more gradual change – both in making the move to e-learning and in moving into the global market – would avoid many of the problems that were encountered.

4.2.2 Cultural Assumptions

The first wave of global providers used the Internet as a conduit that enabled the delivery of a particular sort of education. UNext claimed to 'collaborate[s] with some of the world's leading universities to bring you the best in online graduate business education through Cardean University'; Fathom Knowledge Network Inc. was established 'with the goal of providing high-quality educational resources to a global audience through the Internet'; while the UKeU adopted the slogan 'delivering the best of UK education online'. These slogans imply an assumption that global needs can be met by exporting approaches that have worked in one culture to be used and accepted in another. This view can be supported in terms of existing practices in education where established university systems such as those in Australia, the USA and UK attract students from other countries to study for existing qualifications. However, the Internet does not require students to relocate and base themselves in the other culture physically and so the transfer of education in isolation continues to be impacted on by local aspects. At the same time the Internet and communications technology is causing change to happen in many cultures and may offer an opportunity for those education providers who can match their offerings and approach to this new culture. Initiatives of this kind that involve mutual exchange and benefits have some chance of success.

The difficulties involved in making a commercial success of global education raises the question as to why providers should consider extending their courses globally. A possible answer is that world needs are not just economic. In Africa, for example, the AIDS/HIV epidemic has caused imbalance in the infrastructure at many levels, including in education. Attempting to reestablish such infrastructure suggests that if new ways to meet local needs from a distance can be found, then it may be possible to offer assistance. The Open University is, for example, committed to partnerships in line with the United Nations' Millennium Development Goals (http://www.developmentgoals.org). Through projects such as *The Ferguson Fund for Africa* (http://www.open.ac.uk/developmentoffice/p2_1.shtml), the Open University has plans to make a contribution to Africa that is sustainable and mutually beneficial and enriching. Their aim is to use this fund to help bring about universal primary education and to support a global partnership for development. The *Teacher Education in Sub Saharan Africa* (TESSA) *Project* is an early step in this initiative that is drawing extensively on a variety of media including ICT to build a new programme for primary teachers. The challenge of finding ways to meet the current needs of African societies requires innovative solutions and using technology in new and different ways has its part to play in building new capacity.

4.3 Approaches to Online Learning

4.3.1 E-Learning, Blended Learning and MobileLearning

E-Learning has emerged as a dominant term to describe using computers and networks to help people learn. It has been defined in broad terms by the UK government's 'e-strategy' (DfES, 2005) as 'using ICT to change how we learn'. This definition allows for cases where people work in isolation with computers and technology such as CD-ROMs or work collaboratively online. In practice, however, much of the popularity of the term is linked to the Internet as a way to connect students, teachers and the organisations that provide learning. E-learning therefore sits alongside e-commerce, e-government and e-business as a way of describing new modes of operating online. The promise of e-learning is that it can change the way we understand learning and offer new opportunities both to those who identify themselves as learners and for learning as it occurs in our everyday lives. Livingstone (1999) in his survey of Canadian workers revealed that for many people there are day-to-day activities where they will learn new information in an informal way, and that there need to be new methods found to support this activity.

Many institutions that previously considered moving to online learning are now taking the realistic view that a blend of online and face-to-face teaching is more likely to succeed. As Parr (2004) points out computer-assisted learning has been shown to be less effective, on average, than other forms of intervention in education. The idea behind the move to blended learning is that it allows flexibility between the different modes of learning so that no one approach is rigidly followed, and the needs of different learners are more likely to be better met. Learners are offered the best of both worlds as it were. This has been found to the case particularly when the teaching and learning model for a course is re-conceptualised, rather than simply adapted from other classroom models.

Mobile technologies, or technologies that people carry with them (e.g. PDAs, tablet computers, mobile phones, digital cameras), provide another avenue for the delivery of learning. As people themselves are mobile, as well as carrying devices they also find additional ways to interact electronically with the world – for example, using museum information systems, library catalogues other organisations' devices and other peoples' personal devices. This notion is emphasised in the *MOBIlearn Project* (http://www.mobilearn.org/) where learning is conceptualised as '[a]ny sort of learning that happens when the learner is not at a fixed, predetermined location, or learning that happens when the learner takes advantage of the learning opportunities offered by mobile technologies'. The idea of mobile learning that is adopted therefore needs to be broader than that of simply channelling information through a single mobile device (which inevitably will involve certain compromises as a consequence of the need to be small and portable. Rather mobile learning needs to be thought about as involving the use of contextual information about location, activity and interest that can offer a basis for supporting further learning relevant to the user provided through more appropriate channels.

As we think through the use of these teaching approaches it is important to consider how these new technologies can lead to a rethinking about how learning can be supported, particularly in relation to finding new solutions that cross existing national divides. The digital adopters are a special category in each society and it is possible that there is a commonality between those who operate internationally through the Internet that can be used to overcome some of the traditional international barriers that have hindered global learning projects.

4.3.2 The Open Approach

In software engineering open source sharing of code has shown itself to be a robust and successful approach to disseminating and developing software. In education there is now evidence of success in following the open source model to provide open access to course materials. Most notably this has been adopted by the Massachusetts Institute of Technology (MIT) to provide free access to its course material under the open courseware initiative (http://ocw.mit.edu/). By doing this MIT has shown that the value of provided education does not rest in the content alone: that having access to course materials is not the same as enrolling in an MIT course. Indeed for some courses the material aspect can be very limited. Nevertheless open access to these materials has enabled examples of transfer of courses across the globe in cases where teachers have adopted the MIT courses as a basis for their own teaching. Examples from the MIT web site of those making use of this OpenCourseWare include educators in Malaysia, Indonesia and Cuba. The African Virtual University (AVU) (http://ww.avu.org/) was set up 'to build capacity and support economic development by leveraging the power of modern telecommunications technology to provide world-class quality education and training programmes to students and professionals in Africa'. It has operations in 19 African countries and seeks to link with other universities worldwide. One of these links has been with MIT to provide a range of computing and engineering courses. However, the analysis emerging from this experience is that the reuse of courses is not sufficient as a model for the AVU; it needs to develop its own versions of online courses and to build the skills to support and adapt these rather than simply reuse those developed by others.

The Open University is reviewing its own approach to distributing material. Within the Open University it is recognised that sections of its material are used within other universities as a common practice. It is also currently possible to buy more or less any set of course materials by bidding for them on eBay. Though this use is not legitimate, it is unlikely to be harmful to the business of the Open University if students of other universities use some of its materials while enrolled on other courses; having the materials is not the same as taking the course. The move from tolerating some reuse to making Open University materials available under an open courseware model or creative commons licence may also cause no harm to the Open University but the risk is higher than it was for MIT. The Open University's material is designed for self-study but in a supported way, and it is possible that some alternative low-cost provider could provide and sell that support to go with the freely available materials. As a public service organisation with aims that include seeking to promote global citizenship the benefits need to be weighed against these risks. Such issues are currently being considered and it seems likely that at least some courses will operate in a more open way. The first such courses are now being made available with interesting early results: one course with insufficient interest to be retained has had over 500 registrations for the freely available and unsupported version.

4.3.3 The Open University as a Model for Global Learning

The Open University has an overall model for distance education, termed Supported Open Learning (SOL) that is adapting to the way the Open University acts as it operates as a supplier of online courses. While the Open University is now very much working online the majority of its courses continue to be predominantly for its home audience or offered in partnership for specific initiatives (such as the ArabOU or the Hong Kong Institute). There are important exceptions to this, in particular the MA in Online and Distance Education which is offered globally and is organised through online provision of integrating material and tuition. Table 4.1summarises the changes that are happening in the Open University as it shifts from producing 'traditional' distance education towards using e-learning delivery of courses.

There is a move from an established and effective system towards one where there is more uncertainty and risk, as well as potential advantages. The option to 'do nothing' and avoid e-learning is not viable for the Open University as the student body has changing expectations. A strategy of gradual change has been adopted to retain a mix of different media rather than seeking a completely online solution as a virtual university. This more gradual approach parallels the adoption of blended learning in campus-based universities.

4.3.4 Supported Open Learning

In Supported Open Learning at the Open University in the UK, a centralised course team is responsible for producing the course materials and an overall design for the student's learning experience. The design is often described within a 'course guide' that explains to the student how they could study the course accompanied by a timetable that sets out expected progress. The student body is usually organised in groups of approximately 20 students assigned to an Associate Lecturer as their tutor. The tutor's role is to support the students through remote contact and in face-to-face tutorial meetings, and to give detailed feedback on their submitted work. This model has proved to be very successful in enabling students to study with the Open University and to allow variation in how students and tutors operate. However,

Table 4.1 Emerging differences between traditional and e-learning courses delivered at the Open University

Traditional Open University courses	E-learning Open University courses
Expensively produced courses: lead time of up to 3 years and specialist production of course material	Variable costs: some rapidly produced courses with simplified designs but also can be additional costs in presenting the course and customising online environments
Good course life: the target life for courses was 8 years with minor updating	Annual updates/changes: learners expect revised versions and the technology encourages change
Well-founded design: models for courses were defined in establishing the Open University and form the basis for many of the courses	Experimental designs: more individual courses and variation across the Open University, sometimes with unexpected strains for staff and students
Well-supported: the established tutor model offers direct comment and available support throughout the course; a tutor is likely to know all their students	Well-supported, but with variation: the same model for support is used in many cases with conferencing and email replacing post and telephone; however courses are trying to control presentation costs by changing the student:tutor ratio
Well-regarded for teaching quality: for example based on analysis of government quality assessment the Open University was ranked 5th for teaching (Times Online, 2004)	Well-regarded, but print usually scores best: typically online courses have similar ratings to other courses for overall satisfaction but the most highly rated media are usually printed guides produced specifically for a course (Kirkwood, 2003)
Equality of experiences: materials provided by the Open University were meant to be sufficient for the course, everything that was needed came in the box of materials. http://www.open.ac.uk/johndanielspeeches/chea.htm	Need to accept different experiences: designing online means that learners are expected to use resources to help them carry out the activities, and the large and changing nature of the Internet means learners will use different resources some of which may not have existed at the time of design

while this approach still applies as a general description there are now many variations in the support model especially as applied in e-learning. For example, there are now cases where the course guide and material supplied to the students has been reduced so that the emphasis is on working collaboratively in groups guided by their tutors, either using activities designed by the course team or related activities designed by the tutors. Conversely on some courses tutor involvement has been reduced with the online activities providing the primary guidance while tutors provide backup support with responsibility for 200 students rather than 20.

4.3.5 An Open University Global Course

The MA in Online and Distance Education is a qualification consisting of independent courses that are produced in the Institute of Educational Technology. It attracts relatively low numbers of students, particularly in the context of the Open

University. This smaller student cohort has provided an opportunity for the course to operate more flexibly and to be used as a platform for innovation. For example, one of the courses in the MA, 'Applications of Information Technology in Open and Distance Education' (http://iet.open.ac.uk/courses/), is aimed at graduate professionals working in education or training and attracts around 60 students a year from all over the world. The course was developed by a small team of five academics who all had experience of designing and tutoring online courses. Members of the team had been involved in the design and evaluation of Open University undergraduate courses that had used computer conferencing and were particularly aware of the strengths and weaknesses of the online medium. The course is accessed through a web site and is primarily online – that is, the learning activities and resources are accessed on the site, and students communicate through the conferencing system and work in small, collaborative groups. There are also set books, video and audio on CD-ROM, a CD-ROM of multimedia extracts, software and access to journal articles. The assessments are submitted online and returned to students electronically.

The approach for the course is built around tasks. This enables a relatively robust approach as learners will adjust the way they perform the tasks to match with the groups they are in and the resources that are available. This means that there is uncertainty as to what will happen but also flexibility in the course for the students. The tasks are in many cases collaborative with the aim of building up a community among the learners. This is an effective approach with high completion and satisfaction ratings. When the principles of the course were analysed by tutors and course team members (Ross et al., 2004) it was found that the task-based approach had made considerable impact as it had given learners greater ownership and group involvement and the opportunity to create their own paths to meet the requirements of the course. They noted that this approach meant that tutors had to be very flexible and allow space for what might happen as student activities would vary each time the course was run (e.g. learners could draw on resources not known to the tutor, or that may not have existed when the task was written). At the same time it was recognised that supporting what is expected to happen rather than attempting to force things to happen by exerting too much control was a necessary guideline for tutors. This holding back by tutors is not necessarily appreciated by learners who often remain unaware of how tutors are in fact supporting them.

4.3.6 Global Issues

The MA at the Open University is global in that people in all countries can register and take part in the course. Its tutors are also distributed at various locations though not as widely as students, and its model of using online integration means that no face-to-face meetings are needed and electronic submission ensures that assessment deadlines are fair. However, the course is only offered in English, the producers of the course are all based within the British Open University and while they have a diversity of backgrounds, they essentially operate with a curriculum and pedagogic basis that is founded on UK values. Just as this chapter tries to give value to a worldwide audience even while writing from the perspective of the UK, so these courses have a similar bias. The way in which the course meets the needs of the global audience is based on addressing the following items:

1. Using a task approach that adjusts to individual and group contexts
2. Offering support for those not familiar with the academic writing required for assessment
3. Reviewing for unnecessary referencing to UK concerns

Of these three aspects, Item 2 has been extended in recent times and has proved of benefit to all learners, not just those who come from other cultures. This approach, however, still requires the learners to adapt to the assessment offered by the provider. Item 3 does not ensure that cultural bias is absent though it goes some way towards achieving this. Item 1 then holds the key to providing a course that can adapt to circumstances by setting out an approach where the students are challenged to carry out tasks but allowed to vary exactly how these tasks are achieved. The community aspects of the course depend on staff and students being willing to collaborate on group tasks and to be open to sharing results, progress and reflections – not necessarily something that is easily achieved. The experience of the course has shown that it has been effective for people from a wide range of backgrounds and that many students find great benefits from the task-based approach. It does need to be acknowledged that even this approach does not remove all cultural bias from the course as it appears to be adopted more readily by those used to questioning the teacher's position than those who have operated in systems where the teacher is expected to have the right answer. The implicit assumption that it is desirable to be able to question is itself culturally based and may not be the best approach in the global context. In spite of this limitation, a task-based approach has shown inherent flexibility and is one that avoids the need to frequently change materials and tutor methods.

4.4 Representing Designs

The limited success of global e-learning to date suggests that we need to capture the essence of good designs in a way that allows as much as possible of the learning experience to be transferred to the students' control while at the same time limiting dependence on particular aspects of culture. One possible way to achieve this involves separation of the resources (as learning objects), the design structure (as learning design) and the design rationale (as a pattern) within a framework that recognises the need for people support and the value of global collaboration. Such an approach will not be a solution for all cases but rather for those where part of the intention is to share views and allow diversity.

4.4.1 Learning Objects

Learning objects has emerged as a term to describe materials produced to support learning that can be represented electronically and separated from the way in which they are first used. The International Workshop on Wireless and Mobile Technologies in Education (IEEE) working group on learning object metadata have defined learning objects as 'any entity, digital or non-digital, which can be used, reused or referenced during technology supported learning. There are other definitions of learning objects (see, e.g. Polsani, 2003; Rehak & Mason, 2003) but much of the work on them has focused on reuse (Littlejohn, 2003). In practice, work at the Open University has shown that reuse is not sufficient as a focus, as there is limited motivation for the producer. Rather it has been found that the learning object approach can best serve as a working method during the design process to help divide online courses into discrete sections and to reintroduce flexibility for both the designers and the learners.

Using learning objects for design means that we adopt a technique that helps people author flexible modular pieces of learning that can be well described and carried out in a reasonable amount of time (typically a few hours of activity). Weller, Pegler and Mason (2003) suggest a number of principles for using learning objects in e-learning courses in higher education: that the learning objects should remain autonomous and should in general avoid references to other sections, have sufficient self-description to be understood, contain a task for learners, give opportunity for reflection and collaboration and provide indications of resources with an expectation that alternatives can be found. It would seem sensible to use this relatively informal description flexibly omitting some aspects (for instance collaboration) where necessary and bending or breaking the rules according to the demands of the courses and their students.

A potential disadvantage that Weller et al.'s (2003) study identified was the lack of educational narrative that becomes evident when autonomous objects are collected together. They argue that

> it remains to be seen whether the removal of explicit connections may render the material *more* meaningful for students, since it places the responsibility for making such connections with the student. ... It is also in keeping with more constructivist sympathies, that there is not one set of connections to be made between concepts, i.e. those of the educator, but rather a multitude and every individual will create their own meaningful overarching narrative. (Weller et al., 2003)

If, on the other hand, narrative objects are created to overcome this problem then it would not be expected that these would be reusable (Pegler, 2005), an expectation which removes one of the main advantages claimed for learning objects. It would seem that while the potential of learning objects for use in educational settings is clearly evident, educators still have a considerable way to go in finding out the most efficient ways to create and use them, and just what kind of value they do offer the various stakeholders involved in using them.

4.4.2 Learning Design

As suggested above, a learning object approach offers advantages in dividing courses up into sections but the overall structure that indicates how learners are to use the different objects can get lost. Introducing narrative objects partly addresses this difficulty but only in an informal way. Other work that has focussed on ways in which the design of learning can be represented suggests another possible way forward. The IMS Learning Design specification (Koper & Tattersall, 2005) is a development of the Educational Modelling Language (Hummel et al., 2004) designed by The Open Universiteit Nederland to enable all aspects of online courses to be described; not just the materials but also the order in which activities take place, the roles that people undertake, key criteria for progression and the services needed for presentation to learners. The IMS Learning Design specification does not detail how the course material itself is to be represented but rather how to package up the overall information into a structure that is modelled on a play, with acts, roles (actors) and resources. The work was developed into a specification through collaboration within IMS to address the need for a more structured approach to representing learning. It develops the concept of content packaging, where different digital resources are gathered together with a listing of each resource describing their location, but it enhances this approach by providing an ordered presentation of the different entities within the unit of learning. IMS Learning Design is intended to support all pedagogies but it has a particular advantage over other approaches in that it enables the representation of collaborative activities that involve different roles for learners and tutors and need synchronisation in various ways.

4.4.3 Learning Patterns

By building on work on architectural patterns (Alexander, 1979), Goodyear et al. (2004) have developed a concept of learning design patterns as a way to capture knowledge from designers and share them with practitioners. These patterns are viewed as the source for advice when reproducing the general form but without the expectation that any cases will be exactly the same. Thus a pattern 'describes a problem which occurs over and over again in our environment, and then describes the core of the solution to that problem, in such a way that you can use this solution a million times over, without ever doing it the same way twice' (Alexander et al., 1977, p. x).

Patterns applied to learning seek to identify what can be provided as useful background, guidance and illustration in describing a set of interrelated descriptions for ways to assist learning online. A pattern is seen as something that will not be reused directly but can assist the informed teacher to build up their own range of tasks, tools or materials that can draw on a collected body of experience. This produces a difference of position between what is needed to implement Learning

Design as the aim of patterns is **not** to supply a complete solution but rather to give enough guidance and expect human intervention and variation in each reuse.

The format for a Learning Pattern (adapted from Goodyear et al., 2004) is:

1. A picture (showing an archetypal example of the pattern)
2. An introductory paragraph setting the **context** for the pattern (explaining how it helps to complete some larger patterns)
3. Problem **headline**, to give the essence of the problem in one or two sentences
4. The **body** of the problem (its empirical background, evidence for its validity, examples of different ways the pattern can be manifested)
5. The **solution**. Stated as an instruction, so that you know what to do to build the pattern
6. A diagrammatic representation of the solution
7. A paragraph linking the pattern to the smaller patterns which are needed to complete and embellish it

These patterns are then integrated into a pattern language by providing related components such as a *discussion group* pattern that draws on patterns for *discussion role, facilitator and discursive task* (Goodyear et al., 2004).

The strength of the patterns approach is shown in communities adopting them that have emerged in areas of architecture and computer science. In such communities design patterns are drafted, shared, critiqued and refined through an extended process of collaboration. It is evident that patterns have the potential to make a contribution to the sharing of techniques between developers of learning activities.

In contrast to Learning Design, patterns offer informality and are open to different interpretations and different implementations at the detail level. This can lead to problems with imprecise vocabulary, but it can also be seen as an easier, less formal way of constructing these descriptions and a way that encourages users to engage with and challenge the contents of patterns rather than use pre-packaged designs.

4.4.4 Applying Objects, Designs and Patterns

The division into objects, designs and patterns provides different levels of formality for course descriptions and the chance that different groups and cultures can work in different ways with material. This has been demonstrated at the Open University on a small scale where learning structures and resources have been reused across different levels of courses, in staff development and with global learning groups. This approach has yet to be shown to work on a larger scale but it does align with the Internet culture by allowing for different levels of interest, sharing of experiences, alternative routes and selecting from and managing growing resources. The approach also matches well with open structures both in providing objects, designs and patterns and in drawing from other sources and cultures.

4.5 What Is Needed for Global Learning

The problems that have been found in trying to provide global online courses mean that there is no easy recipe for success. However, study of the actions of organisations involved in online learning and the experience of producing global courses at the Open University suggest that there are lessons to be learned about what is needed for global learning. These lessons can be categorised as relating primarily to course design and relating to the production process.

Lessons for course design:

- *A task-based approach helps robust learning*

A task-based approach to learning design allows the learner to adjust how they respond depending on available resources, the community of learners and their own background. The learner also needs to take an active position that will help them to ground knowledge through reflection and exchange with others. Such a task-based approach does mean that each presentation is different and that there are risks that some tasks will not work with some groups. However, the adaptivity provided by the task outweighs the possible disadvantages.

- *Working with learning objects creates more flexibility*

Learning objects have been promoted as a solution for reuse and exchange of content. A structured approach to describing small sections of learning does indeed have advantages when sections need to be transferred between courses; however, the main advantage is in making the course more modular and able to be separated into different activities which allows students to follow optional paths. Optional work has often been found detrimental in distance learning as it may be either completely omitted by the learner, in which case the investment in producing the material is wasted, or students may opt to carry out all the optional activities leading to overload and dilution of their effort. A learning object approach may not entirely avoid these problems but in practice it does mean that students can select a personal path through a course.

- *Mixed media is stronger than single media*

Adopting different ways to reach the learner has proven to be a benefit for courses operating at a distance. The dominant medium has undoubtedly been printed text and feedback consistently shows that material produced for a course and printed for the student has the highest rating. However, it is also evident that the inclusion of a variety of materials provides motivation and support for students with different preferences. With the move to online courses a mix in media needs to be retained and supported by offering a variety across tasks and opportunities for a range of interactions with others. It needs to be remembered that approaches to technology are also evolving amongst learners – evidence of this can be seen in a gradual acceptance of e-books as an alternative to print materials and reports that are now emerging of students preferring to read on-screen.

Lessons for producing courses:

- *Representing designs helps understanding and transfer of materials*

Generating new courses that operate online has changed the production dynamic in universities. It has led to more variety and shorter time-scales for production of courses. In many cases the quality of the result has been pleasing but the strain on the developers has been significant. The practice of recording designs in ways that represent elements has many advantages, although it may be hard in practice to determine which is the 'better' way to achieve a particular goal. This practice allows commonality to be revealed and offers insight into ways to clarify the stages in online activities. It has proved a useful method both at a high-level in terms of models for courses as well as in terms of models for tasks and activities.

- *Ongoing evaluation of innovations is needed to guide future developments*

Studying what happens in courses is vital and the Open University has followed an approach of developmental testing when introducing new initiatives into courses. For example the technology used in the introduction of synchronous communication tools to support language learning was piloted and the tutorial design that would use the technology examined by studying how small groups of students took part in sample activities. This developmental approach is now being augmented by innovations being trialled as courses move into practice. For example a first year course on using the Internet was launched with a pilot year of 900 students before scaling up to operate as one of the largest online courses in the world with 10,000 students in its largest year of operation. Gathering information from students, tutors and developers becomes part of the operational approach with more the 30,000 students giving feedback on their courses each year.

- *Keep the human in the loop*

The model advocated in this chapter has aspects that could be automated (e.g. the selection of different learning objects, the tailoring of different paths for learners and the building of tutor groups). Such automation can be useful but it should not eliminate the human element from the learning. It is very difficult to allow for all options in automation and implemented systems tend to make simplifying assumptions that may not be valid. For example, the concept of learning styles suggests that individuals may be categorised and steered towards material that is visually more or less rich according to preference. However, learners like to vary what they use and also explore the alternatives. Providing for learner choice avoids the need to predict accurately and helps the students have ownership of their learning. The same argument applies for each of the roles in learning: the designer needs to explore options rather than be constrained by a fixed library of designs; the tutor to work out the best kind of guidance rather than pass on pre-written advice.

4.6 Conclusion

In this chapter the opportunities e-learning has to offer higher education in the global arena have been considered and reasons why those opportunities are difficult to realise in practice explored. It is clear that e-learning has many benefits to deliver to teachers, learners and organisations in our global community, and that producing e-learning for the global community involves a wide range of technical and educational choices. At this early stage of the evolution of e-learning there are no obvious solutions and no easy recipe for success. But building knowledge of developments and the trends and methods that show promise in this area, and learning about innovative practices undertaken by institutions who have already experimented in this field is a way forward for those involved in e-learning or taking it up as a new challenge.[1]

References

Alexander, C. (1979). *The Timeless Way of Building*. New York: Oxford University Press.

Alexander, C., Ishikawa, S., Silverstein, M., Jacobson, M., Fiksdahl-King, I., & Angel, S. (1977). *A Pattern Language: Towns, Buildings, Construction*. New York: Oxford University Press.

Conole, G., Carusi, A., & De Laat, M. (2005). Learning from the UKeU experience. ICE Conference Higham Hall. Reprinted as an E-Learning Research Centre Publication, University of Southampton. Retrieved July 30, 2006 from: http://www.elrc.ac.uk/download/publications/ICEpaper.pdf.

DfES (2005). Harnessing Technology: Transforming Learning and Children's Services. Retrieved July 30, 2006 from: http://www.dfes.gov.uk/publications/e-strategy/docs/e-strategy.pdf.

Goodyear, P., Avgeriou, P., Baggetun, R., Bartoluzzi, S., Retalis, S., Ronteltap, F., &Rusman E. (2004). *Towards a Pattern Language for Networked Learning. Proceedings of Networked Learning 2004*, Lancaster University, England, pp. 449–455.

House of Commons, UK e-University Report. (2005).Third Report of Session 2004–05. Report Together with Formal Minutes, Oral and Written Evidence. Retrieved July 30, 2006 from: http://www.publications.parliament.uk/pa/cm200405/cmselect/cmeduski/205/205.pdf.

Howcroft, D. (2001). After the Goldrush: Deconstructing the Myths of the Dot.com Market. *Journal of Information Technology*, 16, 195–204.

Hummel, H. G. K., Manderveld, J. M., Tattersall, C., & Koper, E. J. R. (2004). Educational Modelling Language and Learning Design: New Opportunities for Instructional Reusability and Personalised Learning. *Journal of Learning Technology*, 1 (1), 111–126.

Kirkwood, A. (2003). Understanding Independent Learners' Use of Media Technologies. *Open Learning*, 18 (2), 155–175.

Koper, R. & Tattersall, C. (Eds.) (2005). Learning Design: A Handbook on Modelling and Delivering Networked Education and Training. Berlin/Heidelberg: Springer.

Littlejohn, A. (Ed.) (2003). Reusing Online Resources: A Sustainable Approach to E-learning. London: Kogan Page.

Livingstone, D. W. (1999). Exploring the Icebergs of Adult Learning: Findings of the First Canadian Survey of Informal Learning Practices. *Canadian Journal for the Study of Adult Education*, 13 (2), 49–72.

[1] This chapter draw on a broad range of experience gained in working with my colleagues at the Open University and from collaborative projects with other organisations.

Parr, J. (2004). A Review of the Literature on Computer-Assisted Learning, Particularly Integrated Learning Systems, and Outcomes with Respect to Literacy and Numeracy. Ministry of Education, Wellington, New Zealand. Retrieved July 30, 2006 from: http://www.minedu.govt.nz/print_doc.cfm?documentid = 5499

Pegler, C. (2005). Objects and Issues – A Sunday Supplement View of Continuing Professional Development in Higher Education. *Open Learning*, 20 (1), 51–64.

Polsani, P. R. (2003). Use and Abuse of Reusable Learning Objects. Journal of Digital information 3 (4). Retrieved July 30, 2006 from: http://jodi.tamu.edu/Articles/v03/i04/Polsani/

Rehak, D. R. & Mason R. (2003). *Keeping the Learning in Learning Objects*. In A. Littlejohn (Ed.) Reusing Online Resources: A Sustainable Approach to E-learning (pp. 20–35). London: Kogan, pp. 114–115.

Ross, S., Kukulska-Hulme, A., Chappel, H., & Joyce, B. (2004).Taking E-moderating Skills to the Next Level: Reflecting on the Design of Conferencing Environments. Journal of Asynchronous Learning Networks, 8 (2).

Times Online. (2004). The Sunday Times University Guide Table: Best Marks for Teaching. From: http://www.timesonline.co.uk/article/0,,8405-1246628,00.html

Weller M. J., Pegler C. A., & Mason R. D. (2003). Putting the Pieces Together: What Working with Learning Objects Means for the Educator. Paper Presented at the E-LearnInternational, February 2003, Conference, Edinburgh. From: http://iet.open.ac.uk/pp/c.a.pegler/ukeu/edinburgh.doc

Chapter 5
Mobile Learning: The Significance of New Mobile and Wireless Communications Technologies for Education

Gerard Goggin

At present, the popular perception of mobile telephones in the UK, including the education sector, is generally negative: they are perceived as a nuisance and distraction (Stone, 2002, p. 262).

The image of schoolchildren staring out of the classroom window, minds preoccupied with daydreams, could be supplanted by one of students staring forward – not daydreaming but interacting with vibrating gadgets, chattering with offsite friends and accessing materials from outside the classroom. Tomorrow's mobile technology may be the perfect tutor in the local/global biomachine that many futurologists anticipate (Katz, 2004).

5.1 Why Have Mobiles Been Neglected in Education?

As of 2002, there were more mobile (or cell) phone subscribers in the world than there were people who have fixed telephones. Mobile phones are now widely used for data as well as for voice communications, and are playing a significant role in commercial, social and cultural settings. In some countries, mobiles are already an important mode of using the Internet – in Japan, for instance, the development of the Internet has been very much bound up with cell phones (Coates & Holroyd, 2003; Funk, 2001; Gottlieb & McLelland, 2003). In the years ahead, it is very likely that mobiles will take centre stage for using Internet and online communications.

With the phenomenal diffusion of mobiles around the world – including in many developing countries – and the directions now being taken with the convergence between mobiles, the Internet and computing, what is striking is the lack of attention accorded mobiles in education. For most people, thinking about mobiles and education is still principally a question of control and regulation. In schools, debate ensues about how to control use of mobiles for voice and text communications during class; and about how to proscribe or regulate inappropriate uses of mobiles in

---

G. Goggin
Centre for Critical and Cultural Studies, University of Queensland

J. Zajda and D. Gibbs (eds.), *Comparative Information Technology,*
DOI: 10.1007/978-1-4020-9426-2_5, © Springer Science+Bussiness Media B.V. 2009

relation to such things as criminal activities (e.g. drug-dealing), or when using mobiles for bullying or harassing other students. Parents, schools and governments are concerned about whether students should be allowed to bring mobiles to school, and if this is allowed, what the rules should be to govern how, when and for what reasons mobiles can be used. In universities, lecturers worry about mobiles ringing in lectures, or students text messaging during class. With the availability of camera phones, questions arise as to how to avoid inappropriate taking and storing of student images. Across educational settings, there is frequent concern expressed, particularly in the media, about whether the pervasive, always-connected condition of mobile-possessed students causes too much distraction and diminishes the quality of the learning experience.

The censorious tone regarding mobiles and education that still dominates discourses on this subject needs to be seen in the larger context of moral panics about mobiles (or 'mobile panics'). Like other new technologies and media forms before them, mobiles have become the subject of moral panics. There are health risks (radiation, driving), criminality (using phones to commit crimes), deviance (gangs and gate-crashing parties), threats to privacy (shouting on mobiles in public places) or sociability (mobiles in restaurants, or interrupting face-to-face conversation), environment and aesthetics (siting of towers), sexuality (illicit and licit) and availability of inappropriate or offensive content (such as pornography) over the mobile phone. While purporting to be about specific social or cultural threats, mobile panics, like other classic moral panics and folk devils (Cohen, 1972), appear to be closely associated with the regulation of subcultural groups by dominant groups – not least the time-honoured target of young people (Cohen, 1972; Hall et al., 1978). The negative perceptions associated with mobile phone usage are particularly resonant in an arena where the development and fostering of the capacities and minds of young people are of central concern. These perceptions usually overshadow consideration of the educational benefits mobile phones have to offer.

When discourses about the use of the Internet in schools are compared with that about mobile phones, strong differences are immediately evident. The advent of the Internet in everyday life from the early 1990s onwards, like the rise of the computer before it, has been of intense fascination to those involved in education. Visions of wired schools, universities and other learning sites have been a staple of policy developments, professional debates and narratives of use. There is a voluminous literature and much practitioner, stakeholder and student reflection on these subjects (e.g. see Dutton & Loader, 2002; Frechette, 2002; Hazemi et al., 1998). There are, of course, those who criticise the use of the Internet for education (Brabazon, 2002), or note the baleful influence of technology on culture and education more generally (Postman, 1993), but there is significant evidence of dialogue occurring. In the public domain the Internet, like the mobile phone, is often associated with a variety of ills (pornography, overuse by young people leading to poor health, excessive playing of games and so on), yet it is also very much prized as a technology that is an invaluable resource for education with the potential to reshape or transform educational practice. When it comes to mobile and wireless communication devices, the picture is very different and much less optimistic.

Against this background, the present chapter aims to take a fresh look at the potential mobile phones have for use in educational settings. In discussing this pervasive and far-reaching new mode of information and communications technologies, an overview of the history of the development of mobile phones is outlined; illustrative case studies of the uses of mobiles in educational practices and institutions across a number of countries are examined; and the distinctive nature of 'm(obile)-learning' educational practices are analysed. The chapter concludes by identifying some of the major issues for educational theorists and practitioners engaged in fruitfully integrating mobiles into education in the global arena.

5.2 Overview of the History of Mobile Phone Development

In 2003 there were an estimated 1,340,667 mobile or cell phone subscribers worldwide (up from approximately 91 million in 1995, and 1.158 billion in 2002), or 53.49% of total telephone subscribers (International Telecommunications Union, 2005). Once the province of business people, realtors or tradespeople, the mobile is now firmly established as the treasured possession of teenage, and even pre-teen, girls and boys. The beginnings of mobiles lie in Marconi's work in the late nineteenth century in wireless telegraphy. The first commercial service was offered in St. Louis, Missouri, in 1946. The real breakthrough, however, occurred with the 1947 invention of the 'cellular' way of efficiently using radio frequencies by Bell Labs (Agar, 2003). However, it was not until 1977 that the first cellular mobile system was trialled by Illinois Bell in Chicago. Cellular licences were auctioned by the Federal Communications Commission (FCC) in the USA in 1982, and 1984 saw the first handheld cellular phone, a Motorola 8000. In Europe, the Nordic countries adopted a common system. The 'first generation' of mobiles phones offered commercially around the world from the mid-1980s were based on an analogue system.

Essentially analogue mobile phones offered portable (or mobile) voice communications. Handsets were originally very large and bulky, and gradually became smaller and easier to carry. Once greater ease of use, and cheaper handset and call prices led to mobiles being more widely adopted, they began to become an important feature of technologically mediated communications. Mobiles could be associated with an individual person, rather than a household. They allowed people to make calls where they were able to find reception and network availability, rather than be restricted by the length of telephone cord or reception distance of a cordless phone (Ling, 2004).

As the predecessor of mobile phones, fixed telephones had long had a role in education, principally in distance education. Distance education students at universities were able to consult their teachers via the telephone for discussion or enquiries. Students on remote rural farms or properties enrolled in the School of the Air in Australia, for instance, communicated via the telephone with their classmates or teachers. In addition to being used one-to-one for discussion with a tutor or teacher, 'bridge' technology allowed a number of people on different telephones in different locations to speak with each other at the same time in what is called an 'audioconference' or 'conference call'.

Unlike fixed phones, analogue mobile phones do not seem to have been widely used in distance education, perhaps because of issues of cost and of quality of reception and transmission. The emergence of using mobiles for educational purposes really did not begin until second-generation mobiles were widely adopted. Second-generation mobiles are based on a digital, rather than analogue, standard. The digital mobile phone as it developed through the 1990s had an extended range of features – such as storage of messages and phone numbers, and call number display (Lindholm et al. 2003) – which also took advantage of 'intelligent telecommunications networks'. The comparative advantages are more efficient sharing and use of scarce radio spectrum, vastly improved security of communications with data encryption, better technical quality of communications and greater potential for data as well as voice communications. Digital technology in mobile phones also made possible something much talked about with respect to new media more generally: multimedia, or communication and cultural exchange through text, image, sound and touch, as well as voice.

The most prominent and pervasive of the new dimensions of digital mobile communications is text messaging. Text messaging allows phone users to key-in characters via the alphanumeric keyboard of their device, compose short messages and send these to other phone users. The widespread adoption of text messaging from 1993 onwards was roughly contemporaneous with the explosion in another form of writing and text, namely electronic mail over the Internet (Goggin, 2004).

Text messaging was a feature of the GSM standard, and early on proved far more popular than the Wireless Access Protocol, an attempt to allow Internet access, including email, over mobile phones. As the capabilities of digital mobile phones were steadily augmented and elaborated, a new term developed to describe them – 2.5 (or second and a half) generation mobiles. 2.5G services especially centred on multimedia applications, such as the ability to receive and send images or short videos, as well as audio capabilities (the most popular of which is probably downloading music to customise the ringtone of a phone). In the middle of the first decade of the twenty-first century, mobile messaging and other mobile data services had become a lucrative segment of the industry in their own right (Goggin & Spurgeon, 2005). As a result, the narrative of an upward march through progressively advanced 'generations' of mobile phone was put into question.

The third generation (3G) of mobile networks and phones were premised on technical systems and standards that promised to finally make 'picture' phones a commercial reality. Third-generation phones offered the possibility of interactive video communications wherever the user happened to be located. Its promoters faced a number of challenges, not least the cost of licences and relatively slow takeup. On the horizon now is the fourth generation (4G) of broadband mobile networks and devices, promising very fast rates of data transfer allowing a full-length video or song to be downloaded, and much higher quality video communications.

There are many other mobile communication devices that are articulated, or overlap, with mobile phones: walkie-talkies or pagers, for instance, or portable digital assistants (PDAs), Blackberries, computers with wireless access and digital cameras. In the realm of digital technologies especially, there are many devices that have multiple functions and distinctive cultures of use – and there is considerable debate about whether these devices will converge into hybrid equipment or keep a separate function.

There is the potential through wireless connection technologies such as Bluetooth for mobiles to connect with many other sorts of devices. Indeed, there are very real possibilities for mobiles to connect to all sorts of objects in a user's environment that are identified, or tagged, with Radio Frequency Identification Devices (RFIDs) that emit a signal and are addressable over radio spectrum by other devices (Konkel et al., 2004; Siegemund & Flörkemeier, 2003). Nokia, for example, launched a phone enhanced with a RFID reader in 2004. There are, too, the cyborg-like possibilities of wearable, pervasive networked computing (Falk & Björk, 2003; Fortunati et al., 2003) which are well worth noting as their potential is still as yet not fully realised.

5.3 Uses of Mobiles in Education

Thus far there is only a slim body of educational practice and scholarly literature devoted to mobile telecommunications. It is fair to say that the bulk of studies are reports on and discussion of various experimental projects that deploy wireless and mobile technologies, often published in proceedings of computing technology conferences and technology-themed journals (e.g. Inkpen, 1999; Malliou et al., 2002; Ring, 2001; Sharples et al., 2002; Stone et al., 2003a; Thornton & Hauser, 2001). There are a number of important studies that move beyond the application of existing mobile technology to educational settings, and focus on the need to understand the contexts of use and to systematically relate these to the design of devices, and software and content management (such as Divitini et al., 2002; Sharples, 2000; Stone et al., 2003a). There is another group of studies that explicitly addresses, evaluates or counters the perceived disadvantages and poor image of mobiles (e.g. Katz, 2003; Stone, 2002). As yet, however, there are few studies that scrutinise the theoretical bearings of mobile learning (although, an important collection of perspectives of this kind is collected in Nyíri, 2003c; see also Nyíri, 2002).

As mobile phone culture consolidates its place across a wide cross section of society, there is growing evidence to suggest that educators are becoming interested in these technologies, and their social, cultural and theoretical implications – in spite of their negative press. New possibilities for education are emerging with the diffusion of feature-rich, high screen quality 2.5 and 3G mobiles that are being used by consumers who wish to use them and can afford to do so. Demand for mobile technologies from users is also being keenly observed and promoted by a fast growing host of telecommunications and IT companies, software developers, service and content providers, educational media companies and educational institutions themselves. Some representative case studies of the use of mobiles in different regions and cultures are offered here to gain some sense of the range and type of possible educational uses for mobile phones that are currently emerging.

5.3.1 Range and Type of Educational Uses for Mobile Phones

(a) Mobiles for Class or Course Administration

Mobiles are now being widely used to provide results of exams or courses by authorities. In Australia, for instance, a number of the state education systems provide matriculation results via SMS.

(b) Mobile Technologies for Libraries

Wireless access for laptop and portable computers is now being widely provided in the libraries and campuses of universities in many wealthy countries. There have been some trials of providing library information via SMS and WAP technologies in a number of countries. Stone et al. note:

> The Wiener Stadt-und Landesbibliotek in Austria has been reported as being one of the first in Europe to offer WAP-enabled catalogue access. Finland's ATP Origo system is reported to be capable of dealing with overdue books and renewals via SMS, and proposes using WAP for search, renewal, and request facilities. (Stone et al., 2001, p. 3)

With the growth in mobile commerce in the early 2000s, especially through the relatively well-proven if rudimentary technology of SMS, some libraries have moved to offer information to borrowers such as notifications (building on the now widespread use of email to alert borrowers to overdue or recalled items) using this method.

(c) Extending the Scope and Possibility of Current Education Practice in Formal Institutions

The *MOBIlearn* project funded by the European Commission explores how mobile technologies could be utilised to enhance learning in various contexts. The project involves the development of a mobile-learning architecture, and is being undertaken by a consortium of partners from Europe, Israel, Switzerland, the USA and Australia. One of the three application areas identified for mobile learning from a questionnaire developed by the MOBIlearn team (http://www.mobilearn.org/results/questionnaire/questionnaire.htm) is the following:

> Master in Business Administration (MBA) schools will extend the reach and scope of their current blended learning offering by providing learners with personalised and tailored subscriptions to content on mobile networks or Orientation Game, inducting undergraduate students on their entry into the university and supporting ad hoc, situation-based, serendipitous learning.

(d) Young Adults 'at Risk'

A €4.5 million 3-year pan-European research and development programme supported by the European Commission's Information Society Technologies (IST) programme, the *m-learning* project, aims to improve levels of literacy, numeracy and participation in education amongst young adults across the EU:

> m-learning ... is aimed at young adults, aged 16 to 24, who are most at risk of social exclusion in Europe. They have not succeeded in the education system, cannot read and write adequately and have problems with simple calculations except in familiar contexts. They are not currently

> involved in any education or training and may be unemployed, under employed, or even homeless. (M-learning, 2003)

M-learning recognised that many young people were keen users of mobile phones – 'What do many of these young people have in common? A mobile phone' – and tried to investigate 'how the technologies in the hands of these young people, now and in the near future, might be used to engage them in learning activities, start to change their attitudes to learning and thereby contribute to improving their skills, opportunities and lives' (M-learning, 2003). The programme ran from October 2001 to September 2004, and was coordinated by the Learning and Skills Development Agency (LSDA). The participants included universities and commercial companies from Britain, Italy and Sweden.

A key outcome of the project was the development of prototype services and products to incorporate insights about young people's learning into the design of mobile technologies. Early results included work on guidelines for learning, teaching and tutoring in a mobile environment, a matter of key significance if the pedagogical implications of the technology are to be fully addressed. Another outcome has been the development of a 'learning content management service' as a way to enable the organisation and coordination of resources and learning experiences.

(e) Lifelong Learning

A number of recent projects examine the potential for mobile technology to support learning 'anywhere, anytime' (a phrase used by technology companies such as IBM, Microsoft and Hewlett Packard to promote learning with laptop computers [Sharples et al., 2002]). One of the most influential projects, the *HandLeR* project at the University of Birmingham, explicitly seeks to link mobile learning with the philosophy of 'life-long learning' which had gained in popularity among policy-makers in the UK, and elsewhere, during the 1990s:

> [L]earning is not confined to pre-specified times or places, but happens whenever there is a break in the flow of routine daily performance and a person reflects on the current situation, resolves to address a problem, to share an idea, or to gain an understanding. (Sharples et al., 2002, p. 220)

Its proponents note:

> [F]ormal education cannot provide people with all the knowledge and skills they need to prosper throughout a lifetime. Therefore, people will need continually to enhance their abilities, in order to address immediate problems and to participate in a process of continuing vocational and professional development. (Sharples et al., 2002, p. 220)

They feel, however, that those experimenting with mobile technologies for education have not given sufficient attention to life-long learning. Accordingly, the *HandLeR* project seeks to develop a prototype of a handheld device designed for children aged 9–11, as an 'exemplar of personal mobile systems for life-long learning' (Sharples et al., 2002). Those involved in the *HandLeR* project postulate the general requirements of design as highly portable, individual, unobtrusive, available anywhere, adaptable to context and skills, persistent (over a lifetime, for instance) and both useful and easy to use (Sharples, 2000; Sharples et al., 2002).

The endpoint of this phase of their project is to claim a proof of concept 'that a handheld or wearable device, with appropriate learning tools and resources, an intuitive interface and high-speed communication could offer a new generation of portable "learning organisers" for people of all ages' (Sharples et al., 2002, p. 21).

(f) Mobile Learning in Fieldwork or Site Visits (Museums, Art Galleries, Cultural Heritage Sites)

In conjunction with the Amsterdam's Montessori School, the new media museum Waag has devised a mobile game, 'Frequency 1550' to teach citizens about the history of their city (see http://freq1550.waag.org/preview.html). Piloted in February 2005, the game is designed to be played on UMTS (3G) handsets offered by the Dutch telecommunications company KPN:

> For one to two days, players roam through the city in small groups. GPS makes it possible to know the position of your team (and of other players or objects). To prove they're the most worthy order of pilgrims, a team will need to demonstrate their knowledge of medieval Amsterdam by doing location-based media-assignments on the city's history. As they wander through the streets of medieval Amsterdam, they get in virtual phone contact with characters that provide information on locations and on the strange disappearing of the holy relic. In the meantime, they're competing with the other teams. GPS technology and mobile phones turn the city into a medieval playing field.

According to the Waag Society's homepage (http://freq1550.waag.org/preview.html) the use of mobile technology makes the game, and learning, interactive:

> UMTS makes it possible for each team to be in touch with their Headquarters (HQ) by mobile video telephone and to exchange multimedia.... Using internet-access, information is looked up and historical references are checked out. HQ also sees the bigger picture, has the overview as to what the other teams are up to and works out the team's strategy.... When the game is finished on the third day, all teams gather at HQ to see who won and collectively reflect on the media produced, the answers given and the strategic decisions taken during the game.

There are at least three key aspects of the technologies used in this. Firstly, there is the capacity for fast data-transfer rates afforded by GPRS and UMTS mobile connections. Secondly, location technology is used (http://freq1550.waag.org/tech.html). Thirdly, a game engine was created, allowing all users to share the same virtual space (i.e. a multi-user environment) and also to up- and download media as they move around the city. The evaluation of this pilot was not available at the time of writing.

Another European example of mobile learning in site visits is part of the *MOBIlearn* project discussed above. *MOBIlearn* identified museums as a representative application area for mobile learning, for citizens 'as members of a culture, to improve the learning experience' (*MOBIlearn*, 2002) while visiting important cultural sites such as a museum. The rationale for this is that 'a museum that manages historical and cultural heritage locations of the city will improve its offerings enabling learning citizens to access context-sensitive art, historical and cultural knowledge with mobile devices while visiting museums and galleries'.

(g) Mobiles for Community Learning and Networks

The *MOOsburg* project in the USA, an existing community-oriented collaborative environment that models the town of Blacksburg (Carroll et al., 2001), used a mobile education paradigm to support a wireless online virtual community (Farooq et al., 2002). One of the target applications for *MOOsburg* is an ongoing project called 'Save Our Streams', aiming to protect the local water environment. The project modelled various scenarios to do with biosampling and data collection in the field, and collaborative discussion of the results, using handheld devices.

(h) Health Information and Training

The *MOBIlearn* project includes health as one of its specialised applications, especially 'access to basic first aid medical knowledge to enable support for anywhere and anytime interventions for non-specialized citizens in basic medical situations' (http://www.mobilearn.org/results/questionnaire/questionnaire.htm). This has its parallels to the various scenarios discussed in the area of telemedicine, where networked communications technology is used to provide information, imaging, instruction or diagnosis, to support lay people or health practitioners in remote locations.

5.4 The Distinctive Contribution of Mobile Learning

Given that the idea of using mobiles in education is relatively new, and that few concrete case studies of its use in the educational context exist, it is not unsurprising that the distinctiveness of their contribution to education has not yet been widely debated. The most useful study to date has been provided by the Hungarian philosopher Kristóf Nyíri in his ambitious three-volume edited collection on mobile learning, democracy and communication. Elsewhere he has discerned 'two familiar approaches to the issue of mobile learning' (Nyíri, 2002):

> The first points out that since the dominant mode of access to the Internet will soon be through wireless devices, e-learning simply becomes m-learning, without any particular changes in content. The second approach stresses that m-learning will characteristically aim at specific kinds of knowledge, namely knowledge that is location-dependent and situation-dependent.

This is a neat and challenging précis of key issues that underpin developing discourses about mobile learning. The first approach Nyiri refers to relating to the transition from e-learning to m-learning is critically important because so many resources and so much intellectual and pedagogical labour has been invested in the imaginative and material creation of digital and networked education. As MacKenzie and Wajcman (1999) and Wajcman (2004) point out developments in technologies are socially shaped, and there are contests and negotiations at stake in the transformations that occur. For example, there has to be a reconfiguration of technology and its social relations if we are to be able to slide or segue seamlessly from e-learning to m-learning. The second approach identified by Nyíri is at the heart of thinking of what is distinctive about m-learning, namely the habitus of networked mobilities and the subjects through these that are in a process of becoming. Rather than knowledge and their teaching and learning being anchored, in particular, well-marked-out institutions and their associated practices (kindergartens, schools, technical institutes, universities, adult and further learning centres, industrial and professional learning sites, training workshops), the radical promise of mobile learning is that it is able to contribute further to the recognition that learning, often the most important learning, happens outside, across or despite these locations; or happens in different ways and spaces inside them. Mobiles have come to imply different possibilities for communication and information exchange, and these new circuits can intersect fruitfully and in new ways with the shifting modes of education.

Nyíri himself signals a critique of these two approaches, and proposes a different perspective:

> I define m-learning as learning as it arises in the course of person-to-person mobile communication. Mobile communication is enhanced everyday communication; and just as our everyday conversation is indifferent towards disciplinary boundaries, so, too, is m-learning. Situation-dependent knowledge, the knowledge at which m-learning aims, by its nature transcends disciplines; its organizing principles arise from practical tasks; its contents are multisensorial; its elements are linked to each other not just by texts, but also by diagrams, pictures, and maps. (Nyíri, 2002; see also Nyíri, 2003b on mobile learning, and Nyíri, 2003a, c on mobile communication and mobile democracy respectively)

Countering critiques of m-learning, he contends:

> The objection that m-learning is likely to provide mere information, rather than knowledge, misses the mark. Information and knowledge are not identical; however, there is an intimate relationship between them: knowledge is information in context. Questions arising in the course of mobile communication seek location-specific and situation-specific answers: the questions create a context, and thus the answers can give rise to knowledge. (Nyíri, 2002)

In defining m-learning as 'learning as it arises in the course of person-to-person mobile communication', and mobile communication in turn as 'enhanced everyday communication' Nyíri is both clearly circumscribing the concept but also making a play for a bold and profound redefinition of it. M-learning is limited to the communication between people using mobiles; but it can lead to a transdisciplinary, multisensorial species of knowledge which draws upon the location and situation of its bearers and creators.

It can, then, be argued that what is distinctive about mobile learning is bound up with the meanings that people in quite different societies, communities, groups, situations and locations attach to the artefacts and practices of mobile devices. For example, the project of marshalling SMS into the enterprise of education has significance, and matters, because of the way people have come to use text messaging. But cultural forces and practices have not been given sufficient emphasis in studies of mobiles, or mobile learning. Neither has the question of the intersection of pedagogies and technologies across and between cultures.

Some cross-cultural questions that have been raised in embryonic and incidental form include Stone et al.'s observation that:

> It is interesting to compare library developments using SMS and WAP to those aiming to use these technologies to support teaching and learning: at the time of writing, much of the reported work in learning and teaching support has taken place in Australasia and the Far East. The library systems, in contrast, appear to have a European bias. (Stone et al., 2002, p. 4)

In a later study of the possibilities of supporting community networks in Tanzania by mobiles, Stone et al. (2003b) offer an important observation:

> There appears to be some potential for using personal wireless communications devices as a means of building capacity in developing countries, but the context of use will be significantly different from that seen in developed countries. (Stone et al., 2003b, p. 2)

They note, for instance, that many applications of SMS for m-learning in Western countries (such as interactivity, provision of information or formation of social and cultural identity) currently assume 'individual ownership of mobile devices'. In contrast, they suggest:

> Shared mobile devices are not likely to afford the same degree of ubiquity at a personal level as individually-owned phones, so the approaches [such as SMS] may not be most appropriate, or would require adaptation for the context of use. As such, we feel that it is better to consider how the wireless networks may be used to enable connectivity to conventional PCs to enable e-learning centres, but also propose these could be used in combination with handheld devices (which could include mobile phones) to enable a blended learning solution. (Stone et al., 2003b, p. 2)

The mobile itself is a relatively recent phenomenon, especially in developing countries where it has provided telephony for the first time (where fixed telecommunications network services were too expensive or difficult to provide). Understanding the diversity of mobile uses in different cultures and societies – and starting to think through their implications and possibilities for pedagogies – provide important challenges for educators and others involved in communications industries.

5.5 Conclusion: Major Issues in M-Learning for Educational Theory and Practice

Given the vast transformations in education over the past 2 decades across most countries, and the sea-change in information and communications technologies that now are firmly part of education, we need to be quite careful about how we situate and envision mobile learning in the future. This is especially so because of the negative perceptions that have tended to dominate discourses about mobile phones in the educational arena and the familiar trap of providing insufficient attention to pedagogies when technological innovations are imported into the field.

The grand promise of mobiles as offering 'anywhere, anytime' learning is clearly shot through with the baggage of technology determinism, not least when enlisted by technology companies themselves to project narratives of use. Clearly, we need to attend to the emerging knowledge regarding social and cultural dimensions of mobiles to counter the 'techno-optimism' now attaching to mobiles that previously attached to the Internet in the 1990s (Lovink, 2002, 2003). On the other side of the mobile learning divide, we need to be firmly sceptical about the dystopian prognostications of educators and administrators who are too busily preoccupied with banning mobiles (along with iPods and other digital music players) to credit their usefulness.

The major issues in m-learning for cross-cultural educational theory and practice that have emerged from this discussion include, firstly, that there is a need to adequately comprehend the cultural bearings and significance of mobile communications technologies. That is, we need to accurately and sensitively understand the dynamic and different practices and their larger implications of mobile cultures among different groups. Who uses mobiles, when, how, for what purposes and in what ways are all questions that still require detailed answers in order to chart mobile culture in different societies, subcultures and groups.

Secondly, armed with such knowledge, there is a need to develop an understanding of the politics of technologies, in order to be able to critically evaluate the goals of mobile learning, in the wider field of education. That is, mobile technologies are being urged upon educators by technology companies. Just as with the field of e-learning, there is a need to place the technology in wider social and political contexts. For instance, in the field of education there have long been debates about how to secure democratic and culturally diverse sustainable education. In the fields of media and communications, there have been comparable struggles over democracy, media and technology (whether these are older imperatives of media ownership and freedom of speech, cultural diversity and sustainability and the role of media, or newer concepts of creative or public commons in Internet and online media). These two sets of discourses around democracy and cultural citizenship in education and media respectively should be brought together so that the stakes and issues involved in mobile learning in a globalised community can be meaningfully identified.

Thirdly, we need to foster many more experiments in mobile learning across many cultures and contexts. Despite the importance of mobiles in the developing world (their role, for instance, in assisting countries to quickly improve telephone penetration rates due to easier and cheaper infrastructure deployment), little research has been carried out into mobile learning in these areas. Given that education can play a role in ameliorating social polarisation, and provide opportunities for gaining technical and cultural literacies in media use, this has obvious significance.

There is much else, of course, that will unfold in the field of mobile learning. But if the blandishments of techno-optimism and the dystopian gloom of the techno-pessimism can be eschewed, and consideration given to the issues raised here, then it is likely that mobile phones, like other technologies, will find a productive and useful place in the world of globalised education.

References

Agar, J. (2003). *Constant Touch: A Global History of the Mobile Phone*. Cambridge: Icon Books.

Brabazon, T. (2002). *Digital Hemlock: Internet Education and the Poisoning of Teaching*. Sydney: UNSW Press.

Carroll, J. M., Rosson, M. B., Isenhour, P. L., Ganoe, C. H, Dunlap, D. R., Fogarty, J., Schafer, W. A. & Van Metre, C. A. (2001). Designing Our Town: MOOsburg. *International Journal of Human-Computer Studies*, 54(5), 725–751.

Coates, K. & Holroyd, C. (2003). *Japan and the Internet Revolution*. Houndsmill, Basingstoke: Palgrave Macmillan.

Cohen, S. (1972). *Folk Devils and Moral Panics: The Creation of the Mods and Rockers*. London: MacGibbon & Kee.

Divitini, M., Haugalokken, O. K. & Norevik, P. A. (2002). Improving Communication Through Mobile Technologies: Which Possibilities? *Proceedings of the Institute of Electrical and*

Electronic Engineers (IEEE) International Workshop on Wireless and Mobile Technologies in Education. Vaxjo, Sweden.

Dutton, W. H. & Loader, B. (Eds.) (2002). *Digital Academe: The New Media and Institutions of Higher Education and Learning*. London/New York: Routledge.

Falk, J. & Björk, S. (2003). *Crossbreeding Wearable and Ubiquitous Computing: A Design Experience*. In J. E. Katz (Ed.). *Machines That Become Us: The Social Context of Personal Communication Technology* (pp. 233–245). New Brunswick, NJ: Transaction Publishers.

Farooq, U., Schafer, W., Rosson, M. B. & Carroll, J. M. (2002). M-Education: Bridging the Gap of Mobile and Desktop Computing. *Proceedings of the Institute of Electrical and Electronic Engineers (IEEE) International Workshop on Wireless and Mobile Technologies in Education*. Vaxjo, Sweden.

Fortunati, L., Katz, J. E. & Riccini, R. (Eds.) (2003). *Mediating the Human Body: Technology, Communication, and Fashion*. Mahwah, NJ: Lawrence Erlbaum.

Frechette, J. D. (2002). *Developing Media Literacy in Cyberspace: Pedagogy and Critical Learning for the Twenty-First-Century Classroom*. Westport, CT: Praeger.

Funk, J. L. (2001). *The Mobile Internet: How Japan Dialed Up and the West Disconnected*. Pembroke, Bermuda: ISI Publication.

Goggin, G. (2004). Mobile Text. M/C: A Journal of Media and Culture 7(1). Available: http://www.media-culture.org.au/0401/03-goggin.html/ [July, 2005].

Goggin, G. & Spurgeon, C. (2005). Mobile Message Services and Communications Policy. *Prometheus: Journal of Issues in Technological Change, Innovation, Information Economics, Communication and Science Policy*, 23(2), 181–193.

Gottlieb, N. & McLelland, M. (Eds.) (2003). Japanese Cybercultures. London: Routledge.

Hall, S., Critcher, C., Jefferson, T., Clarke, J. & Roberts, B. (1978). *Policing the Crisis: Mugging, the State, and Law and Order*. London: Macmillan.

Hazemi, R., Hailes, S. & Wilbur, S. (Eds.) (1998). *The Digital University: Reinventing the Academy*. Springer: London.

Inkpen, K. M. (1999). Designing Handheld Technologies for Kids. *Personal Technologies*, 3(1&2), 81–89.

International Telecommunications Union (ITU) (2004). Mobile Cellular, Subscribers Per 100 People. *World Telecommunication Indicators*. Available: http://www.itu.int/ITU-D/ict/statistics/ [July, 2005].

Katz, J. E. (Ed.) (2003). *Machines that Become Us: The Social Context of Personal Communication Technology*. New Brunswick, NJ: Transaction Publishers.

Katz, J. E. (2004). Mobiles in Educational Settings. Invited plenary presentation. *The Global and the Local in Mobile Communication: Places, Images, People, Connections*. Organized by the Institute for Philosophical Research, Hungarian National Academy of Sciences, Budapest, June 12.

Katz, J. E. & Aakhus, M. (Eds.) (2002). *Perpetual Contact: Mobile Communication, Private Talk, Public Performance*. Cambridge: Cambridge University Press.

Konkel, M., Leung, V., Ullmer, B. & Hu., C. (2004). Tagaboo: A Collaborative Children's Game Based Upon Wearable RFID Technology. *Personal and Ubiquitous Computing* 8(5), 382–384.

Lindholm, C., Keinonen, T. & Kiljander, H. (2003). *Mobile Usability: How Nokia Changed the Face of the Mobile Phone*. New York: McGraw-Hill.

Ling, R. (2004). *The Mobile Connection: The Cell Phone's Impact on Society*. San Francisco, CA: Morgan Kaufmann.

Lovink, G. (2002). *Dark Fibre: Tracking Critical Internet Culture*. Cambridge, MA: MIT Press.

Lovink, G. (2003). *My First Recession: Critical Internet Culture in Transition*. Rotterdam: V2_Publishers.

MacKenzie, D. & Wajcman, J. (Eds.) (1999). *The Social Shaping of Technology*, 2nd ed. Buckingham/England/Philadelphia, PA: Open University Press.

Malliou, E., Stavros, S., Sotiriou, S. S., Miliarakis, A. & Sharples, M. (2002). The AD-HOC Project: eLearning Anywhere, Anytime. *Proceedings of the European Workshop on Mobile and Contextual Learning, 20–21st June*. The University of Birmingham, England.

MOBIlearn. The Vision (2002). Available: http://www.mobilearn.org/download/vision.pdf. [July, 2005].

Mobile Learning for the Learning Citizen (Lifelong Learning Projects Funded Under the Education and Training Action of the IST Programme) Available: http://www.learningcitizen.net/mobile_learning.shtml/ [July, 2005].

M-learning: Learning in the Palm of Your Hand (2003). Ultralab. Available: http://www.m-learning.org/ [July 2005].

Nyíri, K. (2002). Towards a Philosophy of M-Learning. *Proceedings of the Institute of Electrical and Electronic Engineers (IEEE) International Workshop on Wireless and Mobile Technologies in Education*, Vaxjo, Sweden. Available: http://21st.century.phil-inst.hu/eng/m-learning/nyiri_m-learn_philos.htm [July 2005]

Nyíri, K. (Ed.) (2003a). *Mobile Communication: Essays on Cognition and Community*. Wien: Passagen Verlag.

Nyíri, K. (Ed.) (2003b). Mobile Democracy: Essays on Society, Self and Politics. Wien: Passagen Verlag.

Nyíri, K. (Ed.) (2003c). *Mobile Learning: Essays on Philosophy, Psychology and Education*. Wien: Passagen Verlag.

Postman, N. (1993). *Technopoly: The Surrender of Culture to Technology*. New York: Vintage.

Ring, G. (2001). Case Study: Combining Web and WAP to Deliver E-Learning. *Learning Circuits*. Available: www.learningcircuits.org/2001/jun2001/ring.html/ [July 2005].

Sharples, M. (2000). The Design of Personal Mobile Technologies for Lifelong Learning. *Computers and Education*, 34, 177–193.

Sharples, M., Corlett, D. & Westmancott, O. (2002). The Design and Implementation of a Mobile Learning Resource. *Personal and Ubiquitous Computing*, 6(3), 220–234.

Siegemund, F. & Flörkemeier, C. (2003). Interaction in Pervasive Computing Settings Using Bluetooth-enabled Active Tags and Passive RFID Technology together with Mobile Phones. Proceedings of the First Institute of Electrical and Electronic Engineers (IEEE) International Conference on Pervasive Computing and Communications, Fort Worth, TX, pp. 378–387.

Stone, A. (2002). Mobile Telephony and Learning: Nuisance or Potential Enhancement? *Proceedings of International Symposium on Technology and Society Social Implications of Information and Communication Technology*, IEEE, Raleigh, NC, pp. 262–266.

Stone, A. & Briggs, J. (2003). SMS and Interactivity – Some Results from the Field, and Its Implications on Effective Uses of Mobile Technologies in Education. *Proceedings of the Institute of Electrical and Electronic Engineers (IEEE) International Workshop on Wireless and Mobile Technologies in Education*, Vaxjo, Sweden.

Stone, A., Alsop, G., Briggs, J. & Tompsett, C. (2002). M-Learning as a Means of Supporting Learners: Tomorrow's Technologies Are Already Here, How Can We Most Effectively Use Them in the E-Learning Age? *Networked Learning Conference*, March 26–28, 2002, Sheffield.

Stone, A., Alsop, G. & Tompsett, C. (2003a). *Grounded Theory as a Means of User Centred Design and Evaluation (pp. 189–194)*. In K. Nyíri (Ed.). *Mobile Learning: Essays on Philosophy, Psychology and Education*. Wien: Passagen Verlag.

Stone, A., Lynch, K. & Poole, N. (2003b). A Case for Using Mobile Internet and Telephony to Support Community Networks in Tanzania. *International Conference on Online and Open Learning* (ICOOL), University of Mauritius, December, 2003.

Thornton, P. & Houser, C. (2001). *Learning on the Move: Foreign Language Vocabulary via SMS. ED-Media 2001 Proceedings*, Association for the Advancement of Computing in Education, Norfolk, VA, pp. 1846–1847.

Wajcman, J. (2004). *TechnoFeminism*. Cambridge/Malden, MA: Polity Press.

Chapter 6
Connecting Schools to Their Communities: The South-East Asian Experience

Cher Ping Lim and Mykint Swe Khine

6.1 Technologies and School Reform

In the globalised world of education, information communication technologies (ICTs) are playing a major role in changing the ways schools operate and students learn. Many aspects of these educational reform programs have met with resistance from teachers and other school stakeholders (Cuban et al., 2001; Fullan, 1993). More recently, however, in the South-east Asian region, there has been a very positive response to, and enthusiastic uptake of, reforms related to connecting schools to communities through the use of ICTs. Research studies carried out by the authors at schools in Indonesia, Malaysia, Singapore and Thailand have enabled the identification of various examples of forms of electronic connection designed to bring schools and their communities together. It is the purpose of this chapter to explore the nature of these interactions and to analyse some of their more tangible benefits.

6.2 Schools and the Internet in South-East Asia

The rapid spread of the Internet and the extraordinary increase in its usage over the last decade in educational institutions and elsewhere has steadily fuelled the creation of a global information environment. In most countries around the globe the Internet is now having an impact on aspects of everyday life ranging from communication with friends and families to shopping and banking, and everything in between. In many South-east Asian schools there has been recognition that the Internet has the potential to play an important role in facilitating the linkages between schools and their major stakeholders and this has led to some important innovations in

C.P. Lim
Centre of Research in Pedagogy and Practice

M.S. Khine
Nanyang Technological University, Singapore,

J. Zajda and D. Gibbs (eds.), *Comparative Information Technology,*
DOI: 10.1007/978-1-4020-9426-2_6, © Springer Science+Bussiness Media B.V. 2009

school systems. Before providing a description and analysis of the impact of these electronic linkages as they are occurring between schools and their communities, it is necessary to outline the educational and technological landscapes of the school systems in the South-east Asian region – in Indonesia, Malaysia, Singapore and Thailand – that are the focus of this study.

In Indonesia a central goal of the school system is to equip children with the skills, attitudes and knowledge to participate in the modern nation state including developing an understanding of its bureaucracies, its morals and its ideological foundations. In 1993, the government declared a 9-year compulsory basic education program that consisted of 6 years of primary education and 3 years of junior secondary education. For primary education, Indonesians between 7 and 12 can choose between state-run, non-sectarian public schools supervised by the Department of Education and Culture or private/semi-private schools supervised and financed by the Department of Religious Affairs. After primary education, students can choose among vocational and pre-professional junior and senior high schools, where each level is of 3 years' duration.

The goal of the Malaysian education system is to develop the potential of individuals in a holistic and integrated manner. Compulsory education is only at the primary level for 6 years. The national education system consists of pre-school education for 3 years, primary school education for 6 years, secondary school education for 4 years and post-secondary education for 2–3 years. Most primary schools are national or national-type schools. At the secondary level, there are academic schools, technical and vocational schools and religious national schools.

The vision of the education system in Singapore is 'Thinking Schools, Learning Nation' where it describes a nation of thinking and committed citizens capable of meeting the challenges of the future, aiming to offer an education system geared to the needs of the twenty-first century. Compulsory education is similar to that in Malaysia – 6 years of primary education. At the primary level, students go through a 4-year foundation stage, from Primary One to Four, and a 2-year orientation stage from Primary Five to Six. Almost all primary schools are government or government-aided schools. For secondary schools, students go through 4 years before being admitted to pre-university colleges or polytechnics. There are four types of secondary schools: independent, autonomous, government-aided and government schools.

The aim of the Thai education system is to develop Thailand into a knowledge-based society developed on the principle of 'Education Builds the Nation, Empowers the Individual and Generates Employment'. The Thai school system comprises three levels: after 3 years of pre-primary education, there are 6 years of primary education, 3 years of lower-secondary education and 3 years of upper-secondary education. Compulsory education is similar to Indonesia with 6 years of primary education and 3 years of lower-secondary education. Most of the primary schools are under the Office of the National Primary Education of the Ministry of Education, while most public secondary schools are under the Department of General Education, Ministry of Education.

Each of these countries has formulated a national ICT plan for education. This has involved each country in finding ways to meet the technological challenges of selecting and installing a suitable learning management system (LMS), having sufficient bandwidth allocated to e-learning and obtaining state-of-the-art learning tools and materials. Although the technological infrastructure of each country varies (with Singapore and Malaysia being the most developed), each has now established a relatively sustainable infrastructure and has set processes in train for the professional development of educators, and the training of students and parents in the use of the technologies.

6.3 Taking Up the Opportunities of the Internet

Field trips to a variety of schools in Malaysia, Singapore, Indonesia and Thailand reveal that there are many ways in which communities or parts of communities are connected through technologies in this region. Linkages take the form of formal and informal online communication between principals, teachers and parents; online collaboration between students and the local and international community; and online sharing of ideas, problems and information between schools and parents. Lewin et al. (2003) point out that since the early 1990s teachers have planned and facilitated online collaboration between students and the local and international communities. Electronic communications between parents and schools on the other hand is a more recent development.

The channels used to enhance communication between parents and schools include e-mail communication between teachers and parents; updating school web sites with frequently asked questions to provide parents with information about school policies, programs and activities; log-in accounts for parents to access their children's progress records via the school online administrative system; online discussion forums for teachers, principals and parents to engage in dialogues about the visions and activities of the school; and synchronous online communication for parents who are too busy to meet teachers face to face. In addition to these examples of new forms of communications between parents, teachers, students and schools, there is also evidence of expansion into collaborations between students and local enterprises or organizations designed to create linkages with, and/or offer help, to local and wider communities.

Online learning by students from home, *Internet* cafés or community centres is another area commented on in the literature (e.g. Lewin et al., 2003) although not part of the observations reported on here. Sutherland et al.'s (2000) analysis of the *Screen Play Project*, for example, explored the use of the computer in out-of-school settings with cohorts of children from English schools. They found that children's approaches to home computing have definite implications for their use of computers in schools. The study discovered that using computers out-of-school leads students to use different approaches to learning, and gives them access to a range of information and educational resources that have been previously inaccessible to young people. Sutherland et al.'s findings suggest that the role between school and home use of computers may in fact be complimentary – a finding that also has relevance for school and community connections being developed in the South-east Asian region and which would benefit from further exploration.

6.4 Benefits of Linkages Between School and Community in South-East Asian Schools

In this section the links currently being forged between schools and communities in Indonesia, Malaysia, Singapore and Thailand are more fully explicated, and the nature of the benefits of the interactions taking place in each of these locations is further analysed:

1. *The Internet bridges and strengthens the home–school connection and, if properly harnessed, promotes parents' activities and involvement in the school.*

Although there has always been a need for free-flowing information between schools and parents, both parties are often denied critical information about the children (both at home and in the school) due to outdated modes of home–school communication. Such a mode of communication used to focus mainly on formal, scheduled school activities that were offered to all parents, such as parent-meet-teacher day or back-to-school night (Weiss et al., 1998). The informal channel of communication, if any, was confined to suggestion boxes situated outside the school general office or telephone calls when a student was hurt or had repeatedly committed an offence. This lack of home–school communication between parents and teachers has meant that it has sometimes been very difficult to make informed decisions in particular situations about the child that will better meet his/her needs (Epstein, 1996).

The Internet has made a fundamental change in this antiquated mode of communication; it has facilitated the linkages between schools and homes by enabling teachers and parents to play a greater role in the students' learning experiences. The bond between schools and home is able to be strengthened through increased interaction and communication as is evidenced in the following instances.

Malaysia: One of the deliverables of the Smart School Integrated Solution is a feature in the computerized Smart School Management System (SSMS) that enables parents to remotely access their own children's records in the school to keep track of their progress. (The Malaysian Smart School was launched in July 1997 by the Prime Minister as one of the Multimedia Super Corridor's (MSC) Flagship Applications. The aim was to capitalise on leading-edge technologies and the rapid deployment of the MSC's infrastructure to jump-start deployment of enabling technology to schools. This was done by creating a group of pilot schools in 1999 that served as the nucleus for the eventual nationwide roll-out of Smart School concepts, resources, skills and technologies.) This integrated management software covers nine areas of school management, namely, financial, student affairs, educational resources, external resources, human resources, facilities, school governance, security and technology. The feature for parents became available in late 2002. Although this feature is not yet being fully utilized by parents, particularly those who have no Internet access, there are plans to encourage greater parental participation through this means.

Singapore: A wide range of school activities involve parents and the community, due partly to school–industry partnerships and the autonomy given to schools in the ICT in education master plans. Moreover, with better connectivity linking the school to the home and community, peers, teachers and parents are able to play a more active role in the students' learning experiences. One example is the *Learning Village Project* in Outram Secondary School, a joint venture between Singapore's Ministry of Education and IBM. Through this MOE-IBM Collaboration, a School-Community Web Collaboration System using the *Internet* has been developed that aims to foster home–school–community connection and partnership. By connecting various stakeholders of education, the *Learning Village Project* has strengthened the school's effort to achieve its mission: 'An Intelligent School and a Caring Family'. The Radin Mas Primary School has, for example, set up a Parent Link web site to promote rapport among parents and between the parents and the school, as well as to foster mutual support in shaping the overall character of the students.

2. *When parents are encouraged to participate in and contribute to change management activities within a school's ICT master plan, change occurs more quickly.*

Research studies have shown that what parents think and believe about various school reform components can affect the effectiveness of change management activities (Tobin & Dawson, 1992; Konzal, 1997). Where positive attitudes of parents towards reform initiatives are developed, it is likely that their support and participation in these activities will be encouraged. Most parents have a positive attitude towards the use of ICT in schools; but as Scott and Hannafin (2000) point out there needs to be a better understanding of parents' views of how ICT should be used in schools for teaching and learning. By involving parents in the formulation and implementation of the school ICT master plan it is likely that a better reciprocal understanding of the views of parents and teachers and will be realised.

Singapore: Outram Secondary School, the old neighbourhood school chosen to pilot the *Learning Village* web-based project sponsored by the Ministry of Education and IBM, has combined a set of *Internet* applications to allow communication and collaboration both within the school and beyond it. This has served to involve parents and other interested members of the local community with the school and its activities.

Parents are given passwords to log in to the site from their homes and offices. Parents can go to the events calendar to check the whereabouts of their children, or visit teachers' home pages to find out more about their teaching methods, student's grades achieved in class, assignments, homework and also lessons for independent study. Parents can also participate in online 'meetings' with teachers and also be involved in their children's online discussions. With this mode of communication and collaboration, parents can offer their ideas for the schools' development and influence its policies. This site is also used to solicit views about the school's opening hours and other similar matters.

Malaysia: Pilot schools in the *Smart School Project* are encouraged to include parents and the community in their change management activities. Parent–teacher associations (PTA) take a keen interest in the development of the *Smart School Project* and have helped by sponsoring trips to the Multimedia Development Corporation (MDC) for students and others to gain an inside view of the work of the MSC. The MSC is a regional launch site for companies developing or using leading multimedia technology and the MDC is a one-stop shop created to manage and market the MSC. Other PTAs have sponsored talks by ICT personnel, and facilitated the schools' participation in ICT-related competitions. The *Smart School* Pilot Project Team also organized a national seminar for representatives of PTAs from non-pilot schools as part of the *Smart School Outreach Programme*. In addition, the team gives talks and presents papers at seminars, conventions and meetings to help disseminate information about the *Smart School Project*.

Thailand: In most cases, parents, alumni and PTAs are great school supporters and many of them are actively making use of electronic communication to further their involvement. School committees comprising students, parents and teachers have been established across grade levels to enable these groups to work together to prepare proposals to obtain support from the school board or PTA for projects designed to improve students' learning opportunities. In many cases parents not only provide hardware and software, but have also become resource persons. Some private schools offer ICT training to parents so that they can guide their children in the use of technology or even learn together.

3. *As the Internet opens up opportunities to collaborate with different organizations and people in local and international communities, schools are able to use these opportunities to strengthen their students' personal and social development and to bring benefits to these communities.*

With appropriate support and autonomy, schools are capable of innovative *Internet*-based projects to improve the bonds between themselves and their communities (Kerawalla & Crook, 2002). Some South-east Asian examples and the distinctive contributions they are making are described below.

Indonesia: Schools in Indonesia were involved in several projects in the *Asia–Europe Classroom Programme*. An example is the *Ndolalak and Hambo Project* (the title refers to the names of two dances from Sweden and Java that symbolise cultural life in the two countries) created to provide opportunities for cultural understanding and exchange. The Senior High School 7 in Purworejo on Java (Indonesia) and Torsbergsgymnasiet in Bollnäs (Sweden) are attended by students of approximately the same age – about 18–19 years. The purpose of the project was for these students to learn about cultural varieties in Java and Sweden with the aim of their making friends and developing understanding, respect and positive attitudes across cultures. The Swedish group of students belonged to a class who were pursuing cultural studies (art, literature, music, dance, traditions, etc.): they already had personal pen friends in other countries. The Indonesian class, on the other hand, was new to online communication and received a lot of support from their teacher and technical officer. Through e-mail exchanges and online bulletin boards, the students designed web sites and created video for one another.

Malaysia: In the *Face 2 Face Project* under the *Asia–Europe Classroom Programme*, students from Helsinki Business College in Finland and the Garden International School in Malaysia planned to visit each other during the course of the project (October to June). In preparation for these visits, they communicated with one another via e-mail and bulletin board and shared various aspects of their cultures through the web pages that they designed. They also planned the itinerary for their visits using an online open forum. Another project, *Multicultural Exchanger* – a newspaper online – involved Malaysia, Finland, Sweden, Indonesia, France, China, Singapore and Portugal. The students researched, planned and exchanged information before designing the web site for the online newspaper.

Singapore: Parents, industry experts and academics have been invited to work with Singaporean schools to make meaningful contributions to the community (Soh, 2002). One example is the *Service-Learning Programme* at Crescent Girls' School (www.crescent.edu.sg) in which students use ICT in an innovative way to make a difference in the lives of less fortunate members of the community. In 2000, a group of secondary three students set up an e-commerce project, *The Very Special Bazaar Project*, together with members of Peacehaven (a home for the elderly), the Movement for the Intellectually Disabled of Singapore (MINDS) and *The Very Special Arts Project*, Singapore, a programme designed to provide an outlet of expression for people with disabilities. Art and craft pieces were put on sale via the web with an e-commerce engine and the proceeds went to the elderly and the physically and intellectually challenged in these organizations. Two other projects by the school involved the Singapore School for the Deaf (SSD), where hearing-impaired students and Crescent's students co-designed digital art cards to raise funds. They also wrote, illustrated and translated some works into sign language to enrich teaching and learning resources for the hearing-impaired members of the community.

In Radin Mas Primary School, there were also many community projects made possible by the Internet. One such project entitled *Shangrila for the Seniors* commenced in 2001 by Primary five students. The main objectives of the project were to encourage students to care for the elderly and engage them in an entrepreneurial pursuit to help the elderly. The students communicated and interviewed directors of Senior Citizen Centres overseas and locally via e-mail, grandparents and teachers who would be retiring. With that information and the help of the three-dimensional software, the students designed a Senior Citizen Centre for the elderly.

As ICT opens opportunities to collaborate with organizations and people in local and international communities, Outram Secondary School students can use the site to work together on projects, not just with each other, but with counterparts in other schools, even other countries. Official 'mentors' who may have these special expertise or experience to contribute to the school can do so from all around the world. Recently, a class was given the opportunity to put questions to a mountaineer climbing Everest.

These examples demonstrate the nature of the links that are connecting schools and communities through innovative uses of ICT. With support from the ministry, community and commercial sectors it is likely that opportunities for productive and creative interactions between school and community will expand.

6.5 Conclusion

Examples of how the Internet has been used in schools around the Asia-Pacific region have been provided here to suggest the advantages that ensue and their usefulness for parents, students and their communities, whether locally, within their own countries, or globally. As technologies advance, better home–school and community links will be enabled, providing further opportunities for stakeholders to become digitally connected. For parents such links will provide up-to-date and better information about their children's education and opportunities to more fully understand the efforts taken by a school to improve students' learning opportunities. Home–school connections can also provide parents with ways to help their children learn. Using communication channels for this purpose can improve students' academic motivation and engagement with learning tasks which in turn may lead to a higher level of school attainment (Tracey et al., 1999).

Using technologies to connect communities and schools can also contribute to improving the professional growth of teachers and support staff. Connections of this kind allow the setting up of professional links with like-minded staff, thus establishing a community of practitioners. These networks can be used to discuss issues relating to curriculum and assessment or to share and explore any issues that arise where professional exchanges and collaborative interaction is likely to be helpful. Greater interaction with parents also allows staff to see things from a parent's point of view and to better understand and empathise with their concerns. Forging electronic links with community organisations and the wider global community can bring extraordinary benefits ranging from the spiritual to the intellectual to the commercial for all involved. It is evident that a reciprocal culture of appreciation is at present under digital construction in the South-east Asian region – an initiative that deserves every support.

References

Cuban, L., Kirkpatrick, H., & Peck, C. (2001). High Access and Low Use of Technology in High School Classrooms: Explaining an Apparent Paradox. *American Educational Research Journal*, 38(4), 813–834.

Epstein, J. L. (1996). Advances in Family, Community, and School Partnerships. *New Schools, New Communities*, 12(3), 5–13.

Fullan, M. (1993). *Change Forces: Probing the Depths of Educational Reforms*. London: Falmer Press.

Kerawalla, C. & Crook, C. (2002). Children's Computer Use at Home and at School: Context and Continuity. *British Educational Research Journal*, 28(6), 751–772.

Konzal, J. (1997). Attitudes: How Parental Attitudes May Influence Classroom Instructional Practices. Paper presented at the *American Educational Research Association Annual Conference*, Chicago, IL.

Lewin, C., Mavers, D., Somekh, B. (2003). Broadening Access to the Curriculum Through Using Technology to Link Home and School: A Critical Analysis of Reforms Intended to Improve Students' Educational Attainment. *The Curriculum Journal*, 14, 23–53.

Scott, B. N. & Hannafin, R. D. (2000). How Teachers and Parents View Classroom Learning Environments: An Exploratory Study. *Journal of Research on Computing in Education*, 32(3), 401–416.

Soh, V. (2002, September–October). MP2: The Next Masterplan for IT in Education. *Education*, 30–33.

Sutherland, R., Facer, K., Furlong, R., Furlong, J. (2000). A New Environment for Education? The Computer in the Home. *Computers and Education*, 34, 195–212.

Tobin, K. & Dawson, G. (1992). Constraints to Curriculum Reform: Teachers and the Myths of Schooling. *Educational Technology Research and Development*, 40(1), 121–140.

Tracey, K., Penn, C., Fowler, J. H. (1999). Developing an Infrastructure to Support Communities of Learning. *BT Technology Journal*, 17(1), 98–110.

Weiss, H., Kreider, H., Levine, E., Stadler, J., & Vaughan, P. (1998). Beyond the Parent-Teacher Conference: Diverse Patterns of Home-School Communication. Paper presented at the *American Educational Research Association Annual Conference*, San Diego, CA.

Chapter 7
Digital Literacy and Activity Systems in Adolescents

José Luis Rodríguez Illera and Mónica Kaechele

7.1 The Setting for Digital Literacies

This chapter presents our examination of an issue of pressing importance, namely the situation that arises from seeking to understand the digital practices of adolescents today (and those of our children and young people in general), which in many industrialized countries appear to be shaped in contexts far removed from the school. Undoubtedly, this process began some time ago, and has its root in a multiplicity of factors, but here we wish to focus on certain specific aspects that have been exacerbated by recent technological changes. The transformation of time and space are uniquely paving the way for a type of world experience that impacts on the fundamental condition of our survival, production and social ties, while our lifestyles and the rhythms that modulate our lives are being determined by this change; as Giddens has written (1996): "[T]he influence of distant events on those close at hand and on our intimate life have become commonplace. The world we live in today … is a singular world, which possesses a unique framework of experience." Seen in this way, space as a dimension is becoming narrower and more compressed, its corporal nature would seem to have been dispelled: the flows now predominate over the structures, the interconnections over the defined boundaries. Space is expanding and becoming separated from place; social relations are broadening and fracturing "but subsequently they are reconstituted in the form of network nodes" (Lash, 2005).

Both changes – those of time and of space – strike at the heart of the structure of life that has been sustained to date. The work ideal, which logically was sustained within a certain organization that supposed an effort at given "times" and moments in life, now only exists in a limited fashion; the "time" that served as an incentive

J.L.R. Illera
Universitat de Barcelona, Spain

M. Kaechele
Universidad Católica de Temuco, Chili

J. Zajda and D. Gibbs (eds.), *Comparative Information Technology*,
DOI: 10.1007/978-1-4020-9426-2_7,

for effort no longer exists, the logic of work as it was understood in the twentieth century and the experience of work associated with it today live alongside the logic of maximizing our gains in the shortest possible time.

Our relations with others are also being disrupted: not only are they becoming more media-based, transient and replaceable, but they have also been converted into goods which can be attained with the simple click of the mouse. Instability and the pressure of change gain expression in our most intimate relationships, in the building of our ties and our relations with others. Space, in that it is no longer restricted to "place," opens up the possibilities for interconnections that, in conjunction with electronic and communication technologies, are extending the contours of the local world.

Shedding one's body, moving through the network and occupying unimaginable spaces and places has been the revelation for those who have "got wired." Spaces on the network, such as *Second Life*, the proliferation of virtual reality and simulation games are the expression of a part of this discourse. New ways of organizing the physical world are being reconstructed, of crossing once more into the when and where, into generic spaces and spaces of transit, "the non places" as Augé (1998) has christened them. Alongside this vision of the digital society – a vision shared by most of those who seek to imagine it and whose conceptual reconstructions stress its "hypertechnologized" nature, certain zones within it are perceived as detrimental to this dynamic – strangely, these zones are the schools. Primary and secondary schools and their teachers are constantly being labeled as "reactionary," "highly reluctant to change," and "traditional." Schools are often represented (in the discourse of technophiles, though not solely) as being the antithesis of technological progress, their backs firmly turned on the twenty-first century, symbols of early twentieth-century capitalist modernity, and, not unsurprisingly, teaching in the knowledge society is experiencing considerable uncertainty in the schools (Hardgreaves, 2001).

7.2 The Pedagogy and Digital Technology Debate

Schools today are exposed to considerable tension. On the one hand, they need to rethink – as a consequence of the new prospects for learning and the new skills required to form part of an increasingly complex setting – the type of teaching required for a society subject to constant change, while on the other, they have to accept and understand that their pupils have changed. Two situations are creating particular concern in schools: (1) the cultural and social diversity of the students, which has made teaching more complex, and (2) the type of social practices in which adolescents participate and which are increasingly been performed by technology. Today nobody would question that digital technology does not form a part of the daily lives of young people. Various reports and surveys conducted both in Europe and on other continents show just how widely the Internet has penetrated our homes and the everyday acts of communication and entertainment of this sector of the population. The study of the digital practices of adolescents has become a rich field to explore, not only so as to generate an overall view that might help us understand the changes in the context of their schoolwork, but also to rethink the different ways of using technology with the aim of increasing its potential in student learning.

As we begin to understand just how the students go about constructing their everyday practices – using various artifacts and technological devices, and to identify the competences/skills/values that they use in specific contexts – we can generate a dialogue that facilitates the effective inclusion of technologies in schools and the necessary modification of school thinking. To date, the information made available provides, in the main, data related to the type of technology that young people typically consume (computers, cell phones, video game consoles) or the type of services that they request (music and video downloads); however, little is known about how they experience this new form of everyday life with different types of technology and its implications for the development of adolescents, nor the practices that they construct in this local (context), corporal (physical), and virtual setting. We need to further our understanding of how the new artifacts have transformed (if that is indeed the case) typical juvenile practices – of play, entertainment, study – and to identify the flows of interchange, and the spaces in which the practices associated with these technologies are formed. The more qualitative studies report findings such as:

(a) The use of video games produces a greater sensation of power among children and adolescents, with each screen challenge giving rise to intense feelings that can range from anxiety, frustration, and even anger to satisfaction and pride (Balaguer, 2002).
(b) The use of tools of communication and entertainment predominate, while to a lesser extent for school work tools are used for seeking information, and setting up online study groups for team problem solving (Jure, 2004).
(c) The logic of adolescents is articulated around specific moments and circumstances, with a predominance of interrupted discourse. The practices of adolescents do not point towards the establishment of lasting ties. What interests them is having active meeting points (Jure, 2004). Young people can multitask: listen to music, talk, and download, which is characterized as the logic of the Internet, the logic of zapping, or the multiplicity of windows that can be explored simultaneously (Jure, 2004).
(d) The emergence of new consumption and production practices, with consumption practices being dominant. Children and adolescents only perceive the element of play of the devices they handle with the greatest assiduity. Although the entertainment factor is recognized as important in cell telephones, the communicative factor is its prime use, as shown by the fact that messages and calls are its most valued attributes.

The conclusions drawn from these studies can really only be understood in the general framework outlined above. The logic of the Internet, the central position occupied by the relationships, the instantaneity and the multiplicity of voices are in essence the historic, social, and cultural framework in which young people move today. The digital practices of adolescents are practices constructed in a way of understanding the world which cannot be reduced to the technology that they use, but which at the same time are not independent of it.

7.3 Digital Literacies as Forms of Social Practice

To understand these new everyday habits of young people, and to understand how they differ from those in the school culture, it is not enough simply to rely on the descriptive data provided by the surveys. These tend to adopt a somewhat one-dimensional conception of the use of technology, as if we were dealing with a basic literacy involving new machines and programs. Digital literacy is conceived as the learning of multiple applications and little attention is paid to the social and cultural conditions in which the processes of their use and appropriation are carried out (as might be deduced from the word literacy). In the most usual discourses, the concept of digital literacy is linked to processes of learning to use computers and their specific applications. The concept has been limited to the individual relationship between a subject and a specific technological device, which limits our possibilities of understanding the phenomenon of technology in a person's normal practices (Rodríguez Illera, 2004), and in turn promotes the illusion that it is possible to replicate, in contexts of different practices, the same technologies with similar results.

Seen in this way, the link between the digital literacy of adolescents involves examining their experiences based around technology as complex cultural practices, associated with specific contexts and not simply to restrict oneself to drawing up a list of technological devices. Technology itself (the use of computers, video games, their percentage uses, etc.) explains little or restricts our understanding of the development of the skills and the personal means of appropriation associated with them.

Undoubtedly the "new" literacies could be incorporated into those "arts of doing" that de Certeau (1980) described in his analysis of the invention of everyday life. Moved by interests of power, strategic in its terminology, with a top-down logic, the uniformity of the technologies suggests common standardized practices centered on the catalogue of physical apparatus (computers, cell telephones, MP3 players, video consoles, etc.) which function in a similar way (operating systems, standardized user interfaces), and which tend to be common, above and beyond any individual, language, or cultural differences. Together with this global logic, the practices are revealed as tactics, highly personal and contextualized forms of appropriation and use of digital technologies in the spaces created by the strategies. The distinction drawn by de Certeau, we believe, can help us consider how the digital technologies are used, taking us beyond the findings of the surveys that examine their use among young people and which reveal some group differences in the process of uniformity mentioned above; in other words, understanding them as new literacy practices, in which a new skill is learnt, but in which the objectives of the practice are modified by the interaction with the technology. These effects that are produced when undertaking an activity with the technology require a complex form of analysis, not just cognitive (Salomon et al., 1991), but also one that looks at the social interactions occurring in the contexts in which the practices are undertaken, and the way in which the types of activity are redefined.

This problem has attracted little attention to date, and so we propose approaching it as a system of activity within the relations that occur in both schools and more informal contexts – both understood as the product of one or more strategies; in other words, as the creation of private space with given rules of behavior. Envisaging these practices that occur in the settings-with-technology as activity systems means attempting to understand them as tactical movements, of defense against institutional strategies, but also of the constitution of shared and relatively autonomous spaces. To understand the difficulties in the school domain we need to analyze school practices, but we also need to understand the nature of the digital practices of young people in their everyday activities, so as to generate a dialogue that opens up opportunities for strengthening the use of technology in the schools. But what exactly is the nature of the use adolescents make of technology in and out of school?

7.4 Research Design

This empirical study seeks to undertake a qualitative analysis, employing a range of data-gathering tools, and using a theoretical framework derived from the Theory of Socio-Cultural Activity (Leontiev, 1978; Engeström, 1987). The analytical advantages of undertaking this study in this framework are primarily twofold:

1. It enables us, within our interpretative analysis, to link various theoretical and conceptual perspectives that we consider important in meeting our overall goal (while at the same time endowing our data with greater weight): namely, the more experiential relationship between the subject and technology (Dreyfus, 1996); the condition of spaces as ecologies (Nardi & O' Day, 1999) and also as human spaces in the anthropological sense of the term; and their link with the approaches proffered by digital literacy seen as a cultural practice (Lea, 2004).
2. In the same way as it allows us to generate a certain theoretical weight, it obliges us in collecting the data to give importance to the agents in their relation with the context, as well as the cultural, social, and economic conditions in which this relationship is framed (Engeström, 1999). In this way the subjectivity of the persons is taken into consideration throughout the study, but this is interpreted as a function of analytical models that allows us to go beyond the interpretations of the subjects.

The settings chosen for this empirical study were a secondary school in the city of Barcelona and a *locutorio* (a cross between a telephone center and an Internet café typically run by immigrants for immigrants) in the Sant Andreu district of the same city. The data were collected by direct observation, interview, and focus group interviews.

The nature of the *observation* differed from one research space to the other. In the *locutorio* it acquired a participative nature as it was necessary to interact with the young users in situ, while in the school the observation was basically nonparticipative.

The interviews were conducted with the secondary school teachers at the end of the observation period. We interviewed the computer coordinator, our key informant, who also provided us with access to this research area. Likewise, we interviewed the school's coordinator of teaching methodology. In the *locutorio* we interviewed a youth who attended the center regularly. We wished to interview the manager of the center, but this was not possible as the post changed hands during the observation period, and the resulting language barrier made it difficult to maintain a conversation with the new incumbent in Castilian.

The Focus Group was organized with students from the classes that we observed. The focus group was interviewed after the conducting of a survey of these students' consumer habits with relation to technology so as to obtain data concerning their habits in specific spaces and at different times of the day.

7.5 Results

Our observation data from the school and the locutorio are organized in four categories: type of technologies used, function for which the technologies were used, convergence of technologies used, and the ways in which they were put to use.

1. **Type of technologies used.** The technologies were divided on the basis of the technological device (see Table 7.1).

The type of technologies that the students use varies with the context, as Tables 7.2 and 7.3 show.

In a typical day the students, in the three age groups defined, use the following supports most frequently: ***computers, cell phones***, and MP3s. The use of these

Table 7.1 Technologies used according to technological device

Device	Software	Device	Software
Computers	Word processing, Paint programs, CorelDRAW (graphics editor), Excel, Data base, Reading and writing software.	Cell phones MP3	Text messages Music, games puzzles
Internet	Simulations, Role plays, War games, Fight games, Car or motorbike racing games, Search engines, e-mail, Instant message service	Television	TV series, cartoons, films
		Game console	Fight games, racing games
		DVD	Films

Table 7.2 Technologies used principally in the secondary school

Secondary school	
Device	Software
Computers	Word processor
	Data base
Internet	Games
	Search engines
	E-mail
	Instant message service
Cell phones	Text messages
MP3	MP3

Table 7.3 Technologies used principally in the *Locutorio*

Locutorio	
Device	Software
Computers	–
Internet	Simulations
	Role plays
	War games
	Search engines
	E-mail
	Instant message service
Cell phones	Text messages
	Telephone calls
MP3	MP3

technologies varies over the course of a day. In the mornings, the number of adolescents using digital apparatus is lower than in the afternoons, when in addition the game consoles are added to the battery of gadgets that they use and there is a greater diversity in the activities that they undertake. Those in the youngest group, the 12-year-olds, reported only using their cell phones and computers in the mornings.

2. **Function of the technologies used.** In this category we considered three uses: communication, entertainment, and information. The following results were recorded (Table 7.4).

There is a clear differentiation in terms of the functions the technologies serve in the two settings. In the school technologies are used predominantly for an information function which includes searching for information as well as copying and pasting information from one resource to another. By contrast, in the daily space communication and entertainment feature as the main functions.

3. **Convergence of technologies used.** A further characteristic that emerges from the observation of the activities of the young people is the high degree of convergence between the various technologies. The relationship between computer, MP3, and

Table 7.4 Function of the technologies used by the students

Function	Associated technologies
Communication	Internet (text messages – e-mail)
	Cell phone
Entertainment	Computers
	Game consoles
	Cell phones
	MP3
	Radio
	TV
	DVD
Information	Internet (search engines)
	Studio software (CD)

cell phone is high. The adolescents in the *locutorio* had their cell phone on one side of the computer and their MP3 on the other. This same relationship was also seen in the secondary school. In a class dedicated to an optional subject, the teacher said: "If it's a mechanical activity of filling in tables or worksheets for example, the kids can use their MP3s without any problem, as long as they get on with their work quietly."

This idea of "getting on quietly" with their work was also observed during class hours as the students listened to music while they completed the exercises given to them by the teacher. In the interview the children pointed out: "In the optional subject it's good because we can work while listening to music and then there is always time for the Internet … but we can't enter chat rooms, nor can we use our cell phones" (Focus Group).

4. **Ways of use.** The fourth category to emerge from the observations in the field was the type of relationships established while using the technology. Three types of use can be identified in the settings observed: individual, connected individual, and collective.

Individual use is defined as the activity carried out by the young person while he or she uses their computer without establishing a sustained link of either a physical or virtual relation with any other person. This type of use was observed principally in the secondary school, where the students worked individually with their computer and at times when quiet, individual work was encouraged. This method of use is associated with a type of specific practice, as we shall see below, which in the secondary school comprises both the predominant conception as to how persons learn and coincides with the norms for undertaking work that will promote learning.

The use which we classify as *connected individual* is the most typical method observed in the *locutorio*, along with the collective use adopted for playing games. Connected individual describes the practice of using the computer for playing, surfing the net, downloading information, while maintaining a conversation on an instant message system. All the young people observed in the *locutorio* use this method of work on the computer.

Collective use. This comprises two types and is characterized by virtual contact and physical contact. Typically it involves groups of five or six adolescents who meet to play. Each sits in front of their own computer but they play together. The young people would also often arrive in pairs and sit beside each other playing and discussing the techniques for playing the game.

7.6 Adolescent Digital Practices

In the above sections we have outlined the types of technology that young people use, the way they use them, and the purposes for which each is used. From this analysis we can identify two distinct patterns of use that are defined by two systems of activity which allow them to deploy their different repertoires. We shall call these patterns: (1) explicit learning pattern, which is associated with the secondary school's system of activity; and (2) learning pattern linked to the playing of games, which is marked by the activities that they do outside school. The *result* of this learning is the introduction of these young people in institutions of further education or in the job market, depending on their interests or their possibilities. In both cases learning involves training for the work to be undertaken. This goal which guides the school's work is mediated by a range of technologies that make up the school's "ecology," in which the students can acquire given digital experiences, though at the same time others are excluded.

The framework of the school's activity system can be broadly represented as follows (Fig. 7.1).

In this activity system, technologies acquire sense in that they serve the *goal* established by the activity; the *rules* laid down by the disciplinary guidelines of the school, the timetables, the organization of the curriculum, and the academic norms are ideally established to guarantee student learning; the *division of labor*, which recognizes the role of everyone in the system, also ideally seeks to facilitate student learning.

Using the category of information ecologies developed by Nardi and O'Day (1999), we find that in the *school ecology* technology basically serves the function of *representing* information. All the available technology is used for this purpose, while cell telephones and MP3s, used to a lesser extent officially, are subversive technologies, reserved for communication and entertainment. Technology in the school is recognized principally as a tool that enables the student to obtain or represent information. Because of this characteristic, the teachers recognize the difficulties they face in integrating it in the syllabus, unlike the work with the multimedia projector or Internet searches. Moreover, technology is also seen as a subject in its own right, one that students should learn so that in the future they can employ it in the productive workplace. Thus, it acquires the same significance as, for example, learning to read in which a context is reconstructed for learning different languages (if we might call them this) such as *Access*, *Excel*, the logic of the operating system, so that subsequently they can be used in other activities.

Thus it is possible to attain literacy, in terms of denaturalizing the use for which the software was designed, for example a data base by transforming it into a practice,

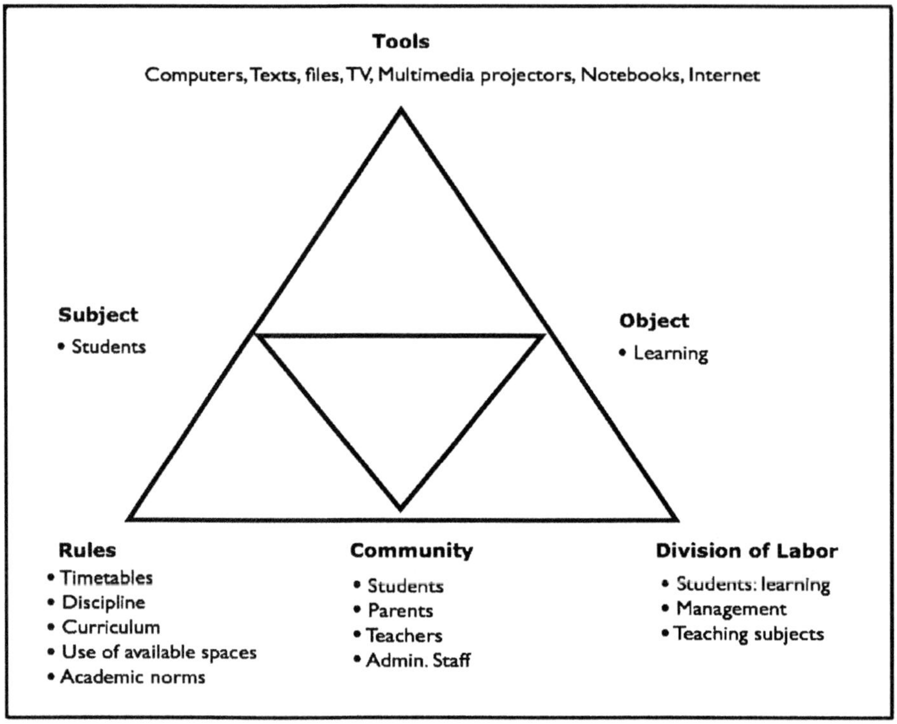

Fig. 7.1 School's activity system

i.e., learning to use *Access*. Seen in this light what is done with the technology and its possibilities of use fit coherently within this concept of the use of the technology. Its inclusion in the programs, and the current project of connecting all the classrooms is a way of understanding that the activity will be strengthened with the computers in the classrooms, but not that the activity itself is going to change.

The norms governing its use indicate that technology is available, as long as it is for coursework: the Internet is accessible for searching for information in the class, for example. All that is not in keeping with this understanding of the "proper" use of the technology is excluded from the practices that can be employed in the school, just as any eccentric practice would be excluded in a context of a socially organized, cultural activity. It is important to realize this in order to understand why the technology works the way it does in each context of use. Equally, and as Table 7.5 shows, the skills developed in this context are primarily concerned with copying and pasting information from one text to another, and general web searches for predefined subjects. The predominant way of working is the individual use of the computer to carry out the specific tasks associated with the learning of the applications.

The other activity system that involves the practices of the adolescents is that centered on their time outside the school, characterized by a high percentage of time dedicated to an activity oriented to socialization through play and connection

Table 7.5 Characteristics of use and associated technologies

Nature of knowledge	Typical methods of use	Type of associated actions	Associated technologies	Character of the technology
Separated from context	Individual	Copy–paste Internet searches writing short texts	Computers and Internet	Primary artifact

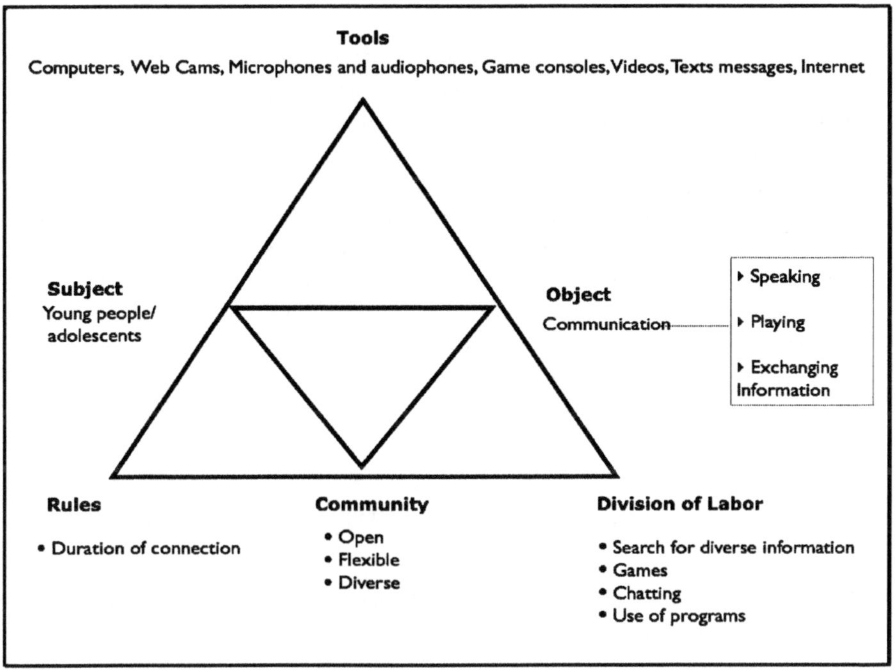

Fig. 7.2 Activity system outside the school

with their friends. The practices derived in this system are organized in different *spaces*, including their *homes* and the *journey* from one place to another. The goal of the activity, as they themselves recognize, is to connect with their friends through the games they play, the exchange of information and by chatting to each other on their computers. As such, the activity can be defined as communication or socialization within the peer group, which can in turn be described as follows (Fig. 7.2).

In this activity system there exists a relatively specialized *division of labor* in which the different users carry out different actions, which involve a transmission of knowledge between the parties that is intense and rich in terms of the skills deployed when using the various tools. In this system the users become members and participate actively – as was the case of Alfonso, who very quickly became a text message user and learnt how to use them and understand their meaning by connecting with his friends from his

Table 7.6 Characteristics of use and associated technologies

Nature of knowledge	Typical methods of use	Type of associated actions	Associated technologies	Character of the technology
Mobilized in action	Collective	Free surfing conversations problem solving associated with games	Computers and Internet	Operations/secondary artifact the technologies organize models of action

home town. In this system we can outline the information ecology employed by the adolescents. The representation of the technology in this system is characterized by the possibility of connecting and playing. Thus, the programs are used for playing games, which expands the recreational time of the young people, allowing them to interconnect with their friends via the screen or by playing certain games together.

In spaces such as the *locutorio*, the computer booth becomes a *physical space* of relationships, and of connecting/mediating communication and play, just like the other devices. Simultaneously, the Internet becomes the base that facilitates the operation, and which determines also the forms and types of communication. Three aspects characterize the setting of interaction: the simultaneous nature of the use of the technologies; the multimode pattern of text, image, and sound that converge in the technology used, and hypertext as a basic aspect of reading (Table 7.6).

7.7 Discussion: The Contradictory Digital Experience

Below, we outline the main points of discussion that have emerged from our study in terms of the questions we raised initially. Some of these points coincide with the research reviewed above; however, there are a number of new areas that need to be explored in terms of what occurs when school systems and the everyday experiences of secondary school students are brought together. Each of our reflections centers around three basic premises: first, that all digital experiences are *always* physical, bodily, experiences; second, that all digital experiences are experienced and built in a socially and culturally organized context; and third, that all human practices can be expanded and transformed.

The patterns of technology uses call into play repertoires of competences and skills which are realized in different contexts according to the predominant activity system.

A critical question is raised in relation to the two activity systems and this needs to be addressed as it has consequences for policies that introduce technologies in school practices. The schools have a dual function: first, it requires the observation of what is studied, knowledge is representational; and, second, it calls for "effort" and "constancy," regarding which the teachers warn that the students on the whole seem to have little "interest in putting in the effort needed to learn."

Learning is the school's work and, as such, it organizes its time and space to meet this objective, which while being compulsory requires the cooperation of the subject in order that the learning might be carried through to fruition. If we examine the other side of the coin, we see that the students inhabit another activity system, characterized by their *being* rather than by their observing the world. The technologies when used in the game activity system constitute a unified experience of knowledge and action. Focusing on this aspect in order that we might picture the potential of transferring these repertoires realized in each system is basic, since otherwise we might end up by only transferring the technology – as is occurring with current tendencies involving the introduction of the cell phone and situations such as those with video games, but perhaps not the competences that are deployed entirely in other activity systems. In other words, the technology does not function as a device that contains within it the skill to be deployed, but rather it functions in an ecology which has its own meaning and which gives meaning to its use. This, however, is an open approach that requires a detailed description of the repertoires that are manifest in each activity system and their corresponding competences.

The digital experience of young people, that is the experience of the incorporeal and instantaneous, transforms their everyday actions and operations, opening up the way to "elaborate" social practices. This is a key question in the debate, as usually the argument concerning the changes brought about by technology in the everyday habits of young people tends to assume that the digital experiences gain an ascendancy over corporal experiences. Certain standpoints would have us believe that the digital experience is only an experience of the mind. However – at least to date – the digital experience has expanded practices of play and communication among adolescents. Among the students we interviewed, technology is not the *object* of their practices, the aims of their activity continue to be having fun, socializing with the group, and the building of their life project. The actions deployed by the adolescents and those associated with technology, such as using their video game consoles and computers, are carried out in a framework of what they themselves describe as having fun and keeping themselves entertained. By contrast, they use instant messaging and their cell phones, above all, to maintain contact with their friends. As García Canclini would put it, young people feel "entertained and wired up" (García Canclini, 2004).

Thus, technology intensifies patterns of communication and acts of leisure, transforming characteristics of entertainment, accentuating digital leisure, and transforming the use of the time available. And it makes the screen in all its dimensions a point of reference for playing games and coexisting with the more usual forms of entertainment. In this sense, the possibilities for playing are broadened and the digital experience of different forms of communication are transformed. The use of text and instantaneous messages, for example, places an emphasis on "short" communicative codes, and young people prefer to send text messages than talk – for a question of costs, with a new code having been created for these platforms.

Each activity system constitutes an information "ecology" that is deployed and realized in the specific actions of use. Young people move between different "ecologies" and their journeys and waiting times are also associated with mobile technologies. It is no surprise that MP3s and cell phones are their most commonly used technologies, and not simply because they cost less, but because they are of great functional value in their everyday practices, as they travel, for example, from one place to another, or as they have to wait in the school for their afternoon classes or travel outside the city. As Nardi and O'Day (1999) write, technologies have a place and name in the lives of people, we inhabit them and they inhabit us. This *habitation* implies interrelationships and dependencies.

7.8 Conclusion

As we have striven to show here, digital literacy and the skills derived from it should be understood in the specific settings in which children and adolescents carry out their practices. Digital literacy, understood as a cultural practice, encourages the development of distinct skills according to the social contexts in which young people are immersed using technology. Likewise, schools not only need to court more technology, but more particularly they need to understand learning in a different way, so that technology might be incorporated within a system in which the latter promotes the development of the necessary skills. In this way it can form a part of, and at the same time critically evaluate, the current context of the knowledge society.

References

Augé, M. (1998). *Los No Lugares: espacios del anonimato*. Barcelona: Editorial Gedisa.

Balaguer, R. (2002). Videojuegos, Internet, Infancia y Adolescencia del nuevo milenio. Retrieved May 25, 2006, from http://www.cibersociedad.net/archivo/articulo.php?art = 6.

de Certeau, M. (1980). *L'invention du quotidien, tome 1: Arts de faire*. Paris: Gallimard.

Dreyfus, H. (1996). *Ser en el Mundo. Santiago de Chile*: Editorial Cuatro Vientos.

Engeström, Y. (1987). *Learning by Expanding: An Activity-Theoretical Approach to Developmental Research*. Helsinki: Orienta-Konsultit.

Engeström, Y. (1999). Activity Theory and individual and social transformation. In: Y. Engeström, Miettinen Reijo & Punamäki, Raija-Leena (Ed.), *Perspectives on Activity Theory* (pp. 19–38). Cambridge: Cambridge University Press.

García Canclini, N. (2004). *Diferentes, desiguales y desconectados. Mapas de la interculturalidad*. Barcelona: Gedisa Editorial.

Giddens, A. (1996). *Las consecuencias perversas de la modernidad*. Barcelona: Editorial Anthropos.

Hardgreaves, A. (2001). *Teaching in the Knowledge Society*. Columbia: Teachers College Press.

Jure, Paula (2004). Juventud y nuevas tecnologías: el pensamiento en red. Retrieved January 1, 2006, from http://www.c3fes.net/docs/jovenes.pdf.

Lash, S. (2005). *Crítica de la información*. Buenos Aires: Amorrortu.

Lea, M. (2004). New literacy studies, ICTs and learning in higher education. In: I. Snyder & C. Beavis (Eds.), *Doing Literacy Online: Teaching, Learning and Playing in an Electronic World* (pp. 3–23). Cresskill: Hampton Press.

Leontiev, A. N. (1978). *Activity, Consciousness, and Personality*. Englewood Cliffs, NJ: Prentice-Hall.

Nardi A. & O' Day L. (1999). *Information Ecologies. Using Technology with Heart*. Cambridge, MA: MIT Press.

Rodriguez Illera, J. L. (2004). Las alfabetizaciones digitales. *Bordón* 56 (3 & 4), 431–440.

Salomon, G., Perkins, D. N. & Globerson, T. (1991). Partners in Cognition: Extending Human Intelligence with Intelligent Technologies. *Educational Researcher* 20 (3), 2–9.

Chapter 8
Digital Literacy and Using Online Discussions: Reflections from Teaching Large Cohorts in Teacher Education

Anne Scott and Josephine Ryan

8.1 Online Application of Preservice Teachers' Beliefs About Teaching and Learning Literacy

There are pressures on Australian literacy teacher educators to incorporate new directions in curriculum policies and to address concerns about the effectiveness of teacher education programs. For example, Louden and Rohl (2006) reported perceptions about preservice literacy education programs from about 1,000 primary, secondary preservice teachers and lecturers across Australia. One of the study's key findings was that preservice teachers and lecturers held very different perceptions about the value of understanding principles and theory. Beginning teachers rated experiences gained during practicums more highly than their coursework which they saw as theoretical. This finding has significant implications for teacher education programs. Furthermore, there is an expectation from curriculum authorities that *Information Communications Technology* (ICT) will be integrated into all aspects of the curriculum (Victorian Curriculum Assessment Authority, 2006). One way to address the former issue is to have preservice teachers discuss theoretical perspectives in relation to classroom practice. It is also possible to use online tools to facilitate ongoing discussions and provide teacher educators with insights about preservice teachers' views and understandings. Therefore, online discussions have the potential to provide meaningful applications of ICT in literacy education programs.

However, many researchers suggest that online facilitators need to carefully consider all aspects of their instruction to maximize participants' engagement with the content in meaningful ways (Burbules & Callister, 2000; Im & Lee, 2003; Maor, 2003; Oliver, 2006; White et al., 2006; Gibbs & Krause, 2007). Other contextual factors affecting learning outcomes include participants' prior knowledge of, and experiences with, the subject matter and their perceptions of the learning environment (Good et al., 1975). Therefore, some consideration of preservice teachers' beliefs about teaching and learning literacy and their perceptions of online discussions as

A. Scott and J. Ryan
Australian Catholic University, Melbourne Campus

J. Zajda and D. Gibbs (eds.), *Comparative Information Technology,*
DOI: 10.1007/978-1-4020-9426-2_8, © Springer Science+Bussiness Media B.V. 2009

opportunities for learning are relevant in this paper. Consequently, three questions are addressed in this paper:

- What are preservice teachers' perceptions of the value of online discussions in their learning about literacy pedagogy?
- Is there evidence of preservice teachers' deepened understandings about literacy education within the online discussions?
- Which factors need to be considered in the design and implementation of online discussions?

8.2 Preservice Teachers' Beliefs About Teaching and Learning

Although there is no agreed definition of teacher beliefs (Beswick, 2003), Pajares (1992) said beliefs are "based on evaluation and judgment" (p. 313). Beliefs are socially created through a process of enculturation; they are context-specific and personally meaningful. However, beliefs are not necessarily based on objective fact. This is the working definition and the terms *perceptions* and *beliefs* are used interchangeably depending on the context in this discussion.

It is widely recognized that preconceived beliefs filter incoming information and impact on learning (Kardash & Scholes, 1996). Beliefs about teaching, learning, roles of instructors and learners, and uses of technology are all relevant to this study and are discussed. Wai-kit Ma, Andersson and Streith (2005) investigated preservice teachers' perceptions of computer technology in relation to their intentions to use computers in schools in the future. Wai-kit et al. (2005) reported there were two determining factors: *usefulness* and *ease of use*. Specifically, participants' perceived usefulness of the technology-related task led to strong intentions to use relevant technologies in their future workplaces. However, their perceived ease of use of the computer-related tasks were considerations only if the usefulness had long-term benefits.

Scanlon and Issroff (2005) reported that tutors and participants often had contradictory expectations and responses about what it meant to use technology productively. For example, for participants using technology efficiently meant not wasting their time; however, for a tutor it meant to maximize student learning using minimal resources. These differences in perceptions of efficiency impacted "on the ways [participants] used the learning technologies" (p. 434).

Furthermore, Scanlon and Issroff (2005) stated that the move away from traditional teaching approaches towards more self-directed learning necessitated a different view of the roles of tutors and learners. For example, expectations about the types of interactions between students and tutors vary. Evaluation of the course was also more complex. They reported that participants could feel a sense of failure as a result of any of the following: the malfunction of learning tool, student effort, expectation, and/or the course.

O'Reilly and Newton (2002) reported tertiary students' perceptions of the importance of online discussion regardless of whether or not these were assessed.

Findings indicated that students valued the social and the unit-focused support. In other words, students valued belonging to the group and appreciated the peer-to-peer interaction which went beyond conversational levels.

Clearly, it seems important to consider participants' perceptions of using ICT in learning contexts if the aim is to engage the learner in the activity. It seems equally important for instructors to understand how to use technology effectively.

8.3 Online Teaching and Learning

For some years now, at any given time, there are individuals participating in conversations in virtual spaces. New *Information Communications Technology* (ICT) provides seemingly endless opportunities for dialogue. The use of *computer-mediated communication* (CMC) medium is evident in the curriculum of many courses throughout the physical world in universities such as in Australia, New Zealand, South Korea, the UK, and the USA. CMC media includes asynchronous and synchronous online discussions uniting people from various backgrounds and locations to exchange experiences and understandings about a shared focus. Some higher education academics and teacher educators across disciplines employ such tools because these are media often used by Generation X and Y students. The use of CMC within a web-based management system such as *WebCT* enables students not only to access and engage with content materials but also to interact with peers to maximize learning.

On the other hand, some authors argue that the Internet is a new phenomenon because of its virtual nature and the social movements within it (Morris & Langman, 2005; Wong, 2007) and this combined with the CMC require participants to develop complex skills if they are to use the media effectively for learning (Bunz, 2003). Regardless of the motivation for the use of CMC, there seems to be an underlying assumption that its inclusion enhances the learning context. This section draws on literature from the field to explore this assumption.

8.3.1 Perceived Benefits of the Tool

Some writers in the field link online teaching and learning with a constructivist approach to knowledge building (Gabriel, 2004; Im & Lee, 2003; Maor, 2003; Nicols, 2003; O'Reilly & Newton, 2002; Panko, 2002). Gabriel (2004) claimed online learning is a:

- Move away from a transition model of teaching
- Collaborative learning process based on transformative model of learning which enables students to construct knowledge and
- A socially mediated process by which understanding develops through interaction with others

Of course, some argue that many of these points may exist in both traditional and virtual contexts (Burbules & Callister, 2000; Goodyear et al., 2001). Indeed, Goodyear et al. (2001) stressed the similarities between traditional face-to-face and online teaching but argued that the implementation of teaching practices may differ. Goodyear et al. (2001) and Burbules (n.d.) argued that online teaching and learning contexts force educators to rethink the planning for teaching. In particular, Burbules discussed four elements of teaching: course content, communication, projects and assignments, and evaluation and feedback. He stressed that each element had to be considered in the planning stage and that educators needed to identify the purposes of the course content and select appropriate teaching strategies to achieve the desired outcomes. Again, this seems applicable to all teaching and learning contexts not just those web-based.

A key difference between the two approaches, traditional and online, concerned the varied role of the instructor. For Burbules (n.d.) online teaching and learning brought about new possibilities for pedagogy which included decentering the role of the teacher, increasing interactivity and collaboration, emphasizing processes, and viewing learners as coproducers of knowledge. Online teaching and learning can include a wide range of strategies for example, online readings, hypertext, lectures plus multimedia, data, simulations, synchronous and asynchronous modes of communication, and flexible groupings. However, this discussion is limited to the use of CMC or online discussions.

Claims that online discussions make learning interactive and collaborative are noted across disciplines and cultures in tertiary education. For example, Gerbric (2005) discussed some of the challenges and opportunities arising from weekly online discussions for both Chinese and Kiwi learners. Twenty-five participants in this study spoke English as their second language. The content analysis of the online discussions described how students were understanding, evaluating, asking questions, applying theory, justifying, and relating to other comments in the virtual community. Gerbric concluded that the text-based nature of the online discussions helped all students to think more deeply about the topic and the assessment activity provided the motivation for their participation. Online discussions also provided opportunities specifically for particular groups of students. Chinese students found the virtual and text-based nature of the medium allowed them to enter discussions more easily and they felt more comfortable with their written responses than was the case in face-to-face discussions. Kiwi more than Chinese students were highly motivated by their involvement in an online debate. In contrast, some Chinese students expressed concern about disagreeing with comments when they were based on personal experience, as this was seen to be a sign of disrespect.

Similarly, Im and Lee (2003) analyzed postings from 40 South Korean preservice teachers who participated in synchronous and asynchronous discussions over 13 weeks. Findings indicated that these students carefully reflected on what they had learned when they participated in asynchronous task-orientated discussions because they had more time to think and organize their thoughts before contributing. Furthermore, Im and Lee noted that "female students were more active than male students in the online discussions" (p. 166).

Varied structures for online discussions also present different opportunities. For example, Panko (2002) described two case studies. One comprised 14 students who worked in small *closed* group settings and only read their group's postings. The other comprised 22 students who worked in small groups but were encouraged to read the postings of the wider class on a regular basis.

Panko (2002) reported that students in the closed group setting indicated that they felt safe and were able to communicate delicate issues because of the arrangement. The alternative structure held different benefits: access to and reading other groups' contributions offered diversity of views and experiences.

8.3.2 Perceived Limitations of the Approach

For various reasons several authors question the integration of CMC. Nicols (2003) argued that frequently discussions about e-learning are practice-based; descriptions and evaluations of events and activities rather than based on theoretical principles. Nicols used a metaphor of a tree to describe the difference between these two:

> Practice-based research can be likened to the branches of the tree, those parts that are readily visible and most easily appreciated. Theoretical principles can be likened to the roots; they do not provide any practical things for people like shade or fruit and neither are they aesthetically pleasing. However, it is the root system that determines the health of the tree and also the extent to which it can grow. Unless attention is given to elearning theory, the branches cannot stretch out for fear of toppling the entire structure. Unless attention is given to elearning theory, elearning practice cannot develop fully. (Nicols, 2003, p. 1)

Nicols (2003) proposed ten hypotheses for e-learning theory which were debated at the *Teaching and Learning Forum* in 2000; however, due to constraints to this publication these are not included here. Concerned about the reliability of results sometimes drawn from online discussions and the practicality of data analysis approaches, Cotton and Yorke (2006) critiqued three different methods for analyzing aspects of online discussions. They stressed using a systematic approach and a need to measure off-topic and organizational aspects of conversations which should not be regarded necessarily as irrelevant talk. To conclude, Cotton and Yorke proposed a combination of the three methods they piloted by describing five categories:

1. "Lower-level engagement (remember reading understanding applying)
2. Higher level engagement (making inferences, analyzing, evaluating, creating)
3. Social presence
4. Tutor facilitation
5. Off- task discussion" (p. 170)

Finally, questioning the value of online discussions as tools for promoting conversational modes of learning, Thomas (2002) described and interpreted the activities of students. He considered their level of cognitive engagement with the course material, the level of critical and reflective thinking, and level of interaction between students. Thomas (2002) concluded that "while online discussion forums promoted high levels of cognitive engagement and critical thinking, the virtual learning space of an online forum did not promote the coherent and interactive dialog necessary for conversational modes of learning" (p. 361). In support of this claim, Thomas demonstrated that many messages in the online discussion forum received no response; hence, those individuals had no conversations about their ideas.

To address this issue, Thomas (2002) argued that it seemed necessary that tutors structure online discussions to create opportunities for students to interact. One strategy employed to increase interactivity between participants is called the *starter-wrapper* technique (Hara et al., 2000). This technique assigns participants with specific roles in the discussion to be used on a rotational basis. Typically, the starter has the responsibility for the initial contribution to the online task. Another participant, the wrapper, is responsible for summarizing key aspects of the group's postings. Although the starter-wrapper technique promotes this analytical skill in one of the participants, Thomas argued that the technique did little to "eliminate the fragmentation and inherent incoherence embedded within the traditional structure of the threaded discussion list" (p. 364).

This section considered some of the advantages and limitations of the tool for learning. The next section reviews literature which addresses some of these issues and includes those which pertain to the design and implementation of the study.

8.3.3 Planning for Online Teaching and Learning Opportunities

Literature related to productive online teaching and learning experiences are discussed under the following subheadings: Allow Time for Participants to Establish their Identity as a Community of Inquirers; Understand the Changing Role of the Instructor; Provide Timely Feedback; and, Use Appropriate Tasks.

8.3.3.1 Allow Time for Participants to Establish Their Identity as a Community of Inquirers

Salmon (2002) described a five-stage conceptual framework for the development of participants' online discussions. In brief, stages one and two involve participants becoming familiar with the technology and their online peers. At stages three and four participants exchange information and construct personal knowledge. At stage five, participants are ready to integrate new content and deepen their understandings.

Concurring with Salmon (2002), Holmes (2004) identified a period of increased communication between online participants after 10 days of interaction and asserted that input from instructors during this period led to maximized learning opportunities. To illustrate the time needed to deal with issues productively Sutherland et al. (2005) described a successful blend of teaching and learning modes (classroom observation, professional discussions with practitioners, lectures, face-to-face sessions, and online discussions). In the study by Sutherland et al. (2005) preservice teachers spent up to 15.5 h per week participating in the various components of teaching and learning activities.

8.3.3.2 Understand the Changing Role of the Instructor

The role of the facilitator of online discussions has received considerable attention. Goodyear et al. (2001) identified six tasks: welcoming, establishing ground rules, creating community, managing communication, modeling social behavior, and establishing own identity. Similarly, Salmon (2002) argued that the role of the instructor was instrumental in determining the level of participant engagement. She suggested that the instructors' interactions varied according to the five stages described earlier. In stages one and two, the instructor motivates participants and begins fostering a sense of community. In stages three and four the instructor acts as an *e-moderator* (Salmon, 2002) supporting participants as they become engaged with the task. In stage five, the instructor assumes a mentoring role for participants.

8.3.3.3 Provide Timely Feedback

Swan (2001) found that student satisfaction with online components of courses was influenced by frequent interactions from instructors. However, many studies using online discussions had sample sizes ranging from 14–40 participants (Burbules, n.d.; Oliver, 2006; Simpson, 2006). It seems likely that a facilitator/participant ratio is a significant factor in achieving such outcomes.

8.3.3.4 Use Appropriate Tasks

Holmes (2004) suggested that online learning tasks needed to be sufficiently open-ended, engaging, and unambiguous. Similarly, Burbules and Callister (2000) advocated the use of case studies or projects to provide recognizable contexts containing problematic issues that could not be easily solved without further research and/or reading. In sum, there is evidence that designing online teaching and learning experiences is more complex than setting up the facilities and infrastructure to communicate using remote access. It requires a change in the perception and the role of the teacher, requires time to build a sense of community among learners, thoughtful selection of tasks, and significant investment in time (White et al., 2006). Having considered some authors' views about factors influencing online teaching and learning opportunities the next section describes the context, participants' perceptions of the experiences and learning outcomes.

8.4 The Investigation

The discussion in the chapter draws on experiences gained over 6 years (2002–2007). Each year participants comprised about 200 prospective primary teachers enrolled in a compulsory literacy education unit at an Australian tertiary institution. Majority of the preservice teachers were young female adults aged (18–24) who had varied levels of competency with computers. In 2002 many students struggled with logging on especially in the first 3 weeks of the course. In contrast, in 2007 there were less than 10% experiencing similar problems and many of these were international students who it seemed had had different experiences with ICT. The authors of this chapter were also consistently the teacher educators and/or designers of this unit. Both began with basic levels of competency with computers yet neither had prior experiences with online discussions nor knowledge about web-based platforms.

The introductory English education unit addressed literacy education in the early years of schooling over 12 weeks. The unit comprised compulsory components endeavoring to link theory with practice and included: a focussed observation of a 2-h literacy session in a P-2 classroom, weekly online discussions with peers, prescribed readings linked to the content of lecture and tutorial activities. Assessment tasks included: a major assignment requiring critical reflection on theory and practice and a 3-h essay-type examination. Furthermore, preservice teachers were encouraged to work voluntarily for ten literacy sessions in a P-2 classroom in the *Classroom Helpers Program* (Nutbean et al. 2003). There were consistently high levels of participation from preservice teachers (about 95%) in the program.

Each year the design and use of the online discussions component changed. Lecturers' skills with using the medium also developed. Table 8.1 summarizes the focus for the online discussion for each year.

As presented in Table 8.1 online discussions differed in nature and in duration each year in response to feedback from instructors and preservice teachers. However, the general aim of the online discussions remained constant: to provide increased opportunities for preservice teachers to discuss theory and practice. Each year preservice teachers worked in groups with five to eight members. Each group was numbered (1–33) and preservice teachers posted their contributions in their group's folder. Each lecturer was responsible for monitoring contributions of preservice teachers in their tutorials. Depending upon the lecturer's workload, this may have involved up to 21 groups. On average preservice teachers spent about 5 h per week

Table 8.1 Summary of the focus and duration of online discussion each year

Year	Focus for online discussions	Number of weeks
2002	To discuss weekly readings with tutorial members	7
2003	To discuss connections between classroom experiences and prescribed readings	12
2004	To allow preservice teachers to experience three modes of learning (handwritten notes, online discussions, answering multiple-choice items as online quiz items) and then allow them to choose their preferred mode as a means for challenging prior perceptions of teaching and learning literacy	3 weeks for each mode
2005	To focus discussions on a set of topics	5
2006	To promote collaborative exploration of three case studies using defined roles for each group member	6
2007	To promote collaborative exploration of documents, websites, and case studies using defined roles for each group member	10

Table 8.2 Summary of typical online discussion tasks

Year	Examples
2002	What are the differences between shared and guided reading? Why is guided reading an important part of reading instruction? How does the role of the teacher change during the literacy block?
2003	Share your experiences of your focused observation of a literacy session What is phonemic awareness? How is it taught?
2004	Identify an area of literacy education which interests you, e.g., children's literature. Research the area by referring to current philosophies and practices in literacy journals and texts. Summarize the insights you have gained about the area Complete online quiz based on weekly readings
2005	Join an online discussion related to the nine assignment topics and contribute regularly until the time of the submission of the major assignment. Topic 8: What does an early years literacy teacher need to know about teaching children who are learning English as a second language?
2006	Discuss some of the key issues facing the teacher and learners in the fictional scenario. Articulate relevant theories or perspectives based on readings
2007	Deconstructing text-types: Identifying language features in the short texts collected last week. For each text, name the text-type, describe the framework and give examples of the language features being used Starter = begins the task set for the week no later than Tuesday 11:59 pm General member = read contribution posted, respond to it in some way e.g., agree, disagree, pose a question, then add your own. NB: Word limit 200. Post your contribution no later than Saturday 11:59 pm Wrapper = reads all contributions, summarizes key points and adds a personal reflective comment of their own. Post your contribution no later than Monday 11:59 p.m.

working on components of the unit. On average lecturers spent 10 min reading each group's weekly entry. Clearly, over 12 weeks significant time was spent reading and giving feedback to postings. Table 8.2 summarizes typical online discussion tasks used each year.

Although the tasks were refined each year there were always some limitations. In 2002 the tasks were too narrow and could have been completed with a literal summation of the prescribed readings. In 2003 there was greater emphasis on making links between readings and observed classroom practices however, there was no guarantee that observed practices were similar to those advocated in coursework. In 2004 and 2005 completion of tasks required sharing further reading in specific topics yet the reading lacked an authentic context. In 2006 and 2007, cases studies and projects provided authentic contexts and roles provided a structure for distribution of work among group members.

8.4.1 Data Collection Tools and Analysis Techniques

Both qualitative and quantitative data were gathered each year (2002–2007). The following lists the range of approaches and tools used:

- Anonymous written responses to items at the end of the unit using a five-point Likert scale ranging from *strongly agree* to *strongly disagree* on the university's unit evaluation instrument
- Anonymous written comments at the end of the unit using the university's unit evaluation instrument
- Confidential records of preservice teachers' online discussions and
- Lecturers' ongoing critical reflections on the implementation and design of the unit

The process for analyzing online postings was consistent over the years. Transcripts were first read for potential commonalities, and preliminary categories were formed. Key issues were coded, in some cases with subnodes, with the assistance of a qualitative software program, NVivo (Richards et al., 2000). Data grouped into similarly coded sections were inspected for coherence. Discrepant comments were recategorized, or where necessary new nodes created to integrate them. Online discussions were examined for higher or lower levels of engagement with content of the unit and levels of social presence between group members (Cotton & Yorke, 2006). Anonymous written responses from end of unit evaluations provided evidence of preservice teachers' perceived value of online discussions on their learning in this unit.

8.5 Results and Discussion

This section presents data from various sources: aggregated data from the university's evaluation instrument for this unit for each year, and, excerpts from the online discussions posted. First, quantitative data are presented and key trends are identified. Following these are qualitative data presenting evidence of preservice teachers' learning in the online discussions. Table 8.3 presents aggregated data from the completion of the university's unit evaluation instrument by preservice teachers enrolled in the unit over 5 years. Data from 2007 are not available yet. For each year the numbers of evaluation forms returned are presented and frequencies for preservice teachers' responses to the items using the scale ranging from *strongly disagree* (SD) to *strongly agree* (SA) are given as percentages.

Figures in Table 8.3 represent the range of preservice teachers' written responses using the five-point scale. Frequencies reported as percentages seemed appropriate and no further statistical measures were applied as there were no experiment and/or control groups. For example, the figure 4 in the far left top cell indicates that only 4% of the 168 who returned their forms in 2002 *strongly disagreed* with the statement that *the use of online discussions contributed to [their] learning in this unit.*

Several trends are evident in the data. Profiles of results for each of the five-point scale are quite similar over the years. Likewise, profiles of results for the statements each year about the value of online discussions to their learning such as, *My perceptions of teaching and learning literacy have been challenged through completing online discussions* (2004) and *The use of online discussions contributed to my learning in this unit* (2006) are quite similar. Generally, about 46–62% at least *agreed* with such statements and 21–28% either *disagreed* or *strongly disagreed* with the same.

Table 8.3 Preservice teachers' written responses to university's unit evaluation about online discussion components for years 2002–2006

Year	Items on unit evaluation	SD	D	U	A	SA
2002 (*n* = 168)	The use of online discussions contributed to my learning in this unit	4	17	23	45	11
2003 (*n* = 227)	The use of online discussions contributed to my learning in this unit	5	21	28	40	6
2004 (*n* = 169)	My perceptions of teaching and learning literacy have been challenged through completing online discussions	5	23	20	41	11
	My perceptions of teaching and learning literacy have been challenged through completing online quizzes	6	13	23	39	19
2005 (*n* = 137)	The use of online discussions contributed to my learning in this unit	5	18	24	35	17
2006 (*n* = 164)	The use of online discussions contributed to my learning in this unit	5	16	17	37	25
	The use of case studies helped me with my learning	2	7	16	46	29
2007 (*n* = 109)	The use of online discussions contributed to my learning in this unit	1	2	12	54	40
	The use of case studies helped me with my learning	0	4	20	60	25

In each of those years between 20% and 28% indicated they were *unsure* whether the online discussions had been helpful to their learning.

In 2004, preservice teachers completed online discussions and answered quizzes about aspects of the content online for 3 weeks each. The assumption was that by providing some variety in the format for online learning it would allow preservice teachers to indicate which of the modes was more helpful to their learning. Results indicate that:

- 52% at least *agreed* that online discussions had challenged their perceptions about teaching and learning
- 58% at least *agreed* that completing online quizzes had challenged their perceptions about teaching and learning
- 28% either *disagreed* or *strongly disagreed* that online discussions had challenged their perceptions about teaching and learning and
- 19% either *disagreed* or *strongly disagreed* that online quizzes had challenged their perceptions about teaching and learning

This suggests that preservice teachers perceived completing online quizzes marginally more useful to learning than their engagement in online discussions. For the authors, it appeared that participants were challenged to think more deeply during online discussions than in answering multiple choice quiz items. This confirms points made by both Wait-kit et al. (2005) about perceived usefulness and Scanlon and Issroff (2005) ideas about perceptions and expectations differing. Having said that, the highest levels of satisfaction from preservice teachers regarding the value of the online discussions were gained in 2006 when 75% at least *agreed* with the statement, *The use of case studies helped me with my learning*. Preservice teachers were given three case studies and encouraged to work collaboratively on a shared task which rehearsed the process and skills needed to complete the major assessment task. They allocated roles (Hara et al., 2000) among group members to complete the task which included: identifying issues impacting on literacy teaching or learning within the case study scenario, researching the issues identified, and proposing a plan of action. Plans could offer advice suitable for either teachers or parents.

Overall, it seemed that over time facilitators' expertise developed and they chose more suitable tasks. As a result, it seemed that more preservice teachers indicated that online discussions were useful to their learning. It is hoped that such positive experiences lead these preservice teachers to deepen their appreciation for using online discussions for learning (Wai-kit et al., 2005).

8.5.1 Levels of Cognitive Engagement

There was evidence of lower-levels of engagement (remembering, reading, understanding, and applying) throughout all year levels but most prominent in 2002, 2003 when the tasks were not sufficiently challenging and to a lesser extent in 2005 when the tasks were not always set in meaningful contexts.

Higher-levels of engagement (making inferences, analyzing, evaluating, creating) were most prominent during the weeks in which groups collaboratively addressed issues embedded within case studies. The use of assigned roles, on a rotational basis, was also helpful. Each week exemplary contributions were identified and posted in an announcement so that all enrolled in the unit could see what constituted successful entries. There were opportunities for preservice teachers to vary their writing styles from informal chatroom style to formal academic pieces depending upon the task set. Clearly, not all were experienced academic writers. However, contributing to online discussions provided opportunities for members to practise their skills in short bursts regularly without fear of severe penalties for typographical and grammatical errors. Reading postings by more capable writers seemed to provide helpful modeling for less experienced writers. The following excerpt demonstrates the quality of the academic writing produced by many preservice teachers in 2007.

> As Lauren has already mentioned, in the case study we are reviewing, minimal verbal interaction is used between Pete and his parents. They do not take on much of a tutoring role in his learning at home and this in turn has affects (sic) on his learning outcomes. One of the experts stated that there was a considerable difference in the affective quality of the parent-child bond relating to both the child's outlook towards reading and the child being able to read fluently. In the same way, this article presents verification that early literacy may be linked with the quality of the relationship the child has with the parent. (Bergin, 2001) A study by Rogoff et al. (as cited in Hamston & Love) said that fathers see themselves as somebody their sons look up to. With this being said, experts reflect in the significance of children learning from observing what others do. With Pete watching his dad make motorbike models and interacting through demonstrations and not verbal instructions, he is more likely to model that type of behaviour. (Contribution from 2007)

In 2007, for the last online discussion preservice teachers were asked to reflect on, and share their thoughts with group members about, "what makes an effective literacy program" The following is one response:

> First and foremost, I concur with Rachel's inclusion of a literacy program which incorporates a range of activities to cater for differing ability levels. This enables students to learn and consolidate their knowledge at an appropriate pace and ability level.
> For a literacy program to be effective one must consider the teacher and the students. … The teacher must have knowledge of each students' literacy abilities in order to help them progress as literacy learners. … Eager students who are instilled with the desire to learn are also of fundamental importance.
> More specifically, an effective literacy program must provide students with ample opportunities to develop their reading, writing, speaking and listening skills. Opportunities … can be gained through guided and shared experiences, as well as explicit teacher modelling of appropriate behaviours and strategies.
> An effective literacy program must incorporate a range of interesting and stimulating activities and resources that can be used to develop children's literacy skills. Instructional strategies and activities such as a Read To, Picture Chat, Cloze Exercise and Show 'n' Tell can be used to provide children with enjoyable literacy experiences and enable them to practise effective reading and writing behaviours. (Contribution from 2007)

Clearly, this preservice teacher was able to articulate her beliefs clearly and concisely. Others in the group had equal opportunities. Shared insights provide specific examples of the knowledge and values gained at the completion of the unit which are otherwise not feasible in face-to-face settings.

8.5.2 Levels of Social Presence

In 2002 there was limited evidence of social interaction between group members beyond a greeting. There was really no need even to communicate organizational arrangements because the tasks set were individualistic. It seemed that most exchanges were complaints and commiserations related to technical mishaps and/or advice for specific issues. Over the years (2003–2007), these elements were still present but infrequent and questions of and encouraging words between peers became more obvious. There was evidence that preservice teachers became engaged in discussions and interacted effectively when they were set appropriate tasks. The following is an excerpt of the discussion from a group who shared an interest in children's literature:

> Hi there, I'm V*. I can't believe that there are not more people contributing to this topic area! What could possibly be more important for teaching children than children's literature? … Since I've been reading to my own children I've been amazed at the amount of fantastic stuff that's out there for kids. (Message no. 622, 2004)
> Sorry to say I don't know all those books V*, though you might like *Roberto the insect architect*, which is a personal favourite. It is written by Nina Laden. (Message no. 625, 2004)
> Some critics believe that children's literature shouldn't be classified as "Literature" because it is basic and undermines the more advanced and detailed forms i.e., Jane Austen etc. I really don't agree as one of u said it is the basis of learning how to read and appreciating texts as a whole. (Message no. 899, 2004)
> Yes that argument re children's books being lit is very interesting, picture books enable children to experience "reading" a book for enjoyment before they are able to read the text. Without this early introduction to literature they would find it harder to understand the concepts of more advanced forms later on. (Message no. 908, 2004)

It seems that preservice teachers were capable of discussing issues enthusiastically with others even though they didn't know each other well and for this task they used a less formal *chatroom* style of writing as their genre. In the chatroom genre there is often little regard for conventional spellings and punctuation marks.

However, there were significant interactions between group members when the starter-wrapper technique was employed in 2006–2007. These included organizational conversations and negotiations about the shared task to be completed. There were signs of team spirit among most groups, boosting morale, and frequent affirmations about people's contributions and resources sharing. The following excerpt was taken from a task which asked the group members to review a web site. This is an extract from a wrapper's comprehensive summary of the group's contribution.

> The *Literacy Educators Coalition* website ... is an Australian-based portal that leads to many practical and informative papers, presentations and commentaries submitted from world-wide sources ... regarding prevalent issues and ideas specifically concerning the field of literacy. As my fellow peers have commented there are many varied contributions; there are those that express personal beliefs, such as Jacqueline Wilson's article 'Literacy Drive is Killing Creativity', as well as researched studies, such as the report referred to in the article 'In Teachers' Hands: Effective Teaching Practices in the Early Years of Schooling' that was commissioned by the Federal Government. (Contribution from 2007)

Complex tasks requiring research and discussion seemed appropriate tasks for small groups to work on collaboratively. Having said that, over the years, two qualities, enthusiasm and excitement, were common to all discussions from preservice teachers when they shared personal experiences as Classroom Helpers. McDonald and White (2005) argued that online forums are ideal for narrative or the sharing of experiences. Records of their discussions suggest that there were useful reflections occurring. For example, one preservice teacher wrote:

> This one child was working with another child who was fairly good at writing, however, the other child (who did not speak much English and could not read) could copy perfectly the words that the other child was writing but still would not have been able to read them back to you. So maybe that raises a question as to whether or not simple copying is beneficial to all children; just because you know what a letter looks like and how to copy it, doesn't necessarily mean you understand it. (Message no. 324, 2004)

It seems that this preservice teacher is capable of critically reflecting on observations of classroom experiences. It also provides others reading the entry with an opportunity for learning without having been present. Bandura (1986) described the *vicarious* capability given situations such as this when people learned from others' experiences.

8.5.3 Challenges Faced

From an analysis of the preservice teachers' written comments on the university's unit evaluation forms, their online contributions, and from the lecturers' reflections on the design of the unit, three issues were classified as ongoing concerns:

1. Access to, and fragility of, technology
2. Challenging preservice teachers' perceptions of the uses of ICT (online discussions) as a tool for learning
3. Monitoring and providing timely feedback

8.5.3.1 Access to, and Fragility of, Technology

Limited access to technology and its fragility also contributed to participants' frustrations with online discussions. Preservice teachers often did not have the appropriate technology at home and access at university was not always easy. On the one hand, such barriers need to be considered given that universities continue to encourage the use of online components in courses yet they may not always provide the infrastructure to support them. On the other hand, it seems likely that those for whom technological challenges are insurmountable are at risk of exclusion (Lankshear et al., 2000). Therefore, institutions need to seek ways to assist those without technological power because educators cannot abandon it.

8.5.3.2 Challenging Preservice Teachers' Perceptions of the Uses of Online Discussions as a Tool for Learning

As discussed earlier, it is important to discuss the roles and responsibilities of facilitators and learners working in an online environment because these impact on the ways technologies are used (Scanlon & Issroff, 2005). It has taken the authors of this chapter a number of concerted efforts to achieve a satisfactory balance.

8.5.3.3 Monitoring and Providing Timely Feedback

Sometimes preservice teachers seemed to get half the intended message provided by the facilitators and it was difficult to prevent them from reinforcing misconceptions among themselves. This excerpt from one preservice teacher who seems to have gained only part of the current advice regarding spelling:

> The journals I have read have emphasised the BIG changes in learning [how to] spell since my primary school days. I am pleased to hear that research has criticised the traditional rote learning method. The approach to spelling these days is far more integrated which is said to provide more lasting learning than previous memorization models. I think children are less conscious that they are actually learning spelling in a whole language approach. They seem to learn to spell subconsciously through immersion and engagement in a rich world of texts. (Message no. 612, 2004)

It was pleasing to see that this preservice teacher realized that it was useful to take words from content being studied. However, in this excerpt the emphasis on teaching implicitly and learning subconsciously are misleading. Providing feedback in a timely manner is always important in teaching. On some occasions it was possible to address misleading information posted by preservice teachers in the lecture and use it as a teaching point. Other times, the lecturer posted a short response. Whatever the approach, there is no guarantee that either would successfully address the misconception.

The issue of monitoring online discussions with 200 participants was an ongoing challenge. As mentioned earlier each lecturer may be involved with up to 21 groups. Even if only 10 min were spent responding to each group this would be very demanding. Over the years, lecturers gave participants clearer advice and expectations for successful online participation. For example, online communications are short (200 word limit), weekly, reflective contributions in response to others' postings and in light of readings and classroom experiences. The most successful way of providing feedback was achieved by posting a copy of an exemplary online discussion for all to read with the permission of the contributors. The lecturer used the example to point out how the criteria had been addressed well. Lecturers noted improved professional discourse among preservice teachers with each case study.

8.6 Conclusion

Given 6 years' experimentation using online discussions it is evident that preservice teachers had increased opportunities to critically explore issues related to literacy education. In many cases, especially in the latter years, there was evidence of preservice teachers' deepened understandings. However, using online discussions requires careful design. Successful implementation considers participants' perceptions of various roles in the learning environment. It requires setting appropriate tasks and providing constructive feedback. As is probably true for other innovative projects, there are periods when the learning curve seems steep and the notion of integrating ICT, which often presents as a fragile technological system, within an already workable design seems senseless. Yet given our role as educators in the twenty-first century when our lifestyles often depend on the efficient use of ICT it seems important that we continue to seek ways to prepare prospective teachers for teaching literacy utilizing opportunities to enable them to grow professionally in a variety of shared spaces.

References

Bandura, A. (1986). *Social Foundations of Thought and Action: A Social Cognitive Theory*. Englewood Cliffs, NJ: Prentice-Hall.

Beswick, K. (2003). Accounting for the contextual nature of teachers' beliefs in considering their relationship to practice. In L. Bragg, C. Campbell, G. Herbert & J. Mousley (Eds.), *26th Annual Conference of the Mathematics Education Research Group of Australasia, Mathematics Education Research: Innovation, Networking, Opportunity* (Vol. 1, pp. 152–159). Sydney: MERGA.

Bunz, U. (2003). Growing from computer literacy towards computer-mediated communication competence: Evolution of the field and evaluation of a new measurement instrument. *Information Technology, Education and Society*, *4*(2), 27–46.

Burbules, N. (n.d.). The new possibilities of online pedagogy. Retrieved 17 August 2006, from http://faculty.ed.uiuc.edu/burbules/papers/onlinepedagogy.ppt

Burbules, N., & Callister, T. (2000). Universities in transition: The promise and the challenge of new technologies. *Teachers College Record, 102*(2), 271–293.

Cotton, D., & Yorke, J. (2006). Analysing online discussions: What are students learning? In L. Markauskaite, P. Goodyear & P. Reimann (Eds.), *Proceedings of the 23rd Annual Australian Society for Computers in Learning in Tertiary Education Conference: Who's Learning? Whose Technology*? (pp. 163–171). Sydney: Sydney University Press.

Gabriel, M. (2004). Learning together: Exploring group interactions online. *Journal of Distance Education, 19*(1), 54–72.

Gerbric, P. (2005). Chinese learners and computer mediated communication: Balancing culture, technology, and pedagogy. In H. Goss (Ed.), *Proceedings of the 22nd Annual Australian Society for Computers in Learning in Tertiary Education Conference: Balance, Fidelity, Mobility: Maintaining the Momentum?* (Vol. 1, pp. 241–251). Brisbane: Department Call for Teaching and Learning Support Services, Queensland University of Technology.

Gibbs, D., & Krause, K.-L. (2007) (Eds.). *Cyberlines 2.0: Languages and Culture of the Internet*. Melbourne: James Nicholas Publishers.

Good, T., Biddle, B., & Brophy, J. (1975). *Teachers Make a Difference*. New York: Holt, Rinehart & Winston.

Goodyear, P., Salmon, G., Spector, J., Steeples, C., & Tickner, S. (2001). Competencies for online teaching: A special report. *ETR & D*, 49(1), 65–72.

Hara, N., Bonk, C., & Angeli, C. (2000). Content analysis of online discussion in an applied educational psychology course. *Instructional Science*, 28(2), 115–152.

Holmes, K. (2004). Analysis of asynchronous online discussion using SOLO taxonomy. From http://www.aare.edu.au/04pap/hol04863.pdf

Im, Y., & Lee, O. (2003). Pedagogical implications of online discussion for preservice teacher training. *Journal of Research on Technology in Education*, 36(2), 155–170.

Kardash, C., & Scholes, R. (1996). Effects of pre-existing beliefs, epistemological beliefs, and the need for cognition on the interpretation of controversial issues. *Journal of Educational Psychology*, 88(2), 260–271.

Lankshear, C., Snyder, I., & Green, B. (2000). Teachers and Technoliteracy. Managing Literacy, Technology and Learning in Schools. Sydney: Allen & Unwin.

Louden, W., & Rogl, M. (2006) "Too Many Theories and Not Enough Instruction": Perceptions of Preservice Teacher Preparation for Literacy Teaching in Australian Schools. *Literacy*, 40(2), 66–78.

Maor, D. (2003). The teacher's role in developing interaction and reflection in an online learning community. *Education Media International*, 40(1), 127–137.

McDonald, L., & White, P. (2005). Blended learning. In J. Clark & M. Maguire (Eds.), *Challenges for the Profession: Perspectives and Directions for Teachers, Teaching and Teacher Education* (pp. 428–436). Proceedings of the 12th International ISATT Conference, Sydney.

Morris, D., & Langman, L. (2005). Networks of dissent: A typology of social movements in a global age. *Information Technology, Education and Society*, 6(2), 5–25.

Nicols, M. (2003). A theory for eLearning. *Educational Technology & Society*, 6(2), 1–10.

Nutbean, M., Ryan, J., & Scott, A. (2003). Forging partnerships between schools and universities: The CLaSS classroom helper initiative. *Learning Matters*, 8(1), 42–45.

O'Reilly, M., & Newton, D. (2002). Interaction online: Above and beyond requirements of assessment. *Australian Journal of Educational Technology*, 18(1), 57–70.

Oliver, R. (2006). Exploring a technology-facilitated solution to cater for advanced students in large undergraduate classes. *Journal of Computer Assisted Learning*, 22, 1–12.

Pajares, F. (1992). Teachers' beliefs and educational research: Cleaning up a messy construct. *Review of Educational Research*, 62(3), 307–332.

Panko, M. (2002). *Small group learning in online discussions: Staying in your own backyard or peering over the garden fence?* Paper Presented at the Australian Society Computers in (ASCILITE).

Richards, T., Richards, L., Fraser, D., & Barrington, T. (2000). *NVivo: NUD*IST for Qualitative Research* (Version 1.2) [CD Rom]. La Trobe University/QSR International Pty Ltd, Melbourne.

Salmon, G. (2002). *Online learning workshop*. Paper Presented at the Conference Proceedings, 17th Australian Council for Computers in Education: Linking learners, Hobart.
Scanlon, E., & Issroff, K. (2005). Activity theory and higher education: Evaluating learning technologies. *Journal of Computer Assisted Learning*, 21, 430–439.
Simpson, A. (2006). *Student Voices, Teachers' Vibes and a Researcher's View: Book Raps as a Model of E-Literacy*. Darwin: Australian Literacy Educator's Association.
Sutherland, L., Marcus, G., & Jessup, A. (2005). From face-to-face to blended learning: Issues and challenges in redesigning a professional course. In A. Brew & C. Asmar (Eds.), Proceedings of the 2005 Annual International Conference of the Higher Education Research and Development Society of Australasia: Higher Education in a Changing World (pp. 551–558). Milperra, NSW: The University of Sydney.
Swan, K. (2001). Virtual interaction: Design factors affecting student satisfaction and perceived learning in asynchronous online courses [Electronic version]. *Distance Education*, 22(2), 306–331.
Thomas, M. (2002). Learning with in incoherent structures: The space of online discussion forums. *Journal of Computer Assisted Learning*, 18, 351–366.
Victorian Curriculum Assessment Authority. (2006). Victorian essential learning standards. Retrieved 9 February 2006, from http://vels.vcaa.vic.edu.au/index.html
Wai-kit Ma, W., Andersson, R., & Streith, K. (2005). Examining user acceptance of computer technology: An empirical study of student teachers. *Journal of Computer Assisted Learning*, 21, 387–395.
White, F., Daly, M., & Scott, K. (2006). Student evaluations of e- learning technologies in undergraduate psychology: A blended model for the future. In L. Markauskaite, P. Goodyear & P. Reimann (Eds.), *Proceedings of the 23rd annual Australian Society for Computers in Learning in Tertiary Education conference: Who's learning? Whose technology*? (pp. 863–870). Sydney: Sydney University Press.
Wong, A. (2007). Cyberself: Identity, language and stylisation on the internet. In D. Gibbs & K. Krause (Eds.), Cyberlines 2.0: Languages and Cultures of the Internet. Melbourne: James Nicholas Publishers.

Chapter 9
Development of IT-Infrastructure for Rural Connectivity: A Pro-poor Approach to E-Governance for Rural Development in India

Karunamay Subuddhi

9.1 Globalization and ICT: Introduction

The most important force driving the contemporary global society is information and communication technology (ICT). The inventive march of human efforts in ICTs in the global culture has shown new dimensions to the development work, knowledge and information exchange, and many other networking facilities. Informationalization has changed the structures of social action as well as institutional sites of cultural processes in several ways. In the "information society," the information intensity of all activities has led to new forms and substances in the organization of society, economy, the labor market, and culture. Information has become one of the primary goods, which, in a particular minimum, is required for everybody. Increasingly, access to computers and the Internet is becoming a basic necessity to achieve specific training and education, especially distant education or adult education. According to John Rawls (1971) and Amartya Sen (1985), certain primary goods, such as rights, freedoms, life-chances, and particular basic income, are so essential for survival and self-respect that they cannot be exchanged for other goods. In the case of information while it is a nonmaterial good, it has the potential to materialize in the shape of an information product and process. As a nonmaterial primary good, information has an important special quality. It is possible to exchange this good without losing it.

This has an equalizing effect on the use of information. With differential appropriation of information by the individuals, groups, and classes (as they have different material, social, and cultural resources), however, two distinct patterns have emerged in the global context. First, informationalization results in increasing relative differences of information processed and skills to be developed, rewarding some and not others, and widening cleavages both within and between countries. Second, while the digital divide between the urban-based information elite and very poorly connected rural people within specific countries, and between developed

K. Subuddhi
Indian Institute of Technology, Mumbai

J. Zajda and D. Gibbs (eds.), *Comparative Information Technology*,
DOI: 10.1007/978-1-4020-9426-2_9, © Springer Science+Bussiness Media B.V. 2009

and developing countries is extending, requirements for policy decisions to remove the barriers of connectivity and to bridge the digital divide is also gaining ground. To escape the deepening of the digital divide, special efforts are now being made to bridge the "information gaps" and to support particular groups that are lagging behind in computer access and that are underserved in terms of computer applications. The impressive capabilities of ICTs are often paraded by management and communication consultants and by some policymakers as producing the transition to a new paradigm of global business opportunities. For some optimistic thinkers, whatever now is organizationally and legally possible can be technologically implemented because of the versatility of the technological medium. There is already "a shift away from the centrality of organizational unit to the networks of information and decisions" (Castells, 1989, p. 142). With the application of ICTs, some assert, there is now an enormous potential to create favorable conditions for restructuring the modern state (Pollitt, 1990; Hoggett, 1990). In the past, much of information was constructed by governments for the administrative control of increasingly large populations.

9.2 IT-Led Penetration in Rural Areas and Knowledge Management

The role of information technology (IT) in knowledge management is now a widely accepted fact in the context of the globalizing world. Revised concept of development communication has led to a reexamination of the advantages of traditional media as vehicles for information, persuasion, and entertainment of people. Since the mid 1970s2001, there has been a steady growth in ICTs and their application in rural development. In response to public demand the technology required for social innovation is also developing very fast (Melkote & Steeves,). There is now a growing trend to build the capacity of entrepreneurs in the developing world, who are working in the rural areas to serve the poor. Though its penetration is still very low in many developing countries and it is still very much an urban-based ICT, it has now emerged as a major platform "allowing increased transparency, efficiency and accountability" (Bedi et al., 2001, pp. 16–36) across the globe. Its advantages are now being accrued not only to the individuals but also intermediaries such as small and medium enterprises, NGOs, development officers, rural health centers, and other development-related organizations.

In the context of rural development the Food and Agriculture Organization (FAO), for instance, has recently asserted that "people oriented" and "beneficiary centric" model of development can very well be possible if people are involved and motivated, and information and knowledge are shared. The new technologies can establish dialogue with rural people by involving them in the planning process to improve the quality of their life. It can also overcome the barriers of illiteracy, language, intercultural differences, and physical isolation. The cornerstone of this strategy is capacity-building activities for rural and agricultural organizations and to enable the communities to freely network with other communities and other knowledge resources, making available at hand the best practices followed in similar situations all over the world. From the remotest field areas, one can contact development workers, professionals, and others all over the world and get instant help.

The relevance of ICT is more pronounced in a supranational–global context as developing economies are increasingly at the mercy of the international organizations who sometimes profess to act as a countervailing force to international trade and financial interests and at times undermine the role of representative local bodies.[1] This has brought about the problems of accountability of the institutions, accompanied by information asymmetries amongst bargainers that lead to costly delays and stalemates in modern economic setup (Bardhan, 2001, pp. 475–480). Market forces generally succeed in bringing together certain interests at specific levels but they fail when the transaction costs are high. With the necessary political orientation and support of the state, some argue, however, that ICT can help aligning the key actors and reduce the problems of alienation, fragmentation, and dislocation of knowledge. For interorganizational coordination special efforts need to be made to support and protect all organizations of workers' and for a "social safety nets for workers" (Hensman, 2001; see also Koushik, 2004, pp. 123–124; Gupta et al., 2000, p. 85). Knowledge can become a means of power, if coalitions or networks of relevant actors evolve.[2] It may also promote participatory and consultative "good governance" while harnessing the democratic potentials of these new technologies at the local level (Held, 1987, p. 285). In view of this expected role of ICTs, an attempt has been made to identify the potential benefits and limitations of the technology approach based on some experiences of ICT programs for poverty alleviation in the rural areas.

9.2.1 Global Rural Network and the Rural Poor (GRN)

ICT and its continued relevance for rural development in the developing countries are best marked in the emerging global network and IT-led development initiatives by the national and global agencies. The activities represent a combination of awareness raising, capacity building, and the expansion of the use of new technologies.

---

[1]Technology planning is no more a local affair. National technology planning is influenced greatly by the trade-related policies developed by the World Trade Organization (WTO), a successor to the GATT. Some critics caution that unless the developing countries are well prepared and coordinated, there would be greater dependence on the developed countries for technological development.

[2]An instance of such an effort is "The Global Knowledge for Development" (GKD), which has helped people solve their problems, forge partnerships, and become allies in the global quest to make developmental information and knowledge available to all (www.globalknowledge.com).

Despite a strong claim for giving emphasis in certain crucial aspects (minimum needs) of rural development first,[3] the infrastructure for the new ICT in the developing countries is not disregarded by the concerned agencies. Its likely net social benefit of applications draws one's attention to the use of these technologies for the promotion of intermediate and appropriate technologies for poverty alleviation and sustainable livelihood. Developed nations such as the USA and Canada assist in setting up community Internet access, especially in rural areas. The British government runs "Rural net" for communities in rural areas to enable rural people avail of the new opportunities all over the world. Along with laying the necessary infrastructure, similar initiative needs to be taken in other countries. Some efforts by developing nations are already made for rural development using the latest technologies. For instance, the online financial services provided by ICICI, a leading bank in India, and its Net-enabled telephony used for online banking appeared in India at about the same time as in Western countries. Efforts are being made to collaborate with global agencies for community Internet centers in India. The Government of Maharashtra has entered into an agreement with WorldTel, a private limited company incorporated in the UK, to work on developing statewide Internet connectivity and reach through Internet community centers. Besides, the e-ASEAN Task Force is developing a broad and comprehensive action plan, covering the necessary physical, legal, logistical, social, and economic infrastructure needed for evolving an ASEAN e-space in the world of ICT (ICT), and developing competencies within ASEAN countries to compete in the global market (Bedi et al., 2001, p. 172).

The development experts have recognized the potentiality of high returns of investment by incremental improvements in the efficiency of participants in the unorganized sector in the recent past. The artisans who produce the most authentic and finest crafts are those with the least access to the global markets. Under an online initiative called The Virtual Souk, since 1998, a financially sustainable, decentralized, and locally controlled Web-e-commerce operation is helping the poorer sections of the people to organize themselves for achieving the economic targets (Maurice Hazan, The Virtual Souk, E-commerce for Unprivileged Artisans' @ www.elsouk.com). The promise of digital development is that it might have the same reach as the original Internet boom of the mid-1990s – only this time, the most underprivileged communities, those who had missed out on earlier waves of technology, might be able to "leapfrog" over their more developed competitors.

---

[3]In south Asia, for some critics, where most rural populations lack running water and sanitation systems, where electricity is still a scarce and intermittent resource, where roads are poor and education a luxury, these new technologies truly appear to be far removed from the everyday concerns of the poorest sections of the countryside. Despite these feelings amongst many critics, Economic development experts ranked improvement in telecommunication infrastructure as most important in the context of rural development (Ontario Federation of Agriculture *Internet and Rural Development Recommendations for Strategy and Activity*, @ www.fao.org, 1995). There are some scholars in India who are very optimistic about the prospect of IT revolution and India's ability to unleash its vast economic potential. (Jagdish Bhagwati, 'Confederacy of Doers', *India Today*, special millennium issue, October 2000).

As the reach of the Internet and wireless communication technologies continues to expand at unprecedented rates around the world, concerns are growing about ways and means of bringing rural communities into the fold as well. A number of approaches have emerged, such as building bridges via globally dispersed online communities or via locally based community networks www.indianfoline.com. Numerous journals, Web sites, professionals, organizations, and events have been addressing such pressing issues. A growing list of notable community networking initiatives for capacity building, information sharing, and online marketing has emerged.[4] Since April 1997 the Rockefeller Foundation, through its Communications Office in New York, has been promoting a series of meetings among communication specialists to reflect on communication for social change at the hinge of the millennium. They contributed to the creation of a position paper that has been widely distributed in print and through various Web sites, in English, Spanish, and French, enabling development experts to realize that much of the ideal communication processes that involve people could be found in a number of grassroots experiences in a variety of forms in many developing countries.

Rural Support programs for connectivity are essentially designed with a view to provide an enabling environment and capacity building for sustainable growth and development. ICTs are setting the stage for such interventions. In 1997, the World Bank initiated the World Links program (www.worldbank.org/world links) in response to developing countries' demand for strategies to prepare the youth for coping with the global trend. Its principal capacity-building objective is to provide developing countries with sustainable solutions to problems mobilizing the necessary technologies, skills, and educational resources to prepare students and teachers to enter the Networked World. Over the last 7 years, World Links has worked with several countries to bring underprivileged schools into a global school network.

---

[4]For most comprehensive listing of projects in the Indian context see Web pages of the India Digital Divide project of the World Economic Forum's *Global Digital Divide Initiative*, which was launched at the January 2000 meeting in Davos, Switzerland? India digital divide initiative hosts a public Web sites to "raise awareness on the digital divide in India and to collect and showcase projects and activities that have been carried out in India that help bridge the digital divide between India and the rest of the world (see betty.hansom@uconnvm.uconn.edu). For description of initiatives and evaluation of the ICT projects see the printed edition of the Global Information Technology Readiness Report 2001–2002 as well as other companion publications of Oxford University Press. http://www.oup-usa.org/reports/[see also the listing of the association of progressive communication http://www.iicd.org,http://www.apc.org,, and the UNDP's Human Development Report 2001 http://www.undp.org/hdr2001]. India's National Association of Software and Service Companies (www.nasscom.org), Inomy.Com (www.inomy.com) and many of their Web sites host important statistics and information on India's Internet economy. BytesForAll.Org (www.bytesforall.org) is a voluntary online community that shares information with other Web-oriented advocates across south Asia. The NGO Voices serves as a research and capacity-building resource for community radio, and is beginning to experiment with the interface between Internet and radio. Mahiti.Org (www.mahiti.org), a branch of the NGO Samuha provides IT services for NGOs in Bangalore.

Over the last few years, a growing list of notable community-networking initiatives for capacity building, information sharing, and online marketing has emerged in the developing countries. These include: FarmNet (for agricultural workers in Uganda), Nabweru and Buwama telecentres (for economic empowerment of women in Uganda), Rural Multipurpose Community Telecentres (libraries and online centres in Benin, Mali, Mozambique, Tanzania, and Uganda), MahilaWeb (for information sharing about women and gender in Nepal), Pakissan (for farmers in Pakistan), PeopLink (artisans portal for 22 developing countries), Tortas (e-commerce portal for homemade cakes made by Peruvian women), Bankilare (a community network in Niger), Across Borders (connecting Palestinians in refuge camps), MarketWatch (price information service in Mongolia), Nairobits (Web services centre for slum children in Kenya), Street Children Telecentre (for IT skills in Ecuador), Mountain Forum (for knowledge sharing on mountainous region communities in over 100 countries on topics like renewable energy, agro-industry, potato research Virtual Souk for underprivileged artisans in the Middle East and North Africa), Multipurpose Community Telecentres (in four farming and fishing villages of northern Mindanano in the Philippines), GrameenPhone (in Bangladesh), HealthInfo (for IT among health workers in Ethiopia), Village Leap (for selling scarves made by Cambodian women), Metrocomia (outsourced Web services centres in about a dozen countries in Africa, Latin America, and Asia), the Communications Boat Project (to bring IT tools via boats to Amazonian communities), and some others.

Examples in India include TaraHaat (for e-marketing in rural areas), AkashGanga (for dairy cooperatives in Gujarat), Warna Wired Village Project (for sugarcane farmers in Maharashtra), HoneyBee Network (documenting grassroots innovations for knowledge on sustainable natural resource management), and Gyandoot (community centre network in rural Madhya Pradesh). The National Informatics Centre is proposing a "Rural Studio" initiative for developing reusable software components and services for the rural development sector, and IndianVolunteers.org networks volunteers interested in such initiatives.[5]

Various uses and applications of ICTs in rural areas of developing countries include aspects, such as finding markets for farm produce, fisheries catches and handicrafts, negotiating prices, arranging transport and delivery of inputs, obtaining information on market prices, consumption trends and inventory, financial transactions, rural ecotourism, expanding educational opportunities, promoting telemedicine, supporting self-help group for global market, serving as a research tool participatory bottom-up approaches to development, and so on.

[5]Online trade and commerce in small towns and rural areas in India have grown five times in the last year (see *Times of India*, Rural India joins the Online Trading, February, 11, 2006).

9.3 ICT for Rural Development in India: Governmental and NGO Initiatives

Since Independence, the scientists, intellectuals, demonstrators, educators, designers, and interpreters, and many other types of expert bodies (both from governmental and nongovernmental organizations) have been using science and technology as instruments for rural development and for political discourse to encourage the individual initiatives for the acquisition and dissemination of knowledge.[6] The Government of India (GOI), through the successive 5-year plans, had set up scientific organizations and introduced many rural development programs of varied nature, some of which were exclusively meant for poverty alleviation. But technology as a solution to the problems in rural India and experiences of the past technological projects failed in many ways because of the inadequacies on the part of the planners to capture the state of underlying structural relationships that impeded in the process of development. The illiteracy, localism, and language acted as barriers to transfer the technology to the rural areas. Many of the experiments remained within the four walls of the laboratories. With institutional measures for critical appraisal and scientific development and decentralization of administration, while some progress was made in the rural development initiatives during 1970s and 1980s, due to concentration of resources (material, social, and economic) in the particular regions, inequalities increased between different groups and between the developed and underdeveloped regions.

Strategically, Government of India's (GOI) initiative for electronic governance in 1980s was a critical move in the state and centrally sponsored poverty eradication programs by connecting officials, nonofficials, and the poor rural people. Like other developing countries, India also has gone through the process of political and economic liberalization and economic growth under the advice of multilateral lending agencies, as part of structural adjustment policies, in the last 2 decades. Having completed the first phase of the economic reform, India, is moving on to the next phase of reform in the field of governance. To overcome some of the problems of implementation of reform process that was initiated in the early era of global integration, India took few initiatives after 2000. A Core Group on Administrative Reforms (CGAR) was constituted in 2003 under the Cabinet Secretary to monitor the administrative reform and for follow-up actions of the recommendations made by the Commission on Review of Administrative Laws (which was set up in 1998). Government of India's Department of Administrative Reforms (DAR) initiated a "Minimum Agenda for e-Governance" for the use of information technology, documented, and disseminated the best practices in the areas of e-governance (Singh, 2005, pp. 54–56).

Efforts were made to develop supportive info-infrastructural facilities such as telecom and IT for making the e-governance more operational for implementation of antipoverty programs and to enhance the potential for grassroots innovations.

[6]This was made clear by the science policy resolution in 1958 and in *The Proceedings of the Third National Conference of Scientists, Technologists and Educationists*, which was held in 1970.

Recognizing the complementarities of different services and the potential use of electronic media (Bhatnagar, 2000, p. 4) the planners have tended to reorganize associated departments and programs in to some particular units for better coordination. For instance, many of the Rural Development programs are now subsumed under IRDP (Integrated Rural Development Program) during the ninth 5-year plan. Furthermore, Planners are increasingly more aware of the information asymmetries amongst bargainers that lead to costly delays and stalemates in modern economic setup.

Slowly but steadily Indian villages are getting wired up. An ambitious IT Action Plan with 108 specific recommendations was submitted to Parliament and approved in July 19, 1998. Three general objectives were specified: to build a world class infrastructure; to increase software and IT services exports to $50 billion by 2008; and to make IT available to all Indian citizens by 2008. One of the important recommendations of the first IT plan was to expand access to IT services, especially to rural areas. Some important steps were proposed to boost IT for agricultural and integrated rural development. A *Wired Villages* pilot project was launched in the state of Maharashtra, and efforts are being made to replicate it. Public Teleinfo Centers (PTIC) were proposed with multimedia capability and access to the Internet, to government and community information systems, and to market information. Finally, a major promotional campaign has been on the agenda to encourage computer applications and Web content in Indian languages. The government is playing a "catalytic and enabling role" to "take IT to the masses" and to recommend new development programs (see www.asia.internet.com;www.mit.gov.in).

While initial domestic stimulus for ICT and ICT service industries has mostly come from government and public sector expenditure (see Roy, 2005, p. 148), the potential use of computers in rural development administration in India, however, came through applied research of some academics during 1979–1980 and since then a general awareness of computers was being created through various efforts made by the governmental and nongovernmental agencies. The National Informatics Centre (NIC) – a central government department was set up to implement a national program called District Information System of National Informatics Center (DISNIC) to computerize all district offices for which free hardware and software were offered to the states (Report of the Working Group on District Planning, 1984). NIC developed uniform software called Public Grievance Redress and Monitoring System (PGRAMS) as an effort towards capacity building for good governance (Singh, 2005, p. 56). In a separate program at the national level in India called "Computerized Rural Information Systems Project" (CRISP), the Rural Development Ministry in India and NIC collaborated to develop software for planning and monitoring of IRDP sometimes in late 1980s. The technological convergence of information technology, telecommunication, and entertainment electronics opened up new vistas in the life of the common man, reducing the rural–urban differences to a minimum. The national Information Infrastructure (NIC) evolved as a network of networks including nationwide computer networks known as NICNET under the planning commission. Investment required for the growth of ICTs has been a feature of every central and centrally sponsored and state plan projects (Bhatnagar, 2000, p. 5). The department of education, under the ministry of human resource development, has set up an Educational Multimedia Center at the National Council of Educational Research and Training (NCERT) to catalyze IT usage across all segments of the schools.

Backed up by political leadership, increasingly, governments in the developing world seek to tie e-government with their overall economic and social developmental objectives to reduce corruption, to increase transparency and quality of service. The new Indian government, elected in 2004, led by the Congress and its allies, has focused on the Common Minimum Programme (CMP) in which the emphasis is on the needs of the poor (Roy, 2005). The Indian telecom network is emerging to be the core area in which the new Indian government has increased the share of foreign investment in the telecom sector. The new government's IT Ministry has a plan to set up statewide information kiosk network connecting 6 lakh villages in India in the next 3 years. The government has acknowledged the importance of vernacular content in increasing the use of the Internet. The department of IT is already working with C-DAC to launch the Indian translation browser that would translate Web pages into vernacular languages.

Although the Federal Government has played an important catalytic and enabling role, most of the specific projects designed to spread IT to rural India have been organized by state governments, nongovernmental organizations, corporate sponsors or, quite often, some combination of these sources. Eighteen state governments have followed the initiative of the federal government in announcing IT policies. These vary greatly in orientation, priorities, and level of activity. A few examples illustrate the orientation in ICT applications initiated by governmental and nongovernmental organization.

9.3.1 E-Governance and Rural Development: Some Micro-level Experiences

The idea of connecting rural India to the world has increasingly drawn attention of the digital pioneers, scholars, journalists, nongovernmental organizations, and the corporate sector. Several initiatives, both governmental and nongovernmental, have already been taken, although many of such initiatives are in the form of pilot projects testing newer approaches. India is gradually becoming a laboratory for small experiments to link isolated rural pockets to the borderless world of knowledge.

In the e-governance initiative, Andhra Pradesh has been foremost in developing citizen-oriented services. The "networked mandals" (rural districts) of Andhra Pradesh are already promoting the IT mindset amongst eager villagers. India now has its own agriculture and rural marketing portals and sites that are offering information aimed primarily at the farmer. Web sites like www.ikisan.com offer information both in English and Telugu languages. Similarly, www.tarahat.com proposes to open up a new village market via the Internet. Another instance of the new project is the central government's initiative to start a process of allotting a Corporate Identity Number (CIN) to identify each community registered in the country. Computer-aided Administration of Registration Department (CARD), by the Andhra Pradesh Government, is another example of such initiative (www.andhra-pradesh.com). The Andhra Pradesh Government's Twin Cities Network Services (TWINS) project, which was launched in December 1999, is also an experiment for providing single-window services to the rural areas. This model is expected to provide effective government services to the citizens. Bhoomi – Computerization of land records, initiated by the government of Karnataka, India, is a striking example where land titles are delivered online to millions of farmers in just no time bringing out a change of the earlier practice where bribes had to be paid and which took weeks to obtain a land title. E-government has now a direct impact on reducing a number of intermediaries that citizens need to interact with in order to get government service.

RajNidhi Information Kiosk was set up on March 23, 2000, when President Clinton visited a remote village of Rajasthan to observe the functioning of a gram panchayat. The RajNidhi project is part of the state government's vision of e-governance aimed at using the information technology to replace the traditional form of government and to overcome the deficiencies of the present system by introducing more open, transparent, and responsive service delivery system. The help centre of RajNidhi provides information, such as the process of obtaining electricity and water connections, their current rates, and the places where bills for these services can be deposited. This also provides different forms and procedures for obtaining various certificates such as caste certificate and the certificate for the place of residence. Moreover, information regarding ration cards, adding of names to the electoral list, and the other services can also be obtained from RajNidhi. Through its user-friendly interface RajNidhi enables the citizens to communicate their suggestions and complaints directly to the chief minister and other senior officers of the state (www.rajgovt.org).

The Taluk Automation Software (TAS) in Tiruvarur district of Tamil Nadu has transformed the Revenue Department by introducing Internet facilities to the villagers. They have used mostly local people to carry out their jobs. Local people's efforts have it possible to conduct annual settlement of village accounts (Jamabanthi) online. This has facilitated the village administration very much. The district has set up a data warehouse of land records at the Collectorate from where the general public can access the records, including orders passed by the various talukas. In addition to this there is *Anbupani*, e-governance software for automating Old Age Pension (OAP), Widow Pension, Physically Handicapped Pension, and related schemes in all Taluk offices.

A quiet revolution is taking place in Dhar district of Madhya Pradesh (M.P.), where the Gyandoot program has been successful. It is a community owned, self-sustainable, and low-cost rural Internet model. This has attracted worldwide attention. Its 31 village centers have been wired through an Internet network. Local rural youth act as entrepreneurs for running cyber cafés-cum-cyber offices on commercial lines without salary or stipend. The computers of this network have been installed in gram panchayat buildings. They have been called "Soochanalayas" (information kiosks). The "Soochanalayas" provide user-charge-based services to the rural people. The operators of these information kiosks are local people with minimum educational skill. The entire expenditure of the Gyandoot network has been borne by panchayats and the community with no expenditure burden on the government. Backed by necessary ICT infrastructure and the political will the M.P. government has decided to transfer nearly all the powers previously exercised by gram panchayats to gram sabhas or periodic meetings. It has thus gone from representative democracy at the grassroots to direct democracy. Such a change in the attitude of the government has yielded better results (see Manor James, Madhya Pradesh experiments with direct democracy, *Economic and Political Weekly*, March 3, 2001).

Warana Wired Village Project is another instance of the successful application of ICTs in some 70 villages of Kohlapur district of Maharashtra. The project has been jointly implemented by the government of India the National Informatics Center (NIC), the government of Maharashtra, and Warana Co-operative Society. The project was initiated to serve the information needs of the farmers for different crop cultivation practices of major crops, sugarcane cultivation practices, pest and disease control, marketing information, dairy and sugarcane processing information, etc., right up to the village level. The NIC was involved in setting up the hardware and software and establishing the connectivity through Wide Area Network (WAN) links such as VAT and dial-up connections. Besides this information retrieval, there are two client-based applications to serve the farmers' needs: the Dairy Information System and the Sugarcane Information System.

9.3.2 Services and E-Commerce Support

The *Sustainable Access in Rural India* project (SARI), a collaborative and interactive research initiative seeks to show that viable markets exist for information and communication services in rural poor areas by inventing and deploying innovative technologies, assessments, and business models. The ultimate goal is to link these activities to sustainable human development objectives. SARI's founding partners include the e-development group at the MIT Media Lab, the TeNeT Group at IIT-Madras, and the I-Gyan Foundation. The key research areas include: (1) technology, applications, and content; (2) assessing social and economic impacts; and (3) business models for financially viable and self-sustaining access, through the development and introduction of appropriate and enabling technologies and applications to foster economic development and for improving health and learning in the rural areas in a financially sustainable way, even as it reaches into the poorest and most disadvantaged communities (see http://cyber.law.harvard.edu/itg/projects/current_projects.html).

The Centre for Knowledge Societies, Bangalore (www.cks-b.org) has collected socioeconomic data on many of the projects undertaken by the center. It is basically considered as people's project as local people's needs, contexts are taken care of for meaning intervention through ICTs (Arunachalam, 2004). It is an important Pan Asia's collaboration with the M.S. Swaminathan Research Foundation, which began in 1997. It aimed to assess and document the impact of ICTs in fostering sustainable agricultural and rural development and bridging the gap between the "haves" and the "have-nots." In the second and third phase of this collaborative effort between 2001 and 2004, with additional funding from CIDA (Canadian International Development Agency), the MSSSRC foundation has established additional village knowledge centers (VKCs), deployed ICTs more widely throughout the region, enhanced connectivity in rural Pondicherry, and assessed the potential sustainability of the projects for poverty alleviation and for improvements in the education and health sector. The social and economic impacts of ICTs are assessed systematically through surveys, interviews, and participatory rural appraisal techniques to determine their effectiveness in poverty alleviation in rural Pondicherry. Some of the ICT-based programs being implemented in the villages include the development of an ICT-enabled integrated health system, computer-assisted learning centers for rural children, a multimedia indigenous knowledge directory for Pondicherry, Web-based information on food security, and a training course in knowledge management for local women, and so on. The MSSRF is also experimenting with the use of open source software. The experience of this research project is now being integrated into the National Virtual Academy for Food Security and Rural Prosperity, a new initiative of the MSSRF for ending hunger and eradicating rural poverty in India.

The Honeybee Network and multimedia database, supported by Society for Research and Initiatives for Sustainable Technologies and Institutions (SRISTI) and IIMA, started in 1990. This Honeybee project demonstrated how database developed by this agency could influence public policy. The project started with the basic objective to help people value their own local indigenous knowledge regarding any products and to connect people to people as bees connect to other bees while pollinating (see Gupta et al., 2000, pp. 84–97). The project helped empowering the local communities and innovators enabling them to share their knowledge with others across large spatial distances, languages, and cultures without being literate. It is observed that exposure to the Honeybee-database helped innovators to overcome inertia and generated a desire amongst the poor people to experiment particularly relating to traditional knowledge regarding pest control and veterinary science. Involving through research in farmer's field and laboratories, and by extending financial and technological supports, the Honeybee-database, supported by SRISTI and IIMA, have demonstrated that "by building upon the knowledge of poor people we can enrich not only the local repertoire of ideas but also trigger initiatives, some of which may transform into innovations" (Gupta et al., p. 97).

SPOTS is an e-commerce support system that brings together spot market employers and employees by utilizing an agent-based matching and negotiation mechanism. n-Logue Communications (www.n-logue.com), incubated out of the TeNet group, is providing connectivity for a series of new projects across India, including those in Madurai and Nellikuppam in Tamil Nadu, and Sikar, Rajasthan. The company works on a commercial basis in partnership with various local partners, including entrepreneurs and nongovernmental organizations.

Tarahaat.com (www.tarahaat.com), promoted by Delhi-based Development Alternatives, is an extremely ambitious commercial project to provide online services to a large number of rural communities in North India. One of the more innovative aspects of this project is its highly interactive and graphics-intensive interface system, which allows semiliterate and neo-literate users enhanced access to products and services. The organization had initiated information centers in several locations in Bundelkhand, Madhya Pradesh, and Bhatinda, Punjab, of which the latter are still functioning. While the project will provide a menu of services that is similar, in many ways, to other rural ICT projects, its current business model requires an astonishing influx of capital before it becomes self-sufficient.

The movement of cooperatives from Co-ops to e-Cops is now making cooperatives much stronger by bringing members together and closer to the customers. Amul is one of the largest milk cooperative movement in India with its 10,000 village cooperatives throughout Gujarat. Today, Amul operates India's first national cyber store in some 120 cities, and an "Amul Cyber store Gifting Service" capable of serving consumers in more than 220 cities of India. India's "National Dairy Development Board" has taken initiative for effective use of the computers for helping the cooperative unions connecting the villagers who sell milk to the union office. Special efforts have been taken to sideline the middlemen.

The Asian Centre for Entrepreneurial Initiatives (AsCent; www.toeholdindia.com) has made an early attempt to introduce CAD/CAM technologies to artisans in north Karnataka, alongside online advertising and sales. Keltron, a public sector undertaking of Kerala, India, is taking up a project to support the dying community of artisans and traditional handicrafts using ICTs. Keltron is planning to set up a major portal for supporting artisans working in traditional crafts and handicarafts in Kerala as a support to marketing their products. Kerala has a very rich traditional art form, and handicrafts made of various material including sandalwood, bamboo, timber, rubber wood, handloom, coir, coconut shells, mud, brass metal, etc. However, these artisans are facing extinction today for want of demand in the domestic market. Unless supported, these artisans would switch to other professions and along with them these traditional art forms will die as these have been inherited from one generation to another.

Another successful e-Commerce initiative keeping in view the need of rural poor is ITC's e-Choupal – literally the "electronic village meeting place" is an example of doing business with poor villagers in Madhya Pradesh. It is an attempt to source soybeans from widely scattered and subsistence farmers who traditionally depended on the *mandi*, a place where the farmers brought their produce to be auctioned. In the traditional system, due to asymmetry in the access to information and choice between the farmers, the traders and processors of soybeans, farmers were always in difficulties in enforcing the contract. ITC, through e-Choupal initiative was successful in eliminating many of these constraints by providing access to information the farmers can independently obtain. Similar initiatives are being taken elsewhere, covering other products and services – such as wheat sourcing in UP and IT-enabled services, namely, telemedicine, ecotourism, traditional medicine, and traditional crafts sourcing goods and services from the rural areas (for details of e-Choupal initiative and profitable rural transformation.

Info-infrastructure has enabled the farmers to reduce their transaction cost, making it possible for them to save more than what they could do in the traditional system. The model is centered on a network of e-Choupals in the villages, which are information centers armed with a computer connected to the Internet. A local farmer called the *Sanchalak* (coordinator) runs the e-Choupal with the help of a Samyojak (collaborator).

9.4 Evaluation

The info-infrastructure in India and the strategic coordinated use of ICT in rural areas has brought about significant changes in the rural developmental practices. ICT-supported services aimed at meeting the requirements of information relating to three broad areas of rural development programs, namely, decision support to government and nongovernmental organizations, improving services for the citizens, and empowering citizens through the access of information and knowledge. The various types of applications have focused on automating the process of delivering services to citizens to bring about transparency in the system.

Some of the micro-level projects, that we have described, have successfully used ICTs and the lessons learnt from these experiences are very promising. We observed an appearance of a new paradigm of governance based on intergovernmental networks exchanging information and knowledge at the global scale and operating in the digital economy. This shift from government to e-governance for rural development depicts a mode of developmental administration in which power to determine public affairs cannot be exclusively assigned to a single organization, such as centralized governmental agency. In fact, the success of local development would depend on the determined and combined efforts of policymakers in partnership with local actors and nongovernmental organizations (i.e., private industry, academia, research institutes, community groups, civic and voluntary organizations) as stakeholders in valued engagements.

The official guidelines of the IT policies stipulated the action plan with greater attention on participation and transparency involving intermediaries both from governmental and nongovernmental organizations. As valuable partners, governmental and nongovernmental agencies are involved in innovations and indigenous economic development. However, all this would require an organizational culture to design and solve problems based on grassroots level experiences and life events, and must be adapted and integrated with the local needs.

Major problems in the rural areas are linked to the gaps in knowledge and imperfections in information.[7] The inadequate communication channels between poor and intermediaries (both official and nonofficial agencies) adversely affected the

---

[7]For details on these aspects, see for instance, Chakravarty, 1994, p. 32; Koushik, 2004, pp. 102–120; Subuddhi, 2002, pp. 3914–3915, 3918–3919; Maheshawari, 1985, pp. 115, 164; Graves & Reddy, 2000).

democratic process and constrained the process of forming coalitions between poor and development agencies. In a number of studies it is revealed that ICT reinforce inequalities rather than bridging the gaps that exist between men and women, rich and poor regions in accessing the ICT facilities (see Heeks, 1999). IT-mediated processes involve issues of power, class, gender, race, culture, economy, and ideology. According to some recent estimates prepared by the Centre for Knowledge Societies, it is revealed that ICT-access is likely to increase socioeconomic opportunities for dominant caste landholding elites, as the services are precisely calibrated with the cultural assumptions and economic needs of the land-owning dominant caste.

Poor (non-elites) rural communities lack certain kinds of social networks and access to social, intellectual, or financial capital, and therefore find it more difficult to take advantage of rural ICT networks. Indirect social discrimination is more difficult to address, as the elite and urbane personalities who often design rural ICT projects are likely to encounter and work with rural elites when they visit the field. Incompatible cultures and resource constraints make a huge difference in finding common ground in communication, a problem that has been discussed extensively by scholars writing about participatory action research (Gersch, 1998).

So, therefore, the challenge is to create conditions for reversing the polarities. Driven on by the hype from ICT vendors and the media that makes ICTs an icon for modern development, technological enthusiasts are pushing ICTs vigorously under the guise that technology per se is development.[8] In fact, there is a need to separate the technology from the information it produces. It is necessary to examine people's capabilities to receive, process, use, and transmit information. Some prior knowledge and certain amount of trust between receiver and source is necessary to locate and evaluate the importance, utility, and relevance of the information received (Heeks, 1999). As the poor are constrained structurally by different social and geographical conditions, there is a need to develop supportive programs and the redistributive policies more effectively responding to the needs of the different communities.

Development agencies have to overcome many hurdles to the use of Information Technology in rural areas. The vast majority of Web sites are in English, a language that more than 95% of Indians do not speak. Moreover, there are problems related to inappropriate software, expensive hardware, and weak infrastructure. In each of these fields, while the landscape is slowly changing, underprivileged groups, such as dalits, adivasis, artisans will be relatively disabled from taking advantage of the opportunities offered by rural connectivity.

[8] In several instances, advocates of ICT applications for rural development tended to underplay the larger social/political/economic resource inequality issues in the process of marketing the ICTs as the new weapons in the war against underdevelopment (see Heeks, 1999, p. 18; Panos, 1998a).

Achieving the better future will require a new development model, one that goes beyond the conventional focus on free-market capitalism, entrepreneurship, and global trade expansion – although such factors will play important roles. Nor will traditional, top-down development directed by governments and financed by foreign aid be adequate. Instead, what may be desirable is a bottom-up model that makes credit, communications, information, energy sources, and other self-help tools directly available to communities and individuals in poor regions, empowering them to take charge of their own development.

There is a clear consensus among development professionals that training and capacity building are key components for the success of e-governance. India's Dhan Foundation, have developed programs to assist their self-help groups in applying for loans from banks and government programs (http://www.dhan.org). Mechanisms and legal provisions for billing, settling accounts, issuing credit/smart cards, and transferring funds determine the appropriateness, cost, and quality of certain services (e.g., e-commerce, national, and international remittances). This business backdrop is a combination of government policy, the legal and regulatory environment, and practices within financial institutions, and therefore depends on diverse stakeholders to ensure its effectiveness.

Education and health are critical application areas if the Internet is to directly address core development objectives in rural areas, and they also can help with economic self-sustainability through powerful public–private collaborations. The World Links project (http://www.world-links.org/), for instance, has been developing an after-school community telecenter program in Uganda. Under this program, schools in rural Uganda that are equipped with computer labs and VSAT-based Internet connections are opening up their labs to outside clients in the afternoons and evenings on a cost-recovery basis. Funds are then used to cross-subsidize daytime educational use. In capacity-building initiative in rural India, Pratham (www.pratham.org), Akshara, and the e-Learning Center together represent the most important attempt to create IT-enabled learning software for underprivileged children. They have developed educational games, which are now being tested in several rural areas through the Centre for Knowledge Societies, Bangalore. For instance, eGurucool (www.egurucool.com) and Zee Interactive Learning Systems (www.zils.com) represent commercial attempts to provide online educational resources coupled with products ranging from in-class instruction to interactive CD-ROMs, to cable TV programs. These products are predominantly in English, although efforts are being made for regional language translations. The Centre for the Development of Advanced Computing (C-DAC; www.cdacindia.com) has been working on Indian language fonts and software for over a decade. Most state-sponsored IT initiatives, as well as many rural ICT projects, now use their fontographic standards, if not their text-processing software. In another significant development, a machine language translation project based in Hyderabad called Anusaraka www.iiit.net/anu/anu_home.html) promises to allow Indian language users translation between various Indian languages, as well as access to English language resources on the Web.

9.5 Conclusion

From the above analysis, we conclude that ICTs are necessary but not sufficient condition for development, unless they are integrated with the national, local, and international bodies. Indeed, ICTs currently have a far greater enabling value in building capacity within intermediary institutions than in directly affecting the poor. These intermediary organizations in turn have championed the causes of greater democracy, social equality, bridging the gaps between what the poor have and what they would need in order to use ICTs.

References

Arunachalam, S. (2004). Information and communication technologies and poverty alleviation. *Current Science*, 87(7), 1–12.

Bardhan, P. (2001). *Social justice in the global economy. Economic and Political Weekly*, February, 3–10, pp. 475–480. Bedi, K. et al. New Delhi: Sage(2001). *Government@net.*

Bhatnagar, S. (2000). *Information Technology and Development Foundation and Key Issues*. In S. Bhatnagar & R. Scheware (Eds.), *Information and Communication Technology in Rural Development: Case Studies from India* (pp. 1–12). Washington, DC: World Bank Institute.

Brown, M. M. (2001). Can ICTs address the needs of the poor? *Choices*, 10, 4. Retrieved October 2005, from http://www.undp.org/dpa/choices/2001/june/index.html.

Castells, M. (1989). *The Informational City: Information Technology, Economic Restructuring and the Urban Regional Process*. Oxford: Oxford University Press.

Chakravarty, S. (1994). *Problems of Plan Implementation*. In T. Byres (Ed.), *The State and Development Planning in India* (pp. 132–1450). Oxford: Oxford University Press.

Gersch, B. (1998). Gender at the crossroads: The Internet as cultural text. *Journal of Communication Inquiry*, 22(3), 306–321.

Graves, M., & Reddy, N. K. (2000). *Electronic Support for Rural Health-Care Workers*. In S. Bhatnagar & R. Scheware (Eds.), Information and Communication Technology in Rural Development: Case Studies from India (pp. 14–24). Washington, DC: World Bank Institute.

Gupta, A., Brij, K., & Patel, K. (2000). *Networking Knowledge-Rich, Economically Poor People*. In S. Bhatnagar & R. Scheware (Eds.), Information and Communication Technology in Rural Development: Case Studies from India (pp. 84–97). Washington, DC: World Bank Institute.

Heeks, R. (1999). *Information and Communication Technologies, Poverty and Development*. Development Informatics. Working Paper Series, No. 5. London: UK Institute of Development Policy and Management.

Held, D. (1987). *Models of Democracy*. Oxford: Polity Press.

Hensman, R. (2001). Globalization and Informalisation. Economic and Political Weekly, March, 31, 1074.

Hoggett, P. (1990). *Modernization, Political Strategy and Welfare State: An Organizational Perspective. Studies in decentralization and Quasi Markets 2*. Bristol: SAUS/University of Bristol.

Koushik, P. D. (2004). *An Agenda: Electronic Governance for the Poor*. In K. Keniston & D. Kumar (Eds.), Experience in India: Bridging the Digital Divide (pp. 98–126). New Delhi: Sage.

Maheshawari, S. (1985). *Rural Development in India: A Public Policy Approach*. New Delhi: Sage.

Melkote, S., & Steeves, L. (2001). *Communication for Development in the Third World: Theory and Practice for Empowerment*. New Delhi: Sage.

Panos, M. (1998a). The Internet and Poverty: Real Help or Real Hype? Retrieved October 2005, from http/://www.oneworld.org/panos/briefing/interpoy.htm.
Pollitt, C. (1990). *Managerialism and the Public Services*. Oxford: Blackwell.
Rawls, J. (1971). *Theory of Justice*. Cambridge, MA: Harvard University Press.
Report of the Working Group on District Planning (1984). Volume 2. New Delhi: Planning Commission.
Roy, S. (2005). *Globalisation, ICT and Developing Nations: Challenges in the Information Age*. New Delhi: Sage.
Sen, A. (1985). *Commodities and Capabilities*. Amsterdam: North-Holland.
Singh, A. (2005). *Administrative Reforms Towards Sustainable Practice*. New Delhi: Sage.
Subuddhi, K. (2002). Science and Technology for Rural Development. Economic and Political Weekly, September 21, 3914–3920.
The Proceedings of the Third National Conference of Scientists, Technologists and Educationists (1970). *The Committee on Science and Technology*. New Delhi: Government of India.
Times of India, February 11, 2006. 'Rural India Joins online trading party'.

Chapter 10
Context Is Everything: An International Perspective of, and Its Challenges to, Research and the Evaluation of Educational Technology

Ellen B. Mandinach

10.1 Situating Educational Technology Policy: The Need for a Paradigmatic Shift and ICT Skills

The emergence of information communication technology (ICT) has forced researchers, policymakers, and educators to rethink the intersection of ICT and education to help create an informed citizenry within the global community (International ICT Literacy Panel, 2002). Correspondingly, advances in ICT have created a need for new links to cultural and social reform and how such changes can be studied internationally (Crossley, 2001). ICT also have spurred countries to review and ultimately change how teaching and learning activities occur across all levels of educational systems. From the introduction of more learner-centered approaches in pre-college environments to distance learning at the college level, ICT has opened many possibilities for examination in the comparative education community (Watson, 2001b).

This chapter reviews the international technology literature and describes a methodology based on the principles of systems thinking as a potential way to gain a richer contextual understanding of the complex process of implementing technology in educational settings. Much has been written about educational evaluation methodology, with a growing literature on the evaluation of educational technology (Heinecke & Blasi, 2001). Only within the past few years has attention been paid to the global nature of educational technology (Education Week, 2004; International ICT Literacy Panel, 2002; Kozma, 2003d; Martin et al., 2004; OECD, 2004a, b; Pelgrum & Anderson, 2001; Plomp et al., 2003a). Many publications, papers, and policy pieces examine technology in specific countries (Plomp et al., 2003a), but fail to address issues comparatively, as is the ongoing trend in student achievement through the work of TIMMS (Mullis et al., 2004; Mullis et al., 2003; NCES, 2004) and PISA (OECD, 2000, 2002a, b, 2003, 2004c). Much can be learned from the examination

E.B. Mandinach
The CNA Corporation, Alexandria, VA, USA

J. Zajda and D. Gibbs (eds.), *Comparative Information Technology,*
DOI: 10.1007/978-1-4020-9426-2_10,

of policies, practices, and implementation of technology in specific countries, but a lack of consistent methodologies makes comparisons and trends difficult to discern. Educational technology, and education more generally, are deeply contextualized and systemic in nature, making cross-national comparisons even more challenging.

Thus the argument presented here is that it is necessary to gain a deep understanding of the contexts that influence and the systemic nature of educational technology not just within but across countries as well. Work in this area must recognize the importance of examining the dynamic interrelations among the components that contribute to technology infusion and use and also acknowledge the similarities and differences across sites from which valuable lessons can be learned, rather than making the competitive and evaluative judgments that result in statements about which countries are better or worse, or more or less effective than others. This is not a new thesis as others have written on the need to address context, perhaps most convincingly the framework presented by the Cognitive Technology Group at Vanderbilt (1996). Just as Brown et al. (1989a, b) purport that knowledge is a situated activity that is best understood within specific contexts and cultures, the same argument can be made for the examination of educational technology.

10.2 ICT Paradigm Shift

There is no debate about the emergence of ICT globally and that its infusion in all domains of work, school, and life is stimulating substantial economic, educational, and cultural change. It is also clear that some countries are at the forefront of the ICT curve, whereas others are only beginning, hoping that ICT will promote development, and still others are struggling (Education Week, 2004; International ICT Literacy Panel, 2002; Plomp et al., 2003a). Kozma and McGhee (2003) found that ICT is breaking down some traditional classroom barriers such as the forms of interactions between student and teacher and instruction. They also noted that teachers still are not using innovative technologies. Instead, they are doing innovative things pedagogically using ordinary technology. In order to become part of the global community, countries are examining their educational systems to determine how the infusion of ICT will enhance the ability to provide an education that will enable students to better function in a global society. Developing countries must make difficult decisions about resource allocation. Oftentimes the decision point is whether to invest in an ICT infrastructure that may stimulate economic, educational, and cultural growth, or provide for the basic necessities for their citizenry.

ICT is seen as a way for developing countries to improve their lot. For the industrialized countries, technology is a matter of survival. In order to take advantage of the emerging technologies, businesses must train their employees, and schools must educate their students in the effective use of ICT to function in a global society. The types of skills necessary to function are changing with the demands and affordances of technology (Honey, 2001; International ICT Literacy Panel, 2002; PCAST, 1997). Just as Kozma and McGhee (2003) note the lack of use of innovative techniques, there also are instances of high-end techniques being used for mundane tasks. Of concern here is not just what students learn but how they learn it. There is a question of the appropriate alignment of pedagogical philosophy.

To use technology effectively, it is widely recognized that a pedagogical paradigm shift is occurring toward learner-centered or constructivist learning (Bransford et al., 2000). Kozma (2003a, c) distinguishes between emergent and traditional practices. The shift takes education away from teachers who dispense knowledge to teachers who serve as mentors, guides, advisers, and coaches who facilitate and enable students to construct their own learning. They monitor student practice. It is no longer sufficient to simply acquire facts and declarative knowledge and regurgitate them on tests. What has become increasingly critical is students' ability to take active responsibility for their own learning; applying information; and acquiring problem-solving skills, procedural knowledge, and lifelong learning skills (Anderson, 2003; Lewis, 2009 & Mandinach, in press; World Bank Group, 2003). The use of ICT and a learner-centered perspective creates role changes for students and teachers, and also requires new skill sets (Mandinach & Cline, 1994; Voogt & Pelgrum, 2003). In a learner-directed environment, knowledge acquisition is seen as any time, anywhere, and at any pace, with infinite resources and immediate knowledge. Moving away from the didactic to the interactive, students engage in collaborative, global learning through intellectual exploration. Teachers no longer serve as transmitters of information. They become "guides on the side" rather than "sages on the stage." Students are no longer passive receptors, but active and engaged participants in learning. They search for information using ICT-supported practices. Curricula, too, change. Although content may remain static, new goals are introduced and taught in new ways.

Kozma (2003c, d) and Plomp and colleagues (2003a) survey the pedagogical practices and policies that impact the infusion of ICT into the educational systems across many countries. Kozma's work indicates that there are consistent innovative practices, including the aforementioned role changes. Consistent across countries is the need for convergence between curricula and assessment, with national curricula preventing significant constraints. Further, ICT is seen as embedded in patterned sets of pedagogical practices, thus necessitating new kinds of embedded and authentic, performance-based measures that use ICT to assess outcomes and processes. There is a wide range of infusion not just of technology, but also of the country's ability to adopt the pedagogical shift. For example, Shimizu and colleagues (2003) note that Japan is highly conservative and slow to make the shift. In contrast, Finland has a highly developed technological infrastructure and professional development plan to enable teachers to make the pedagogical shift (Kankaanranta & Linnakylä, 2003). Singapore has introduced a masterplan for their technological infrastructure and for training their teachers to support learner-centered learning (Mui et al., 2003; Singapore Ministry of Education, 2008; Yong, 2005). The pedagogical shift creates the need for substantial changes within educational systems, including how instruction is delivered and how classrooms and schools function (Mandinach & Cline, 1994).

Anderson (2003) outlines implications of global trends for educational policy and practice, noting the emerging directions created by ICT. He traces the global and societal trends, the issues for educational policy, and finally the current and future impact on educational practice. He notes that ICT is causing rapid emergence of, and a collectivization of knowledge and the need for, increased collaborative learning experiences, on-demand learning, and a focus on lifelong learning skills. Anderson also points to, as cross-national findings, the need for attention to the technology infrastructure and teacher and administrator professional development that addresses the pedagogical paradigm shift. As Law and Plomp (2003a) and Quale (2003) note, attention only to the infrastructure is not sufficient to realize the potentials of ICT. Teachers are the essential component to the paradigm shift. They must embrace it to be able to implement it, and also have the appropriate administrative and policy support and resources.

Law and Plomp (2003a) outline a continuum of pedagogical practices: traditional, some new elements, emergent, innovative, and most innovative. Just as there is a paradigm shift for pedagogy, there is a corresponding evolution in the definition of ICT skills and how they are taught in different countries. As Law and Plomp (2003a) note, the Asian countries tend to teach ICT skills separately, whereas Western European countries and the USA tend to integrate skills into existing curricula. They differentiate learning about ICT, learning with ICT, and learning through ICT. And aptly noted, despite counties having explicit statements about the role of ICT in education, without the appropriate infrastructure or trained practitioners, the policies become only pipe dreams rather than reality. For example, in the Philippines, there is an ICT plan in place, but the country lacks the technology infrastructure to bring it to reality (Ogena & Brawner, 2003). Many parts of the country lack electricity so the only exposure students and teachers may get to ICT is via mobile technology laboratories. Many African nations also suffer the same problems with infrastructure, but the severity of problems differs within and across countries (Zehr, 2004). As Dede (2003) notes:

> In order to fully realize technology's capabilities for reinventing teaching, learning, and schooling, policy makers must engage in a complex implementation process that includes sustained, large-scale, simultaneous innovations in curriculum, pedagogy, assessment, professional development, administration, organizational structures, strategies for equity, and partnerships for learning among schools, businesses, homes, and community settings (Dede, 1998). Creating policy frameworks that foster the development of powerful learning technologies, the delineation of conditions for their successful implementation, and the preparation of teachers and schools for effective usage are all crucial for improving students' educational outcomes and educators' ability to innovate in response to the demands of 21st-century civilization. (p. x)

It is quite clear that the introduction and infusion of ICT in education is highly complex and fraught with challenges. Despite well-intentioned policies, there continues to be a pressing need for attention to infrastructure and professional development. Policies and implementation practices must be aligned and take into consideration local, regional, and national variations. Context does matter. Policies, pedagogical practices, standards, curricula, and assessment must also be aligned. One must consider the instructional goals, integration strategies, and how processes and outcomes will be assessed.

10.3 ICT Skills in the Global Culture

Just as the technological infrastructure is a necessary but not a sufficient component to ICT infusion, ICT literacy is more than just the mastery of technical skills. It includes cognitive skills and the applications of cognitive skills and knowledge. ICT literacy is seen as a continuum of skills and abilities from simple, everyday tasks to complex applications. Policymakers and stakeholders worldwide recognize the importance of ICT skills (Plomp et al., 2003a), and hopefully their recognition is not little more than political rhetoric. For example, the former Prime Minister of Cypress, Costas Simitis, has been quoted as saying: "Those who are illiterate in the 21st century are the people who lack computer skills" (Adamides & Nicolaou, 2004).

Many definitions of ICT literacy exist, most of which are variations on a theme. In 2001 and 2002, Educational Testing Service convened an international panel of information technology business and educational experts to identify the skills needed to function in a global society. After days of discussion and debate, the definition agreed upon was:

> ICT literacy is using digital technology, communications tools, and/or networks to access, manage, integrate, evaluate, and create information in order to function in a knowledge society. (International ICT Literacy Panel, 2002, p. 2)

These skills are now seen as life skills, given the emergence of knowledge societies. Identifying particular skills that must be addressed in educational settings, informal settings, or corporate and military training takes a step toward better preparing students, employees, and citizens to function in the information age, while also addressing the need to decrease the digital divide (Lewis & Mandinach, in press). The more technology is infused, the more essential ICT becomes. As the International ICT Literacy Panel notes, however, the digital divide is not limited to the infusion of technology. The divide also includes the inequities in the necessary skills to make use of the affordances of technology. "Technology skills, alone, without corresponding cognitive skills and general literacy, will not decrease the gaps defined by a digital divide" (International ICT Literacy Panel, 2002, p. 6). This is readily apparent in countries such as South Africa where there is a high percentage of adult illiteracy and a fifth of the population has no formal education (Muller, 2003).

The five skills – access, manage, integrate, evaluate, and create – are seen as the foundational skills that form a continuum of cognitive complexity. These skills are essential to ICT proficiency, one of three proficiencies that combine into ICT literacy. Cognitive proficiency is composed of the foundational skills needed to function in everyday life. Technical proficiencies are the basic components of digital literacy. ICT proficiency is seen as the integration and application of cognitive and technical skills. This proficiency is considered to be transformative in that it enables individuals to use the affordances of technology. Individuals can exhibit basic ICT literacy but not have the cognitive capacity to make full and effective use of the technology. Conversely, there are highly intelligent individuals who have no ICT proficiency, thereby not capitalizing on the affordances of the technology. The example that comes to mind is the men of the generation who never learned to type, but are now CEOs of large corporations. By definition, these individuals must be somewhat intelligent, but lack the ability to use technology to transform their work, instead delegating technology-based work to colleagues who have the appropriate skill sets. Thus the transformative power of ICT requires both the cognitive skills and the knowledge of technology.

A second international expert panel was convened to plan a preliminary study that would provide information for a potential PISA ICT literacy assessment. A slightly revised definition of ICT literacy was crafted (Lennon et al., 2003):

> ICT literacy is the interest, attitude, and ability of individuals to appropriately use digital technology and communication tools to access, manage, integrate, and evaluate information, construct new knowledge, and communicate with others in order to participate effectively in society. (p. 8)

The State Educational Technology Directors Association (2002) in the USA modified the original definition to adapt it specifically for educational environments. Their working definition included references to responsible and appropriate uses of technology, learning in subject areas, and the goal to acquire lifelong learning knowledge and twenty-first-century skills.

Many other definitions exist for ICT literacy (Committee on Information Technology Literacy, 1999; Partnership for 21st Century Skills, 2003; Pearson & Young, 2002; Tapscott, 1998), as well as standards (American Association of School Librarians & Association for Educational Communications and Technology, 1998; International Society for Technology in Education, 2002; OECD, 2001), and frameworks for examining ICT skills (Center for Children and Technology, 2002; Honey, 2002). Each definition, set of standards, and framework is slightly different, but there is a great deal of convergence on key themes. All of these documents recognize the centrality of ICT literacy skills. Interestingly, a report by the American Association of School Administrators that describes what skills students will need to function in the twenty-first century fails to address technological literacy (Uchida et al., 1996). Other reports address ICT skills in the workforce (Commission on Technology and Adult Learning, 2001; ITAA, 2000, 2001).

The Partnership for 21st Century Skills (2003) defines not only information and communication skills, but also the thinking and problem-solving skills, and interpersonal and self-directional skills needed to be an effective learner in the twenty-first century. The Partnership distinguishes between information and media literacy skills and communication skills. The former are: "analyzing, accessing, managing, integrating, evaluating, and creating information in a variety of forms and media understanding the role of media" (p. 9). The latter are: "understanding, managing, and creating effective oral, written and multimedia communication in a variety of forms and contexts" (p. 9). It is important to note that the fundamental skills are almost identical to the two previous definitions.

Butler (2000) defines ICT skills within the domain of mathematics in the UK, distinguishing between general skills (e.g., spreadsheet, graph plotting, and scientific calculator) and Internet skills (e.g., video conferencing, World Wide Web). The Swedish Ministry of Education mandates a five-part set of goals for the integration of everyday technology in context: (a) development; (b) technology, nature, and society; (c) what technology does; (d) components and systems; and (e) construction and operation (Mattsson & Svensson, 2004). The Swedish take a broad definition of technology, considering not just hardware and software, but everyday technology in the context in which they are used and integrated into many disciplines. Law and Plomp (2003a) distinguish learning about, with, and through ICT. Learning about ICT refers to ICT as a subject. Learning with ICT refers to the use of applications to enhance teaching and learning activities. Learning through ICT occurs when ICT is completely integrated into the curricula as an essential tool.

In the USA, many states have content standards that include technology. Technology is rarely a stand-alone topic. Instead, ICT is integrated into the standards for mathematics, science, social studies, and languages (see, e.g., Delaware Department of Education, 2002; New Jersey Department of Education, 2002). Work at the EDC Center for Children and Technology (Gersick et al., 2004) explores the skills needed to be considered digitally literate. This work takes a larger view, focusing on tasks that involve multimedia applications. The purpose of the project is to provide teachers with materials to address digital literacy through work on live multimedia presentations. This reflects the appreciation that teachers will be unable to teach with and model appropriate digital, multimedia skills, if they are not trained in their use.

10.4 Recurrent Educational Technology Policy Themes

Plomp and colleagues (2003a) examine educational technology policies across 33 countries. Anderson (2003) summarizes the global and societal trends, issues for educational policy, and educational practice's emerging directions. He lists six policy issues that cross-cut the international landscape: infrastructure development and maintenance; the development of a knowledge-based workforce; equipment renewal; the role of knowledge management in the curriculum; filtering information; and the assessment of collaboration skills.

McMillan Culp et al. (2005) surveyed 20 years of policy documents on education technology in the USA. According to this report, the investment in technology is seen as serving at least three main purposes: (a) as a tool for addressing challenges in teaching and learning; (b) as a change agent; and (c) as an impetus for economic competitiveness. In tracing trends over the past 2 decades, the authors identify several recurrent themes that permeate the many documents and reports that have informed and influenced the conceptualization of educational technology in the USA. These themes are not localized to the USA; they can be generalized or localized to many other countries with perhaps limited contextualization.

The first recommendation is to improve access, connectivity, and infrastructure. As in the countries surveyed in the book by Plomp and colleagues (2003a), there is no question that technological infrastructure is a necessary but not a sufficient condition to the effective use of ICT. Technology is increasingly becoming available in many nations, but many others are severely lacking in infrastructure, thus creating a digital divide. The divide exists not only across countries, but also within, with great disparities between the "haves" and the "have-nots." Infrastructure can range from schools lacking electricity and therefore having to rely on mobile or solar-powered units (Ogena & Brawner, 2003) to complete or almost complete ubiquity.

A second recommendation is to create better software. Over time, the kinds of software or applications developed from integrated learning systems and drill and practice software to a current and increasing emphasis on virtual learning environments. Software often reflects trends in pedagogical philosophy and curriculum standards. It is therefore logical that preferred software or types of applications will mirror the context, philosophy, and constraints of specific countries.

The third theme, and the one that many believe is the most essential requisite, is the provision for quality professional development activities and support for teachers to innovate in their work. Teachers make things happen in the classroom. The better trained they are, the more comfortable they feel with ICT *and* the pedagogical philosophy. The more they recognize an alignment with curriculum goals, the more likely they are to effectively infuse technology into their typical classroom activities. It is essential to note the intimate relationship between the technology and the pedagogy. Giving a constructivist application to a teacher who insists on didactic methods will cause a disconnect and vice versa. Professional development is a central international theme (Kozma, 2003a; Plomp et al., 2003a). All the countries participating in the IEA studies highlight professional development as one of the foundational issues in the infusion of ICT.

Sustained and long-term funding is a fourth recommendation. The infusion of technology and the necessary surrounds are costly. All countries have struggled with how to fund technology and who should pay for it. The common theme identified by McMillan Culp and colleagues (2005) is that funding must be sustained and ideally must come from multiple stakeholders, from collaborations of public and private sectors. Certainly funders will differ across countries based on context, but regardless of the source, money still is necessary.

The fifth theme that parallels the previous one is to define and promote the roles of multiple stakeholders, both public and private. Given the different structures of educational systems around the world, each country has a distinct structure for how local, state, and national governments control education (see Plomp et al., 2003a for a good overview). In the USA, for example, there is a complex mix among the three levels of government, with schools often having to meet sometimes competing accountability measures and standards set by local, state, and federal departments of education. The role of private stakeholders, such as local business and the community, also must be defined.

Increasing and diversifying research, evaluation, and assessment comprise the sixth recommendation. The need for research to determine the impact of ICT on teaching and learning activities has been an enduring theme. The PCAST Panel on Educational Technology (1997) makes the case for a cohesive and diversified program of research. *Teachers' Tools for the 21st Century* (U.S. Department of Education, 2000) describes nine research questions that form a comprehensive program of research. More recently in the USA, there is a mandate to establish that technology in (National Educational Technology Plan, 2004) any educational intervention "works" (What Works Clearinghouse, 2004), and studies such as the National Study of the

Effectiveness of Educational Technology Interventions (Dynarski et al., 2007). Understanding the effectiveness of ICT is important, but the right questions should be asked and appropriate methodologies aligned to the questions. A similar need for appropriate alignment has been noted with respect to assessment as cited above (Dede, 1998; Fensham, 2004; Kozma, 2003d; Sjoberg, 2004). ICT has the potential to transform pedagogy and how teaching and learning activities occur. Consequently, there is a pressing need to develop and use assessment devices that are aligned. Standardized achievement tests are not the best measures of learning in many ICT environments. As Sjoberg (2004) notes, aligned assessments and moving the focus away from international comparative accountability measures such as TIMSS and PISA are necessary steps toward progress.

The final recommendation is the need to review and revise regulations concerning technology. As ICT continues to develop and becomes increasingly virtual, new regulations for security and privacy are needed to protect students, teachers, and users. Copyright, digital plagiarism, and accuracy issues arise and are universal issues.

These seven recommendations are fundamental to the infusion and sustaining of educational technology. There are natural variations across countries, with more or less emphasis on particular themes. The two themes, however, that are most frequently mentioned cross-nationally are the needs for appropriate technological infrastructure and professional development. Without these two components, little progress will be made.

10.5 Finding the Intersection of Educational Technology and Evaluation Among the Disciplines

As mentioned in the introduction to this chapter, there is a need for researchers to focus on the intersection of international/comparative education, evaluation, and educational technology. The IEA policy and practice book (Plomp et al., 2003a) provides an initial step toward a global understanding of the role and emphasis on educational technology across many countries. The SITES-2 module (Kozma, 2003d) is perhaps the best example of the intersection. Its multimethod approach, bringing together qualitative and quantitative data, provides a nonjudgmental but comparative aggregation of cross-national findings from which researchers, practitioners, policy-makers, and other stakeholders can draw implications. The field needs to use the Kozma work as an exemplar that will stimulate future work.

In contrast, in one of the few scholarly articles that should address the intersection of international evaluation and educational technology, Nelson et al. (2003) present a framework that describes the institutionalization of educational technology in terms of technological infrastructure, teacher skills, and curriculum integration. The authors' categorization of the factors that characterize each of the dimensions are overlapping, showing the interrelationships, but also go against common and accepted definitions within the field. Infrastructure generally means the technology per se, not the human capital required to maintain the infrastructure. This is an entirely different set of factors. What is most surprising is that this work appears as a chapter in the *International Handbook of Educational Evaluation* (Kellaghan & Stufflebeam, 2003). Yet, surprisingly, there is only a brief mention of evaluation and citations to a limited number of international studies. Studies such as this make a contribution, but ignore the role of context and the extent to which the findings can be generalized.

One conference (the International Organization for Science and Technology Education, IOSTE) serves as an exemplar for the kinds of discussions that can occur when organizations purposefully provide a forum for an international exchange of ideas (Janiuk & Samonek-Miciuk, 2004). Scholars from all over the world convened to present findings from their own countries, but more importantly, they strived to draw cross-national parallels and implications, focusing on commonalities, while discussing differences caused by contextual factors. It was not about who was doing better. Although this meeting focused more on science than technology, leaders in the field of educational technology and the evaluation of ICT more specifically should create a similar organization and model this forum. Perhaps the closest organization is the European Association for Research on Learning and Instruction (www.earli.org) that has a special interest group for learning and instruction with computers. EARLI promotes just the kind of professional exchange of information that is needed in the educational technology field. There is a pressing need to bring together researchers, evaluators, practitioners, and perhaps also stakeholders and policymakers to focus on the types of ICT typically infused into educational settings worldwide. Only then can fruitful cross-fertilization begin to happen, stimulating an appreciation for methodological issues, the constraints of practice, and the knowledge that everyone can learn from commonalities and differences, without placing judgments on who is doing well or not so well from a comparative perspective. Finally, countries can learn from others, recognizing that indeed context does matter. As Gaskell and colleagues (2004) note, globalization and localization perspectives can be merged into glocalization, thereby creating a rich forum for educational research and evaluation. The time is ripe for the field of international evaluation to adapt a glocalized methodological perspective for the examination of educational technology and ICT.

10.6 Toward Evaluation of Glocalization, Information Technology Development, and Implementation

The notion of glocalization extends to technology development and implementation, ICT policy and infusion, and educational research and evaluation. Each of these components must somehow balance the need to focus on local issues, while also addressing the universality or global nature of technology and context on its impact.

10.6.1 Technology Development

Hardware and software developers must take into consideration the difference in available technology and prospects for future infrastructure within and across countries. This is a major challenge, not only to develop with the present infrastructure in mind, but also with an eye to the future. Developers need more that a crystal ball to predict what will happen globally and locally with respect to technology infrastructure. Take for example the Philippines, as noted above. Ogena and Brawner (2003) note that much of the country lacks even the most basic technological infrastructure to see their technology plan come to fruition. Without electricity, there is little that can be done to power the technology, thus the advent of mobile units. Another example comes to mind from the mid-1980s and television technology. The developers of Sesame Street collaborated with Jordanian Television to create an Arabic version of the program. They wanted the program infused in schools and homes in several Middle Eastern countries and to then study its impact. Although well intended and focused on future development, the creators did not have the necessary infrastructure in place for effective delivery. Many schools and homes did not have electricity and therefore the delivery of the television program was limited (Murphy, 1988).

Such constraints impact the kinds of applications that developers can create for those environments. Another example can be found in India. Many schools have only one phone line, in the Director's office. If the applications intended for use here are web-based and the school does not have a wireless network, all sorts of problems will arise. Students are forced to go to Internet cafés to complete their work. A potentially logical solution could then be stand-alone applications. But that raises other issues such as the need for a technological support phone line and translation challenges. In Russia, the majority of the schools are remote and rural, containing fewer than 50 students across all grade levels and with one or two teachers. Do developers plan for web-based or stand-alone applications in such schools, and how do the demands differ or are similar in the urban schools of Moscow or St. Petersburg? How do the needs of those schools differ or are similar to rural schools of China, Australia, or the USA?

As has been noted above, many countries are focusing educational goals on teaching to tests such as PISA and TIMSS. In the USA, there are pressures to teach on the state and federally mandated tests. The more intense the accountability pressures, the more they are stimulating the development of specific integrated learning systems and drill-and-practice applications that directly relate to standards and accountability measures. The National Educational Technology Plan and study (2004) reflect these foci. Many in the field of educational technology are concerned about this reversal as the trend moves away from promising applications that capitalize on the affordances of the technology.

10.6.2 Technology Infusion and Policy

Just as developers struggle with the balance between the present and the future, educators and researchers also balance the promises and realities of educational technology in real classroom settings. As Lesgold (2000) notes: "The problem we face in inserting new technologies into education is that they partly represent new ways of teaching and partly represent new content that ought to be taught now" (p. 403). Salomon and Almog (1998) extend this point to pedagogical philosophy and change:

> A paradox gradually became evident: The more a technology, and its usages, fits the prevailing educational philosophy and its pedagogical application, the more it is welcome and embraced, but the less of an effect it has. When some technology can be smoothly assimilated into existing educational practices without challenging them, its chances of stimulating a worthwhile change are very small. (p. 224)

This paradox can be seen worldwide and is articulated throughout the chapters in the book by Plomp and colleagues (2003a). Educators at all levels, whether the classroom, the school, the district, the local or state entity, or even nationally, struggle with how best to integrate technology, given the specific needs, objectives, standards, and the local resources and constraints. Many believe that technology's biggest impact is likely to occur with the applications that espouse constructivism and stimulate higher-order thinking and metacognition in contrast to more didactic, drill-and-practice applications. Yet constructivism often is in conflict with the local or national pedagogical philosophy, where direct instruction may be the norm. Or take for example the National Study of Effectiveness of Educational Technology Interventions in the USA as mentioned above. There was a concerted effort to select applications for examination that espouse direct instruction and focus specifically on the acquisition of content knowledge aligned to state accountability measures. Thus, one has to consider how Salomon and Almog's principle will play out in such circumstances, and also the point that Lesgold makes about just how new some of direct instructional applications are. These may in fact be nothing more than a translation of paper-and-pencil activities now delivered through a technological medium. More sophisticated applications may indeed capitalize on the affordances of the technology but be less easily integrated.

Yet the paradox continues in terms of the measurement of impact. The more easily it is integrated, the more likely an application is to be used and the more there is infusion. Thus there may well be enough of the phenomenon needed to measure impact. But the impact may be superficial and not lasting. One has to ask whether it is a "good" implementation of an appropriate application. In contrast, the more difficult the integration due to the sophistication of the application, the deeper is the impact and the more discernible, assuming there is sufficient implementation. This paradox is not easily solved and is certainly part of the ongoing debate in the field of educational technology.

10.6.3 Educational Technology Research and Evaluation

Researchers continue to struggle with the age-old balance between internal and external validity, and the focus on the particular or the ability to generalize findings beyond the specific circumstances. Researchers such as Donald Campbell and Thomas Cook (Cook, 2002; Shadish et al., 2002) have been proponents of strict experimental control to establish internal validity, whereas Lee Cronbach (1982; Cronbach et al., 1972, 1980) espouses the focus on generalizability, attending to issues of context and how they influence one's ability to translate findings to other circumstances. Essentially this may be seen as an early form of glocalization.

It is clear that the conduct of rigorous and relevant educational research is a challenging enterprise, and that the contexts in which teaching and learning occur are nuanced and affected by many controllable and uncontrollable factors. Each situation can be seen as unique, with those factors combining in specific ways. Yet a great deal can be learned drawing invaluable principles from the local or specific and applying them more generally. It is probably the case that some principles must remain completely localized. There are, however, many more similarities than differences within and across countries and therefore principles that can be drawn from the local and made universal.

10.7 Conclusion

It has been argued in this chapter that as globalization takes hold of educational communities around the world, it is becoming increasingly important to understand and appreciate the differences and similarities among countries as they continue to implement technological solutions to their pressing educational and ICT problems. This chapter reviews the international information technology literature and describes a methodology based on the principles of systems thinking as a potential way to gain a richer contextual understanding of the complex process of implementing information technology in educational settings. The challenge, as I see it, in the examination of international educational technology is to apply a glocalized perspective, through which the researchers as well as the policymakers, practitioners, and other stakeholders across the world can learn from one another and advance the field through cooperation rather than competition.

References

Adamides, M. H., & Nicolaou, K. (2004, July). *Is technology "welcomed" in mathematics courses in the 21st century?* Paper presented at the XIth symposium programme of the International Organization for Science and Technology Education. Lublin, Poland.

American Association of School Librarians and Association for Educational Communications and Technology. (1998). *Information literacy standards for student learning*. Washington, DC: American Library Assoication.

American Educational Research Association. (2003). Resolution on the essential elements of scientifically-based research. Retrieved December 1, 2003, from www.aera.net/meeting/council/resolution03.htm

Anderson, R. E. (2003). Introduction. In T. Plomp, R. E. Anderson, N. Law, & A. Quale (Eds.), *Cross-national information and communication technology policy and practices in education* (pp. 3–13). Greenwich, CT: Information Age Publishing.

Arnove, R. F., & Torres, C. A. (Eds.). (2003). Comparative education: The dialectic of the global and the local (2nd ed.). Lanham, MD: Rowman & Littlefield.

Barab, S. (2004, June). Ensuring rigor in the learning sciences: A call to arms. Paper presented at the Sixth International Conference of the Learning Sciences. Santa Monica, CA.

Barab, S., & Squire, K. (2004). Design-based research: Putting a stake in the ground. *Journal of the Learning Sciences*, 13(1), 1–14.

Bennett, D., McMillan Culp, K., Honey, M., Tally, B., & Spielvogel, B. (2001). It all depends: Strategies for designing technologies for change in education. In W. F. Heinecke & L. Blasi (Eds.), *Methods of evaluating educational technology* (pp. 105–124). Greenwich, CT: Information Age Publishing.

Berliner, D. C. (2002). Educational research: The hardest science of all. *Educational Researcher*, 31(8), 18–20.

Berliner, D. C., & Calfee, R. C. (Eds.). (1996). Handbook of educational psychology. New York: Macmillan.

Bhola, H. S. (2003). Introduction: The social and contextual contexts of educational evaluation. In T. Kellaghan & D. L. Stufflebeam (Eds.), *International handbook of educational evaluation: Part one: Perspectives* (pp. 389–396). Dordrecht, The Netherlands: Kluwer.

Bransford, J. D., Brown, A. L., & Cocking, R. R. (Eds.). (2000). *How people learn: Brains, mind, experience, and school*. Washington, DC: National Academy Press.

Brown, A. L. (1992). Design experiments: Theoretical and methodological challenges in creating complex interventions in classroom settings. *The Journal of the Learning Sciences*, 2(2), 141–178.

Brown, A. (1994). The advancement of learning. *Educational Researcher*, 23(8), 4–12.

Brown, A. L., & Campione, J. C. (1994). Guided discovery in a community of learners. In K. McGilly (Ed.), *Classroom lessons: Integrating cognitive theory and classroom practice* (pp. 229–270). Cambridge, MA: MIT Press.

Brown, A. L., & Campione, J. C. (1996). Psychological theory and the design of innovative learning environments: On procedures, principles, and systems. In R. Glaser (Ed.), *Innovations in learning: New environments for education* (pp. 289–325). Mahwah, NJ: Lawrence Erlbaum.

Brown, J. S., Collins, A., & Duguid, P. (1989a). Debating the situation: A rejoinder to Palinscar and Wineburg. *Educational Researcher*, 18(4), 10–12.

Brown, J. S., Collins, A., & Duguid, P. (1989b). Situated cognition and the culture of learning. *Educational Researcher*, 18(1), 32–42.

Butler, D. (2000). Case study 4: The training implications of the ICT resolution in secondary mathematics. In C. Wright (Ed.), *Issues in education & technology* (pp. 115–127). London: Commonwealth Secretariat.

Campbell, D. T., & Fiske, D. W. (1959). Convergent and discriminant validation by the multitrait-multimethod matrix. *Psychological Bulletin*, 56, 81–105.

Center for Children and Technology. (2002). *The evaluation toolkit: A work-in-progress*. New York: Education Development Center, Center for Children and Technology.

Cline, H. F., & Mandinach, E. B. (2000). The corruption of a research design: A case study of a curriculum innovation project. In A. E. Kelly & R. A. Lesh (Eds.), *Handbook of research design in mathematics and science education* (pp. 169–189). Mahwah, NJ: Lawrence Erlbaum.

Coalition for Evidence-Based Policy. (2002). Bringing evidence-driven progress to education: A recommended strategy for the U.S. Department of Education. Retrieved December 11, 2002, from www.excelgov.org

Cognition and Technology Group at Vanderbilt. (1996). Looking at technology in context: A framework for understanding technology and education research. In D. C. Berliner & R. C. Calfee (Eds.), *Handbook of educational psychology* (pp. 807–840). New York: Macmillan.

Cochran-Smith, M., & Lytle, S. (1990). Research on teaching and teacher research: The issues that divide. *Educational Researcher*, 19(2), 2–11.

Cochran-Smith, M., & Lytle, S. (1993). *Inside/outside: Teacher research and knowledge*. New York: Teachers College Press.

Cohen, D. K., & Barnes, C. A. (1999). Research and the purposes of education. In E. Lagemann & L. Shulman (Eds.), *Issues in education research: Problems and possibilities* (pp. 17–41). San Francisco, CA: Jossey-Bass.

Collins, A. (1999). The changing infrastructure of education research. In E. Lageman & L. S. Shulman (Eds.), *Issues in education research: Problems and possibilities* (pp. 289–298). San Francisco, CA: Jossey-Bass.

Collins, A., Joseph, D., & Bielaczyc, K. (2004). Design research: Theoretical and methodological issues. *Journal of the Learning Sciences*, 13(1), 15–42.

Commission on Technology and Adult Learning. (2001). *A vision of e-learning for America's workforce*. Alexandria, VA/Washington, DC: American Society for Training and Development and the National Governors Association.

Committee on Information Technology Literacy. (1999). *Being fluent with information technology*. Washington, DC: National Academy Press.

Cook, T. D. (2002). Randomized experiments in educational policy research: A critical examination of the reasons the educational evaluation community has offered for not doing them. *Educational Evaluation and Policy Analysis*, 24(3), 175–199.

Cook, T. D., & Campbell, D. T. (1979). *Quasi-experimentation: Design and analysis issues for field settings*. Chicago, IL: Rand McNally.

Cronbach, L. J. (1963). Course improvement through evaluation. *Teachers College Record*, 64, 672–683.

Cronbach, L. J. (1971). Test validation. In R. L. Thorndike (Ed.), *Educational measurement* (2nd ed., pp. 443–507). Washington, DC: American Council on Education.

Cronbach, L. J. (1975). Beyond the two disciplines of scientific psychology. *American Psychologist*, 30(2), 116–127.

Cronbach, L. J. (1982). *Designing evaluations of educational and social programs*. San Francisco, CA: Jossey-Bass.

Cronbach, L. J., Gleser, G. C., Nanda, H., & Rajaratnam, N. (1972). *The dependability of behavioral measurements: Theory of generalizability for scores and profiles*. New York: Wiley.

Cronbach, L. J., Ambron, S. R., Dornbusch, S. M., Hess, R. D., Hornik, R. C., Phillips, D. C., Walker, D. F., & Weiner, S. S. (1980). *Toward reform of program evaluation*. San Francisco, CA: Jossey-Bass.

Crossley, M. (2001). Reconceptualizing comparative and international education. In K. Watson (Ed.), *Doing comparative education research: Issues and problems* (pp. 43–68). Oxford: Symposium Books.

Dede, C. (1998). The scaling-up process for technology-based educational innovations. In C. Dede (Ed.), *Learning with technology. 1998 yearbook of the Association for Supervision and Curriculum Development* (pp. 199–215). Alexandria, VA: ASCD.

Dede, C. (2003). Foreword. In R. B. Kozma (Ed.), *Technology, innovation, and educational change: A global perspective* (pp. ix–xii). Eugene, OR: International Society for Technology and Education.

Delaware Department of Education. (2002). Science curriculum framework. Retrieved November 13, 2002, from www.doe.state.de.us/standards/science.

Design-Based Research Collective. (2003). Design-based research: An emerging paradigm for educational inquiry. *Educational Researcher*, 32(1), 5–8.

Dynarski, M., Agodini, R., Heaviside, S., Novak, T., Carey, N., Campuzano, L., Means, B., Murphy, R., Penuel, W., Javitz, H., Emery, D., & Sussex, W. (2007). *Effectiveness of reading and mathematics software products: Findings from the first student cohort* (NCEE 2007–4005). Washington, DC: Institute of Education Sciences.

Education Week. (2004, May 6). Global links: Lessons from the world: Technology counts 2004. Education Week, 23(35).

Ercikan, K., Domene, J. F., Law, D., & Lacroix, S. (2004, April). Identifying the source of DIF using think-aloud protocols: Comparing thought processes of examinees taking tests in English versus in French. Paper presented at the annual meeting of the National Council of Measurement in Education, San Diego, CA.

Fensham, P. J. (2004, July). *Beyond knowledge: Other scientific questions as outcomes for school science education*. Paper presented at the XIth symposium programme of the International Organization for Science and Technology Education, Lublin, Poland.

Gaskell, J., Mehta, J., & Ogawa, M. (2004, July). Globalisation and localization: Competing tendencies or inevitable companions. Paper presented at the eleventh symposium programme of the International Organization for Science and Technology Education, Lublin, Poland.

Gersick, A., Pasnik, S., Brunner, C., Honey, M., & Parris, J. (2004). *Skills for the twenty-first century: Supporting digital literacy in the classroom: Pre-final report*. New York: EDC Center for Children and Technology.

Guba, E. G., & Lincoln, Y. S. (1989). *Fourth generation evaluation*. Newbury Park, CA: Sage.

Heinecke, W. F., & Blasi, L. (Eds.). (2001). Methods of evaluating educational technology. Greenwich, CT: Information Age Publishing.

Honey, M. (2001, July 25). *Benefits of educational technology*. Testimony and statement before the Labor, HHS, and Education Appropriations Subcommittee, United States Senate.

Honey, M. (2002). New approaches to assessing students' technology-based work. In N. Dickard (Ed.), *Great expectations: Leveraging America's investment in educational technology* (pp. 24–28). Washington, DC: Benton Foundation.

Information Technology Association of America. (2000). *Bridging the gap: Information technology skills for a new millennium*. Arlington, VA: Author.

Information Technology Association of America. (2001). *When can you start? Building better information technology skills and careers*. Arlington, VA: Author.

International ICT Literacy Panel. (2002). *Digital transformation: A framework for ICT literacy*. Princeton, NJ: Educational Testing Service.

International Society for Technology in Education. (2002). *National educational technology standards for teachers: Preparing teachers to use technology*. Eugene, OR: Author.

Jacob, E., & White, C. S. (Eds.). (2002). Theme issue on scientific research in education. Educational Researcher, 31(8).

Janiuk, R. M., & Samonek-Micuk, E. (Eds.). (2004). International Organization for Science and Technology Education: XIth symposium proceedings. Lublin, Poland: Marie-Curie Sklodowska University Press.

Jonassen, D. H. (Ed.). (1996). Handbook for research for educational communications and technology. New York: Macmillan.

Jonassen, D. H. (Ed.). (2004). Handbook for research for educational communications and technology (2nd ed.). New York: Macmillan.

Kankaanranta, M., & Linnakylä, P. (2003). National policies and practices on ICT in education: Finland. In T. Plomp, R. E. Anderson, N. Law, & A. Quale (Eds.), *Cross-national information and communication technology policy and practices in education* (pp. 213–231). Greenwich, CT: Information Age Publishing.

Kellaghan, T., & Stufflebeam, D. L. (Eds.). (2003). International handbook of educational evaluation. Dordrecht, The Netherlands: Kluwer.

Kelly, A. E. (Ed.). (2003). Theme issue: The role of design in educational research. Educational Researcher, 32(1), 3–4.

Kennedy, M. M. (1997). The connection between research and practice. *Educational Researcher*, 26(7), 4–12.

Kozma, R. B. (2003a). ICT and educational change: A global phenomenon. In R. B. Kozma (Ed.), Technology, innovation, and educational change: A global perspective (pp. 1–18). Eugene, OR: International Society for Technology and Education.

Kozma, R. B. (2003b). Study procedures and first look at the data. In R. B. Kozma (Ed.), *Technology, innovation, and educational change: A global perspective* (pp. 19–41). Eugene, OR: International Society for Technology and Education.

Kozma, R. B. (2003c). Summary and implications for ICT-based educational change. In R. B. Kozma (Ed.), *Technology, innovation, and educational change: A global perspective* (pp. 217–239). Eugene, OR: International Society for Technology and Education.

Kozma, R. B. (Ed.). (2003d). Technology, innovation, and educational change: A global perspective. Eugene, OR: International Society for Technology in Education.

Kozma, R. B., & McGhee, R. (2003). ICT and innovative classroom practices. Kozma, R. B. (2003a). ICT and educational change: A global phenomenon. In R. B. Kozma (Ed.),

Technology, innovation, and educational change: A global perspective (pp. 43–88). Eugene, OR: International Society for Technology and Education.

Lagemann, E. (2000). *An elusive science: The troubling history of education research*. Chicago, IL: The University of Chicago.

Law, N., & Plomp, T. (2003). Curriculum and staff development for ICT in education. In T. Plomp, R. E. Anderson, N. Law, & A. Quale (Eds.), *Cross-national information and communication technology policy and practices in education* (pp. 15–30). Greenwich, CT: Information Age Publishing.

Lennon, M., Kirsch, I., Von Davier, M., Wagner, M., & Yamamoto, K. (2003). *Feasibility study for the PISA ICT literacy assessment*. Princeton, NJ: Australian Council for Educational Research, Educational Testing Service, and the National Institute for Policy Research of Japan.

Lesgold, A. (2000). What are the tools for? Revolutionary change does not follow the usual norms. In S. P. Lajoie (Ed.), *Computers as cognitive tools: No more walls: Volume II* (pp. 399–408). Mahwah, NJ: Lawrence Erlbaum.

Lewis, A. E., & Mandinach, E. B. (2009). Informal learning on the Internet. To appear inT. L. Good (Ed.), 21st century education: A reference handbook. Thousand Oaks, CA: Sage.

Long, L., Rivas, L., Light, D., & Mandinach, E. B. (2008). The evolution of a homegrown data warehouse: TUSDStats. In E. B. Mandinach & M. Honey (Eds.), *Data-driven school improvement: Linking data and learning* (pp. 209–232). New York: Teachers College Press.

Love, A. J. (2003, January 17–18). *Implementation analysis for feedback on program progress and results*. San Francisco, CA: Evaluators' Institute.

Mandinach, E. B. (2008). Creating an evaluation framework for data-driven instructional decision making *(final report to the National Science Foundation)*. New York and Alexandria, VA: EDC Center for Children and Technology and the CNA Corporation.

Mandinach, E. B., & Cline, H. F. (1994). *Classroom dynamics: Implementing a technology-based learning environment*. Hillsdale, NJ: Lawrence Erlbaum.

Mandinach, E. B., & Cline, H. F. (2000). It won't happen soon: Practical, curricular, and methodological problems in implementing technology-based constructivist approaches in classrooms. In S. P. Lajoie (Ed.), *Computer as cognitive tools: No more walls* (Vol. II, pp. 377–395). Mahwah, NJ: Lawrence Erlbaum.

Mandinach, E. B., Rivas, L., Light, D., & Heinze, C. (2006, April). The impact of data-driven decision making tools on educational practice: A systems analysis of six school districts. Paper presented at the meeting of the American Educational Research Association, San Francisco.

Martin, M. O., Rust, K., & Adams, R. J. (1999). *Technical standards for IEA studies*. Amsterdam: International Association for the Evaluation of Educational Achievement.

Martin, W., Mandinach, E., Kanaya, T., & McMillan Culp, K. (2004). *Intel international interim report*. New York: EDC Center for Children and Technology.

Mattsson, G., & Svensson, M. (2004, July). The identity of the school subject technology: How teachers in primary school and university students in teacher training perceive school subject technology. Paper presented at the XIth symposium programme of the International Organization for Science and Technology Education, Lublin, Poland.

McCandliss, B. D., Kalchman, M., & Bryant, P. (2003). Design experiments and laboratory approaches to learning: Steps toward collaborative exchange. *Educational Researcher*, 32(1), 14–16.

McMillan Culp, K., Honey, M., & Mandinach, E. (2005). A retrospective on twenty years of education technology policy. *Journal of Educational Computing Research*, 32(3), 313–341.

Mosteller, F., & Boruch, R. (Eds.). (2002). Evidence matters: Randomized trials in education research. Washington, DC: Brookings Press.

Mui, Y. H., Kan, E., & Chun, T. Y. (2003). National policies and practices on ICT in education: Singapore. In T. Plomp, R. E. Anderson, N. Law, & A. Quale (Eds.), *Cross-national information and communication technology policy and practices in education* (pp. 495–508). Greenwich, CT: Information Age Publishing.

Muller, A. (2003). National policies and practices on ICT in education: South Africa. In T. Plomp, R. E. Anderson, N. Law, & A. Quale (Eds.), *Cross-national information and communication technology policy and practices in education* (pp. 541–555). Greenwich, CT: Information Age Publishing.

Mullis, I., Martin, M., Smith, T., Garden, A., Gregory, K., Gonzalez, E., Chrostowski, S., & O'Connor, K. (2003). *TIMSS assessment frameworks and specifications 2003*. Chestnut Hill, MA: International Study Center, Lynch School of Education, Boston College.

Mullis, I. V. S., Martin, M. O., Gonzalez, E. J., & Chrostowski, S. J. (2004). *TIMSS 2003 international mathematics report: Findings from IEA's Trends in International Mathematics and Science study at the fourth and eighth grades*. Chestnut Hill, MA: TIMSS & PIRLS International Study Center, Boston College.

Murphy, R. T. (1988). *Evaluation of Al Manaahil: An original Arabic children's television series in reading* (RR88–45). Princeton, NJ: Educational Testing Service. (ERIC Document Reproduction Service No. 395007)

National Educational Technology Plan. (2004). Retrieved July 6, 2004, from www.nationaledtechplan.org

NCES. (2004). TIMSS USA: Trends in International Mathematics and Science Study. Retrieved July 14, 2004, from nces.ed.gov/timss/

Nelson, C. A., Post, J., & Bickel, W. (2003). Evaluating the institutionalization of technology in schools and classrooms. In T. Kellaghan & D. L. Stufflebeam (Eds.), *International handbook of educational evaluation: Part two: Practice* (pp. 843–870). Dordrecht, The Netherlands: Kluwer.

New Jersey Department of Education. (2002). New Jersey core curriculum content standards for mathematics. Retrieved November 12, 2002, from www.state.nj.us/njded/cccs/02s4_math.htm

Newman, D. (1990). Opportunities for research on the organizational impact of school computers. *Educational Researcher*, 19(3), 8–13.

Newman, D., & Cole, M. (2004). Can scientific research from the laboratory be of any help to teachers? *Theory into Practice*, 43(4), 260–267.

Ogena, E. B., & Brawner, F. G. (2003). National policies and practices on ICT in education: Philippines. In T. Plomp, R. E. Anderson, N. Law, & A. Quale (Eds.), *Cross-national information and communication technology policy and practices in education* (pp. 445–463). Greenwich, CT: Information Age Publishing.

Organisation for Economic Co-operation and Development. (2000). *Measuring student knowledge and skills: The PISA 2000 assessment of reading, mathematics, and scientific literacy*. Paris: Organisation for Economic Co-operation and Development.

Organisation for Economic Co-operation and Development. (2001). *Schooling for tomorrow: Learning to change: ICT in schools*. Paris: Organisation for Economic Co-operation and Development.

Organisation for Economic Co-operation and Development. (2002a). *Manual for the PISA 2000 database*. Paris: Organisation for Economic Co-operation and Development.

Organisation for Economic Co-operation and Development. (2002b). *PISA 2000 technical report*. Paris: Organisation for Economic Co-operation and Development.

Organisation for Economic Co-operation and Development. (2003). *Literacy skills for the world tomorrow: Further results from PISA 2000*. Paris: Organisation for Economic Co-operation and Development.

Organisation for Economic Co-operation and Development. (2004a). *An OECD survey of upper secondary schools: A technical report*. Paris: Organisation for Economic Co-operation and Development.

Organisation for Economic Co-operation and Development. (2004b). *Completing the foundation for lifelong learning: An OECD survey of upper secondary schools*. Paris: Organisation for Economic Co-operation and Development.

Organisation for Economic Co-operation and Development. (2004c). The OECD Programme for International Student Assessment. Retrieved July 14, 2004, from www.pisa.oecd.org/.

Partnership for 21st Century Skills. (2003). *Learning for the 21st century*. Washington, DC: Partnership for 21st Century Skills.
Pearson, G., & Young, A. (2002). *Technically speaking: Why all Americans need to know more about technology*. Washington, DC: National Academy Press.
Pelgrum, W., & Anderson, R. (Eds.). (2001). ICT and the emerging paradigm for lifelong learning (2nd ed.). Amsterdam: International Association for the Advancement of Educational Achievement.
Plomp, T., Anderson, R. E., Law, N., & Quale, A. (Eds.). (2003a). Cross-national information and communication technology policy and practices in education. Greenwich, CT: Information Age Publishing.
Plomp, T., Howie, S., & McGaw, B. (2003b). International studies of educational achievement. In T. Kellaghan & D. L. Stufflebeam (Eds.), *International handbook of educational evaluation: Part two: Practice* (pp. 951–978). Dordrecht, The Netherlands: Kluwer.
Popham, W. J. (2003). Are your state's tests instructionally sensitive?: High-quality assessments share three attributes. In Harvard Education Letter (Eds.), *Spotlight on high-stakes testing* (pp. 17–22). Cambridge, MA: Harvard Education Press.
Popham, W. J. (2005, April/May). F for assessment. Edutopia, 38–41.
President's Committee of Advisors on Science and Technology, Panel on Educational Technology. (1997). *Report to the president on the use of technology to strengthen K-12 education in the United States*. Washington, DC: President's Committee of Advisors on Science and Technology, Panel on Educational Technology.
Pressman, J. L., & Wildavsky, A. (1984). *Implementation*. Berkeley, CA: University of California Press.
Preston, R. (2001). Contextual and methodological influences on trends in comparative and international educational research. In K. Watson (Ed.), *Doing comparative education research: Issues and problems* (pp. 69–84). Oxford: Symposium Books.
Quale, A. (2003). Trends in instructional ICT infrastructure. In T. Plomp, R. E. Anderson, N. Law, & A. Quale (Eds.), *Cross-national information and communication technology policy and practices in education* (pp. 31–42). Greenwich, CT: Information Age Publishing.
Reynolds, D. (1999). Creating a new methodology for comparative educational research: The contribution of the International School Effectiveness Research Project. In R. Alexander, R. Broadfoot, & D. Phillips (Eds.), *Learning from comparing: New directions in comparative educational research: Volume One: Contexts, classrooms, and outcomes* (pp. 135–148). Oxford: Symposium Books.
Rossi, P. H., & Freeman, H. E. (1993). *Evaluation: A systematic approach* (5th ed.). Newbury Park, CA: Sage.
Russell, M. (2001). Framing technology program evaluations. In W. F. Heinecke & L. Blasi (Eds.), *Methods of evaluating educational technology* (pp. 149–162). Greenwich, CT: Information Age Publishing.
Russell, M., & Plati, T. (2000). *Mode of administration effects on MCAS composition performance for grades four, eight, and ten* (Report prepared for the Massachusetts Department of Education). Chestnut Hill, MA: National Board on Educational Testing and Public Policy.
Salomon, G., & Almog, T. (1998). Educational psychology and technology: A matter of reciprocal relations. *Teachers College Record*, 100(2), 222–241.
Schmidt, W. H., & Houang, R. T. (2003). Cross-national curriculum evaluation. In T. Kellaghan & D. L. Stufflebeam (Eds.), *International handbook of educational evaluation: Part two: Practice* (pp. 979–996). Dordrecht, The Netherlands: Kluwer.
Schoenfeld, A. H. (1999). Looking toward the 21st century: Challenges of educational theory and practice. *Educational Researcher*, 28(7), 4–14.
Schweisfurth, M. (2001). Gleaning meaning from case studies in international comparison: Teachers' experiences of reform in Russian and South Africa. In K. Watson (Ed.), *Doing comparative education research: Issues and problems* (pp. (211–223). Oxford: Symposium Books.

Scriven, M. (1967). The methodology of evaluation. In R. E. Stake (Ed.), *Curriculum evaluation* (pp. 39–83). Chicago, IL: Rand McNally.

Scriven, M. (2003). Evaluation theory and metatheory. In T. Kellaghan & D. L. Stufflebeam (Eds.), *International handbook of educational evaluation: Part one: Perspectives* (pp. 15–30). Dordrecht, The Netherlands: Kluwer.

Senge, P. (1990). *The fifth discipline*. New York: Doubleday.

Senge, P., Cambron-McCabe, N., Lucas, T., Smith, B., Dutton, J., & Kleiner, A. (2000). *Schools that learn: A fifth discipline fieldbook for educations, parents, and everyone who cares about education*. New York: Doubleday.

Shadish, W. R., Cook, T. D., & Campbell, D. T. (2002). *Experimental and quasi-experimental designs for generalized causal inference*. Boston, MA: Houghton-Mifflin.

Shavelson, R. J., & Towne, L. (Eds.). (2002). Scientific research in education. Washington, DC: National Academy Press.

Shavelson, R. J., Phillips, D. C., Towne, L., & Feuer, M. J. (2003). On the science of education: Design studies. *Educational Researcher*, 32(1), 25–28.

Shimizu, K., Watanabe, R., Shimizu, Y., Miyake, M., Yamade, K., Horiguti, H., Saito, M., Yoshioka, R., Sakayauti, M., Saruta, Y., Ogura, Y., & Numano, T. (2003). National policies and practices on ICT in education: Japan. In T. Plomp, R. E. Anderson, N. Law, & A. Quale (Eds.), *Cross-national information and communication technology policy and practices in education* (pp. 335–355). Greenwich, CT: Information Age Publishing.

Shulman, L. S. (1970). Reconstruction of educational research. *Review of Educational Research*, 40(3), 371–396.

Singapore Ministry of Education. (2008). Mission and vision statement. Retrieved February 5, 2008, from www.moe.gov.sg/corporate/mission_statement.htm.

Sjoberg, S. (2004, July). Science and technology in the new millennium: Friend or foe? Paper presented at the XIth symposium programme of the International Organization for Science and Technology Education, Lublin, Poland.

State Education Technology Directors Association. (2003). SETDA national leadership institute toolkit. Retrieved April 11, 2003, from www.setda.org/nli2002/CD/TLA/index.htm.

Stufflebeam, D. L. (2002). The CIPP model of evaluation. In T. Kellaghan & D. L. Stufflebeam (Eds.), *International handbook of educational evaluation: Part one: Perspectives* (pp. 31–62). Dordrecht, The Netherlands: Kluwer.

Tapscott, D. (1998). *Growing up digital: The rise of the net generation*. New York: McGraw-Hill.

Uchida, D., Cetron, M., & McKenzie, F. (1996). *Preparing students for the 21st century*. Arlington, VA: American Association of School Administrators.

U.S. Department of Education. (2000). *Teachers' tools for the 21st century: A report on teachers' use of technology* (NCES 2000–102). Washington, DC: Author.

U.S. Department of Education. (2003). *Identifying and implementing educational practices supported by rigorous evidence: A user friendly guide*. Washington, DC: U.S. Department of Education Institute for Education Sciences National Center for Education Evaluation and Regional Assistance.

Voogt, J., & Pelgrum, W. J. (2003). ICT and the curriculum. In R. B. Kozma (Ed.), *Technology, innovation, and educational change: A global perspective* (pp. 81–124). Eugene, OR: International Society for Technology and Education.

Vrasidas, C. (2001). Making the familiar strange-and interesting-again: Interpretivism and symbolic interactionism in educational technology research. In W. F. Heinecke & L. Blasi (Eds.), *Methods of evaluating educational technology* (pp. 85–103). Greenwich, CT: Information Age Publishing.

Watson, K. (Ed.). (2001a). Doing comparative education research: Issues and problems. Oxford: Symposium Books.

Watson, K. (2001b). Introduction: Rethinking the role of comparative education. In K. Watson (Ed.), *Doing comparative education research: Issues and problems* (pp. 9–20). Oxford: Symposium Books.

Weiss, C. H. (1998). *Evaluation: Methods for studying programs and policies* (2nd ed.). Upper Saddle River, NJ: Prentice Hall.

What Works Clearinghouse. (2004). Retrieved July 6, 2004, from www.w-w-c.org

Whitehurst, G. J. (2003a, April). The Institute for Education Sciences: New wine and new bottles. Paper presented at the annual meeting of the American Educational Research Association, Chicago, IL.

Whitehurst, G. J. (2003b, August). Psychology and evidence-based education. Paper presented at the annual meeting of the American Psychological Association, Toronto, Canada.

Whitehurst, G. J. (2007, April). Big challenges for education research. Paper presented at the annual meeting of the American Educational Research Association, Chicago, IL.

World Bank Group. (2003). *Lifelong learning in the global knowledge economy: Challenges for developing countries*. Washington, DC: The World Bank.

Yin, R. K. (1995). New methods for evaluating programs in NSF's Division of Research, Evaluation, and Dissemination. In J. A. Frechtling (Ed.), *Footprints: Strategies for non-traditional program evaluation* (pp. 25–36). Arlington, VA: National Science Foundation.

Yong, G. K. (2005, November). Singapore's Ministry of Education. Speech given at the meeting of the International Conference on Computers in Education, Singapore.

Zehr, M. A. (2004, May 6). Africa. Global links: Lessons from the world: Technology counts 2004. *Education Week*, 23(35), 56–59.

Zhao, Y., Byers, J., Pugh, K., & Sheldon, S. (2001). What's worth looking for?: Issues in educational technology research. In W. F. Heinecke & L. Blasi (Eds.), *Methods of evaluating educational technology* (pp. 269–296). Greenwich, CT: Information Age Publishing.

Name Index

Subject Index

GPSR Compliance

The European Union's (EU) General Product Safety Regulation (GPSR) is a set of rules that requires consumer products to be safe and our obligations to ensure this.

If you have any concerns about our products, you can contact us on ProductSafety@springernature.com

In case Publisher is established outside the EU, the EU authorized representative is:

Springer Nature Customer Service Center GmbH
Europaplatz 3
69115 Heidelberg, Germany

Batch number: 10823959

Printed by Printforce, the Netherlands